Chinese Economic Planning

Chinese Economic Planning

TRANSLATIONS FROM CHI-HUA CHING-CHI

Edited with an introduction by Nicholas R. Lardy

Translated by K. K. Fung

M. E. Sharpe, INC.

Dawson

Library of Congress Catalog Card Number: 78-52292
M. E. Sharpe ISBN: 0-87332-117-8
Dawson ISBN: 0-7129-0898-6

Printed in the United States of America

Contents

Part Two

Lectures on Basic Knowledge of
National Economic Plan Tables

Introduction

Nicholas R. Lardy

This volume brings together translations of a series of fundamental articles that are of special value for those who seek to
understand China's system of economic planning. These materials,
which were intended to provide a basic introduction to the principles and techniques of economic planning being introduced during
the First Five-Year Plan, originally appeared in two series in the
journal Chi-hua ching-chi (Economic Planning), the official organ
of the State Planning Commission and the State Economic Commission. The first series of seventeen articles, under the general
title "Lectures on National Economic Planning," appeared in the
journal in 1955 and 1956, while the second series of fourteen articles, entitled "Lectures on Basic Knowledge of National Economic
Plan Tables," was published between January 1957 and February
1958. The present volume contains complete translations of nine
articles from the earlier series in Part One and ten articles from
the second series in Part Two.

These articles are of special importance for those who are interested in the emergence of the People's Republic of China as the
world's second largest economic system in which resource allocation decisions are made primarily by bureaucratic-administrative
means rather than through the operation of the marketplace. Their
special value stems from several sources. First, unlike the So-
viets, the Chinese have not published any books describing in detail
the methodology of economic plan formulation. For an official description of Soviet planning techniques, one can turn to such works
as G. Sorokin's Planning in the USSR: Problems of Theory and Organization[1] and Mikhail Bor's Aims and Methods of Soviet Planning.[2] While these volumes are frequently somewhat turgid and
cast at such a high level of generality that they are not particularly
revealing to Western specialists, they sometimes provide a starting point for studies based on more specialized and less accessible

materials. While the Chinese have not published comparable volumes, the series of articles collected here is similar in its breadth of coverage to these Soviet volumes. The articles selected discuss planning of industry, agriculture, transportation, capital construction, labor and wages, prices and costs, social services, finance, and commodity distribution. A comparable range of topics is covered, for example, in the Bor book cited above.

In some cases, these Chinese articles appear to be somewhat more revealing than the two Soviet studies referred to above. This is particularly true of the articles in the second series, which are more detailed and somewhat more operational than those in the first series. This may be because the Chinese articles were published for a specialized internal audience while the Soviet books cited are addressed primarily to general readers outside the Soviet Union. The articles in Chi-hua ching-chi were specifically intended to introduce general principles of planning and more detailed information on the nature of the plan tables actually used in the formulation of annual plans to the increasing number of cadres specializing in economic planning work. The number of planning specialists was growing, both within the ministerial bureaucracy as well as at the provincial and county levels. Provincial planning commissions were formally established in 1954 in most regions,[3] and evidence of their active role became available in the late fall of 1955, when following the publication of the First Five Year Plan for the Development of the National Economy of the People's Republic of China in 1953-1957[4] in August, provincial five-year plans were first promulgated.[5] Equally important, at this time planning offices at the county level were beginning to play an increasing role in mobilizing and planning the use of local economic resources. By 1955 over 1,400 counties, about two-thirds of the total, had established their own planning commissions.[6] Because of the special purpose of these articles they are frequently more informative than the two Soviet books.

A second reason for the significance of these materials is that they form a meaningful base for measuring the evolution of Chinese planning and development strategy. Perhaps most importantly, they provide a basis for understanding the extent to which China's approach to economic development in the First Five-Year Plan period was based on a simple replication of the Soviet model. The articles reveal widespread borrowing of institutional arrangements and planning principles from the Soviet Union, particularly the use of material balances as a fundamental planning technique. But they also sometimes evince sensitivity to the implications of the different underlying economic conditions in China. For example, the first article on industrial planning makes reference to the standard Soviet planning principle that requires the rate of growth of output of machinery, equipment, and other producer goods to exceed the rate of growth of output of consumer goods. The author, however, goes on to state that this pattern is necessitated not only by the desire to increase the share of total output allocated to investment, but also partially by the constraints imposed by China's agricultural sector. Increased output of consumer goods such as food, clothing, and other daily necessities depends crucially on the growth of the agricultural sector, which supplied about three-fourths of the inputs used in the manufacture of consumer goods. Because of the difficulty of accelerating the growth of agricultural output under conditions of a relatively fixed quantity of arable land, the increased inputs necessary to achieve a relatively rapid rate of growth of consumer goods output would not be available.

This theme of the relative backwardness of China's agriculture as compared with the Soviet Union is explicitly reiterated in the subsequent article on agricultural planning. The Chinese authors are acutely aware of the relative importance of raising yield levels as a means of increasing agricultural output under conditions of relative land scarcity. Furthermore, they appear to understand the importance of the interactive effects on yield levels of modern inputs such as improved seed varieties, improved water control, and mechanized equipment. The total yield improvement is not simply the sum of the partial effects of each of these inputs applied individually, but reflects the interactive effects of these inputs as well. By contrast, the authors of the books on Soviet planning cited above do not even refer to this set of issues, perhaps reflecting the historic Soviet emphasis on increased cultivated area as the predominant source of agricultural growth. The relative backwardness of China's agriculture, as compared with the Soviet Union, is also specifically cited by the Chinese authors as the reason that it will be impossible to develop animal husbandry and industrial crops such as cotton and oil seeds as fast as was done in the Soviet Union. Solving the problem of supplying more adequate quantities of staple foods was to be the first priority for agriculture in China.

Thus articles published as early as 1955 indicate quite clearly that in important respects Chinese planners were already well aware of the limits of the relevance of the Soviet model to their own more backward, more densely populated country. Yet this awareness was still somewhat limited. For example, the article on labor planning that appeared in 1955 is stated to have been "based on relevant materials about the Soviet Union." The author's discussion of China's labor planning appears to be based on the faulty premise that industrial sector growth would be sufficiently rapid to increase the demand for labor in the modern sector by enough to reduce the proportion and perhaps even the absolute number of people employed in the agricultural sector. Less than one year later the leadership had realized that China's relative backwardness would substantially delay the time when the industrial sector would be able to employ an increased share of the total labor force. The draft of the Twelve-Year Plan for Agricultural Development,[7] published in 1956, had as a prime objective the absorption of unemployed urban workers within the agricultural sector — a reversal of the Soviet experience in which the industrial sector employed a gradually increasing share of workers both during the first two five-year plans (1928-1937) and in the post-World War II period as well.

In addition to sharpening our understanding of the extent to which China's approach to economic development differed from that of the Soviet Union even prior to the Great Leap Forward of the late 1950s, these articles provide an important benchmark for measuring the evolution of Chinese planning methods and principles since the First Five-Year Plan period. One can contrast, for example, the policy of linking increases in industrial wages to the growth of labor productivity outlined by Wu Ching-ch'ao in his article, published in 1955, with the quite different policy of freezing industrial sector wages that was adopted in 1957. More recently, under the new political regime led by Hua Kuo-feng, the average industrial wage has been increased for the first time in more than two decades, and statements of the leadership suggest that in the future wage increases will be tied to (although still somewhat less than) productivity growth, as in the years before 1957.

More generally, as we witness in the late 1970s a renewed emphasis on economic growth and modernization, the principles and methods of planning discussed in this volume are of increased relevance. While qualitative information on the system of planning remains relatively scarce, presumably there is currently greater continuity with the planning practices of the First Five-Year Plan than there was either during the period of the Cultural Revolution, when the industrial and transport sectors were dis-

rupted, or with the period of 1974-76, when the transition to the
post-Mao leadership led to a partial paralysis of the planning process as well as significant disruption of industrial production in
some provinces. For despite some important changes since the
1950s, I would hypothesize that there is a somewhat greater degree
of continuity between the system of planning of the 1950s and that
of subsequent years, with the exception of the Cultural Revolution
and 1974-76 periods, than is frequently assumed. Hopefully, the
Chinese will reveal enough information to test this hypothesis
more fully.

In summary, as pure description these materials are unique.
Furthermore, they provide significant materials for analyzing the
degree to which Chinese planning, as early as the First Five-Year
Plan, was sensitive to the fundamentally differing economic conditions in China vis-à-vis the Soviet Union. Finally, they provide a
benchmark for measuring the evolution of Chinese planning principles and practices since the First Five-Year Plan.

While the present volume contains almost two-thirds of the original material contained in the two series, space limitations pre-
cluded the inclusion of twelve articles that were judged to be
either too introductory or too specialized in nature to be useful to
most readers. For those who are interested in these topics, a list
of the author(s), title, and original date of publication of each of
the omitted articles follows: Li Yü-heng, "What Is National Economic Planning," Chi-hua ching-chi (CHCC), 1955, No. 1; Ma Chi-
k'ung, "The Tasks and Principles of National Economic Planning,"
CHCC, 1955, No. 2; Li Yü-heng, "Examination of the Conditions of
Implementation of the National Economic Plan," CHCC, 1955,
No. 4; Li Yü-heng, "Capital Construction Planning," CHCC, 1955,
No. 9; Yü Kuang-hua, "Product Circulation Planning," CHCC, 1956,
No. 2; "Planning Residents Social and Cultural Programs," CHCC,
1956, No. 3;[8] Ch'en Hsi-jun, "Product Cost Planning," CHCC, 1956,
No. 5; Li Yung, "Construction and Installation Plan Tables," CHCC,
1957, No. 6; Ku To-ching," Muncipal Public Utilities Plan Tables,"
CHCC, 1956, No. 7; Ko Hu, "Survey and Design Work Tables,"
CHCC, 1957, No. 8; Li Hui-lin and Li Wen-jui, "Geological Pros-
pecting Plan Tables," CHCC, 1957, No. 9.

I wish to acknowledge the support of several persons in the completion of this book. Most important the late Professor Alexander
Eckstein of the University of Michigan was an early supporter, encouraging both the editor and the publisher to undertake this project. Raymond Powell, of the Department of Economics at Yale

University, was an ever-ready participant in comparative discussions of Soviet and Chinese Planning practices. John Philip Emerson, of the U.S. Department of Commerce, gave freely from his vast knowledge of specialized Chinese economic terminology, particularly in the area of manpower planning. Wei-ying Wan, of the University of Michigan, was instrumental in supplying copies of the original texts of the articles from Chi-hua ching-chi.

Notes

1. Progress Publishers, Moscow, 1967.
2. New York: International Publishers, 1967.
3. Yang Ying-chieh, "Kuan-yü ko-chi chi-hua chi-kuan ti tsu-chih ho tso-yung" (The Organization and Role of Each Level's Plan Organization). Chi-hua ching-chi, 1955, No. 6, p. 4.
4. Peking: People's Publishing House, 1955.
5. For the most comprehensive listing of these provincial five-year plans, see John Philip Emerson et al., The Provinces of the People's Republic of China: A Political and Economic Bibliography. International Population Statistics Reports, Series P-90, No. 25 (Washington, D. C.: U. S. Government Printing Office, 1976).
6. Chou Chung-fu, "Kuan-yü hsien chi-hua wei-yüan-hui ti jen-wu tsu-chih ho tso-yung" (The Responsibility, Organization, and Work of County Planning Commissions). Chi-hua ching-chi, 1955, No. 10, p. 19.
7. Chinese Communist Party Central Committee, "1956-nien tao 1967-nien ch'üan-kuo nung-yeh fa-chan kang-yao (ts'ao-an)" (The Draft National Plan for Agricultural Development, 1956-1967) (Peking: People's Publishing House, 1956).
8. This issue of Chi-hua ching-chi is not available in the West so the author of this article is unknown. The title was, however, listed in the introduction to the first series in Chi-hua ching-chi, 1955, No. 1.

PART ONE
Lectures on National Economic Planning

LECTURE 3: METHODS IN FORMULATING NATIONAL ECONOMIC PLANS

Chung Ch'i-fu*

I. The Basic Method in Formulating National Economic Plans — the Balance Method

After the Party and the state have determined the political and economic tasks of each period, the planning organs must formulate national economic plans that can guarantee the fulfillment of these tasks. These plans must be formulated with scientific methods. These scientific methods must correctly reflect the requirements of a planned (proportional) development of the national economy. The more than 30 years' experience in plan formulation of the Soviet Union demonstrates that the balance method is such a method.

First of all, the term "balance method" itself shows that it is a method used to determine the correct proportional relations among the various sectors of the national economy.

The national economy is a unified entity. The various sectors of the national economy are closely related. The relations among the various sectors of the national economy are objective proportional relations expressed in quantitative terms. For example, when the textile industrial sector wants to produce a certain quantity of cotton fabrics, a certain quantity of spinning and weaving machines will be required from the machine-building industrial sector, and a certain quantity of cotton from agriculture. And to guarantee the production of spinning and weaving machines and cotton, other related sectors are required to supply certain products to the machine-building industry and to agriculture. In this way, the various objective proportional relations for the development of the national economy are formed. The basic difference between socialism

---

*Chung Ch'i-fu, "Pien-chih kuo-min ching-chi chi-hua ti fang-fa." <u>CHCC</u>, 1955, No. 3, pp. 28-30, 22.

and capitalism lies in the fact that the socialist society can develop
the national economy according to objective proportions in a con-
scious and planned way. This then is the basic requirement of a
planned (proportional) development of the national economy.

The special character of the balance method lies in its ability to
bring together the various parts of the national economy for comparison and examination, so as to correctly specify the proportional relations among them. For example, whether the output of
steel by the metallurgical industry can meet the needs of the
machine-building industry and the railway and capital construction
sectors can be determined through the formulation of the steel balance table. Through the formulation of a balance table for steel
and other related balance tables, we can correctly specify the proportional relation between steel production and the tasks in machine building and capital construction. Complicated proportional
relations such as those between social production and consumption
can also be specified correctly through the formulation of corresponding balance tables.

Second, the use of the balance method to formulate plans not only
allows the development of the various sectors to be systematically
integrated, but also facilitates maximum economy and effective
utilization of the material, human, and financial resources of the
country. This is also an important requirement of a planned (proportional) development of the national economy. In contrast to the
inevitable massive waste and destruction of social labor and its
output which results from competition and chaotic production, the
principles of planning and economy are inseparable.

In formulating balance tables, we must have a realistic idea of
the needs and the resources of the country and use the average advanced material consumption quota and equipment utilization quota
as standards for calculation. In balancing needs with resources,
we must also discover means to overcome backward links so as to
tap all possible resource potential. In this way, a better utilization
of material, human, and financial resources can be achieved and a
further increase in output and consumption can be guaranteed.

II. Types of Balance Tables and General Principles
Governing Their Formulation

The concrete application of the balance method is the formulation of various balance tables, the determination of various plan
targets through these balance tables and the determination of

the mutual relations among these various targets.

The balance tables used in formulating plans can be classified into material balance tables, labor balance tables and money balance tables.

Under the socialist system, the production of the social product is still realized in two forms: (a) a physical form, (b) a value form or money form. Insofar as the physical form is concerned, it is a form that must accompany any social production. This is because any social production is itself the production of material goods (producer goods and consumer goods). Therefore, the relation among the various sectors of the national economy must first of all be a relation expressed in material goods. For example, to produce a bolt of cotton fabric requires a certain quantity of cotton. The expression of social production in value terms is due to the continued existence of commodity production and the law of value under the socialist system — thus the impossibility of calculating the total social product and the production and distribution of the national income on the direct basis of labor time. Under the socialist system, however, the nature of the social economy expressed in value terms is different in principle from capitalist production. The value form no longer reflects the capitalist exploitative relation, but reflects instead the socialist relation of mutual cooperation. In this way there exist in the production process of the socialist society not only proportional relations in physical terms but also proportional relations in value terms.

In addition, the production of labor is realized in the socialist production process. A planned allocation of labor among various sectors is one of the basic conditions for the expansion of socialist production.

From this, we can see that in order for the national economic plans to completely reflect social production, it is necessary to specify the following three proportions: (1) physical (material) proportions, (2) value proportions, (3) labor proportions. Corresponding with these is the formulation of material balance tables, money balance tables, and labor balance tables.

The formulation of these three types of balance tables is briefly described as follows:

Material balance tables: They show the proportional relation between production and consumption in physical terms for a type of product or a group of products. Through them, the material relations among the output of various sectors or between the output of consumer goods and people's consumption can be determined.

Material balance tables can be further classified by economic uses into producer goods balance tables and consumer goods balance tables.

The general format of material balance tables is divided into the needs and the sources sections. The "needs" section includes: (1) production and operation needs, (2) capital construction needs, (3) market fund, (4) export, (5) allocation to state reserves, (6) inventory at the end of the plan period. The "sources" section includes: (1) inventory at the beginning of the plan period, (2) output in the plan period, (3) allocation from state reserves, (4) imports, (5) other resources.

Insofar as the producer goods balance tables are concerned, the major items of the "needs" section are the production and operation needs and the capital construction needs. They reflect the major allocation directions of material resources. To ensure the correct coordination of current production and capital construction, it is necessary to specify correctly the proportionate allocation of producer goods between the two uses. The needs of the leading sector should first be guaranteed. This is the most important principle governing the allocation of material goods. The calculation of the needs for material resources must be based on the average advanced consumption quota and reserves quota as standards. Also, these quotas must have an actual technical and economic basis. Only in this way can overestimation or underestimation of needs be avoided.

The major item in the "sources" section is the output of the product in the plan period. The socialist plan is established on the basis of using domestic resources first. Of course, in the industrialization period it is necessary to rely on imports of technical equipment which the country cannot produce enough of or which still cannot be produced. The determination of productive resources should start from the principle of effective utilization of existing productive capacity and be based on the advanced capacity utilization quota. In addition, consideration should be given to the utilization of new productive capacity.

A balanced relation between the output and needs of certain products frequently can only be determined after carrying out repeated balance calculations and examining each of the items in the balance table.

Material balance tables are useful for many purposes. They are used when the output of various types of products are planned. But it certainly is not necessary to compile material balance tables for all products; they are formulated only with respect to major products in the state plan.

Material balance tables are mainly used to formulate industrial and agricultural production plans, transport plans, capital construction plans, supply plans of material resources and technology, and marketed product circulation plans. In industrial and agricultural production planning, material balance tables are mainly used to determine the correct proportional relations between the production and consumption of industrial and agricultural products so as to correctly specify the level of output of industrial and agricultural products. In the transport plans, through the formulation of the transport balance tables for coal, petroleum, metals, timber, food and other bulk goods, it is possible to determine the transport volume of the above-mentioned goods. When capital construction plans are formulated we must compile balance tables of productive capacity and balance tables of fixed assets in the national economy in order to determine correctly the scale of construction of fixed assets. And the formulation of balance tables for equipment and construction materials provides a guaranteed level of supply of material resources for capital construction. In the material and technical supply plan the goal of compiling material balance tables is to ensure that the producer goods required by each department will be distributed and supplied under a unified state plan. Commodity distribution plans are formulated on the basis of material balance tables.

Money balance tables: They express the balance relations between the national income and the sources and the distribution of state financial revenues.

Money balance tables include the balance table of the money income and expenditure of the people, the state budget, sectoral financial plans, the credit and loan plan of the State Bank, and the cash inflow and outflow plan of the State Bank.

The balance table of money income and expenditure of the people is an important means to plan the circulation of retail products. Under the socialist system, personal consumption goods are still mainly distributed through commodity circulation (buying and selling). Therefore, a proper proportional relation between the money income of the people and the supply of marketed products should be maintained. The formulation of the balance table of the money income and expenditure of the people can determine the total purchasing power of the people and balance the supply and demand of marketed products.

The state budget, the sectoral financial plans, the credit and loan plan and the cash inflow and outflow plan of the State Bank are links in the financial system which are compiled in the form of balance tables. They specify the distribution and uses of state revenues.

Labor balance tables: They specify the labor resources and thei proportionate distribution.

Labor balance tables are the basis for formulating labor quantit plans. In the Soviet Union, the formulation of labor plans involves first of all the formulation of labor balance tables of the national economy, sectoral labor balance tables, regional labor balance ta- bles, labor balance tables of the collective farms, and balance ta- bles for skilled workers and specialized cadres.

Labor resources are determined by the age structure of the ex- isting population and its natural rate of increase. And the quantity of skilled workers, engineers, and technicians is determined by th labor reserve system*, and the training plans of the middle-level technical schools and higher-level schools. The needs of each sec tor for labor depend on its output, work load, and labor productiv- ity. Under the socialist system the elimination of unemployment facilitates the most rational utilization of labor resources. In China, potential labor resources are very large. This is a favor- able condition for the development of socialism. But, owing to the constraint of our existing production scale, temporary dislocation between labor resources and needs still exist.

Labor balance tables of the national economy are a synthesis of regional and sectoral labor balance tables. Plans for the redistri- bution of labor among regions are formulated on the basis of the regional labor balance tables.

In formulating material balance tables, money balance tables an labor balance tables, it is necessary to maintain their internal con nections. These close connections are determined by the unified production process of socialism.

Although there are internal connections among the three types of balance tables mentioned above, they are separately formulated Thus they can determine only the various partial proportional re- lations of the national economy. For example, the steel balance ta ble can only determine the proportion between the production and consumption of steel. In order to make national economic planning correspond better to the needs of the law of planned development,

---

*This system is explained in Lecture 10: "Labor Planning," pp. 61-76, be- low. — N. R. L.

and to become a genuine organic entity, it is necessary to coordinate the various partial balance tables and to establish an overall balance relation for the national economy. To do this, we need to formulate national economic balance tables.

The national economic balance tables consist of a series of comprehensive tables, of which the most important are the balance table for the production, consumption and accumulation of the social product, the balance table for the production, distribution and redistribution of the national income, and the labor balance table of the national economy. The balance table for the production, consumption, and accumulation of the social product is the most central balance table in the system of national economic balance tables. It shows the total quantity and composition of the social product. For example, the proportional relation between the first category and second category of social product*, the proportional relation among the various basic sectors (industry, agriculture, capital construction, transport, commerce, etc.) of social product, the relative weights of each of the economic components of the social product, and the relation among the production, distribution, circulation, consumption, and accumulation processes of the social product.

The scientific formulation of national economic plans should start and end with the compilation of national economic balance tables. That is to say, the preliminary draft of the national economic balance table is the basis on which the control figures of the national economic plan are determined. And the final draft of the national economic plans should conclude with the final determination of the national economic balance tables.

Although the balance method is the most basic method to formulate plans, certain conditions must be present before we can use it. These conditions are: (1) a large amount of statistical data and quota data required for the analysis of various important economic processes; (2) unified scientific methods of calculation and units of calculation; (3) a knowledge of Marxist production theory.

---

*Marx divided the social product into the means of production (I) and the means of consumption (II). <u>Capital</u>, Volume II, Part 3. While this division is maintained primarily in theory, Soviet and Chinese statistical practice usually focuses on industry only where gross industrial output is divided into categories A (producer goods) and B (consumer goods). This division is discussed in Lecture 5: "Industrial Production Planning," pp. 12-23, below. — N.R.L.

III. Other Methods for the Formulation of
National Economic Plans

In addition to the balance method, it is also necessary to use other supplementary methods in formulating plans. These methods are of many types. And the purposes of their uses are all different. Of these methods, the most important are the fixed proportions method, and the dynamic relations method. The contents of these two methods are as follows:

1. Fixed proportions method: The quantitative expressions of the proportions in the plan period are based on the quantitative expressions of the corresponding proportions manifested in the growth process of the reporting period.

For example, suppose that during the reporting period the ratio between the amount of coal transported and the amount of coal mined (i.e., the transport coefficient) was 0.9 and that we expect no large changes of this ratio in the plan period. Then we can specify the transport coefficient of coal for the plan period as 0.9. Again suppose the planned amount of coal to be mined is 250 million tons; then we can estimate the amount of coal transported in the plan period by using the constant transport coefficient (0.9) to be 225 million tons (250 million tons $\times$ 0.9 = 225 million tons).

Initial estimates for other similar planned targets, namely those with little changes and little effect on the accuracy of the whole plan, can all be calculated according to the fixed proportions method in formulating the draft plans.

2. Dynamic relations method: The growth rates of the targets in the plan period are based on the growth rates of corresponding targets in the past.*

For example, according to statistical figures on the rate of growth of labor productivity in the Soviet Union before the Second World War, we know that the average annual growth rate of labor productivity in this period was 11 percent. If, after analysis, it is determined that there are no great changes in the conditions that promote labor productivity after the war as compared to before the war, then the growth rate of labor productivity in the postwar Soviet Union can be set around 11 percent.

The above two methods possess the following common features: (1) they view certain economic processes in certain periods as constant or nearly constant; (2) they extrapolate the future from

---

*Chinese applications of this approach are discussed in Lecture 9: "The Material-Technical Supply Plan," pp. 49-60, below. — N.R.L.

the past; (3) their accuracy is low as they rely on estimation.

Although these two methods suffer from some shortcomings, they are indispensable for specifying certain targets when the initial draft plans are being formulated and when adequate data are lacking. Particularly in China today when there are many economic components and when comprehensive, accurate statistical data as well as experience with the balance method are lacking, it is necessary to use certain well-tested estimation methods to formulate plans.

It should be pointed out that the above two methods, though similar in form to the "static coefficient method" and the "dynamic coefficient method" proposed by the opportunists and bourgeois experts who sneaked into the state planning agencies in the early period of Soviet Union's socialist construction, are completely different in essence. The "static coefficient method" and the "dynamic coefficient method" were used to plan the statics and dynamics of Soviet economic growth based on Czarist Russian capitalist statics and dynamics. They determined the proportional relations and the rate of Soviet economic growth according to the proportional relations and growth rate of Czarist Russian capitalism. These methods would hinder socialist industrialization and threaten to restore capitalism.

LECTURE 5: INDUSTRIAL PRODUCTION PLANNING

Ma Chi-k'ung and Tsung Shih*

I. The Basic Task of Industrial Production Planning

Industry is the most important material production sector of the national economy. Industry is the producer of all modern means of production. Only by developing industrial production, especially heavy industrial production, can it be guaranteed that the application of new technology and equipment will transform the various sectors of the national economy, lead to the establishment of social production based on advanced technology, and guarantee the economic independence of the nation and the consolidation of national defense.

In the transition period of our country, large-scale socialist industry is the core of our nation's industry; it is the material basis and leading force that guarantees the socialist transformation of individual agriculture, individual handicraft industry, and capitalist industry and commerce. Without the development of large-scale socialist industry, the socialist society can never be established. Therefore, the Party regards the realization of socialist industrialization as the principal and central link in realizing the general line in China's transition period.

Industrial production planning is the most important component of national economic planning.

The most basic task of industrial production planning in the national economy is to guarantee the gradual realization of national socialist industrialization. That is to say, it must guarantee high-speed development of industrial production, especially heavy industrial production, and establish a complete industrial system that is capable of manufacturing various types of machinery and equipment.

---

*Ma Chi-k'ung, Tsung Shih, "Kung-yeh sheng-ch'an chi-hua." CHCC, 1955, No. 5, pp. 27-30.

It must guarantee the socialist transformation of capitalist industry and gradually transform China's industry into a single socialist industry.

Based on the above-described basic tasks of industrial production planning, the following problems must be correctly solved in formulating the industrial production plan of the national economy: (1) specify the rate of growth of industrial production; (2) correctly specify the proportional relationship between type A industry and type B industry and the relative shares of socialist industry and nonsocialist industry in the gross value of industrial output*; (3) correctly specify the level of output of major industrial products. The degree to which these problems are correctly solved is an indicator for evaluating the scientific nature of industrial production planning.

II. The Rate of Growth of Industrial Production

The rate of growth of industrial production is the percentage ratio of the gross value of industrial output in the plan period to the gross value of industrial output in the reporting period computed at constant prices. It indicates the rate of increase of all industrial production.

In the early period of Soviet socialist industrial construction, the rate of industrial growth was an issue that determined the life or death of the Soviet state. At that time, Comrade Stalin pointed out: "We are fifty to a hundred years behind the advanced countries. We must close this gap within ten years. Either we manage to do just that, or we will be trampled on by others." [1]   Immediate attention to raising the rate of growth of China's industry is also an acute issue in China's socialist construction. This is because, on the one hand, China's original industrial base is very weak. If we do not pay attention to raising the rate of growth of industry, especially the growth of heavy industry, China's socialist construction will be delayed, and we will be unable to increase the people's standard of living for a long time. On the other hand, owing to the present existence of imperialism, a serious threat of war still exists. If we do not develop heavy industry rapidly, we will be unable to further consolidate our national defense. Therefore, an important principle

---

*Type A industry makes producer goods, or those used for further production processes, such as steel. Type B industry makes consumer goods, such as bicycles and clothing. — N.R.L.

in formulating the industrial production plan is to ensure a con-
sistently high rate of growth of industrial output.

The feasibility of a high rate of growth of our industrial production is due to the fact that our country is a people's democratic
dictatorship led by the working class and based on the worker-
peasant alliance. The leading force in the national economy is the
socialist state economy. Therefore, our country possesses immense political and economic superiority. This enables all the elements that determine the growth of industrial production to play
their roles fully.

The elements that determine the growth rate of industrial production are: (1) increases in the use of labor, especially increases
in industrial production personnel; (2) increases in labor productivity; (3) increases in the stock of embodied labor, namely, increases of fixed assets and circulating assets; and (4) reductions
in material consumption.

All products are the fruit of human labor. The four factors described above merely show from different perspectives how labor
is used in industrial production. Increases in labor used and in the
stock of embodied labor indicate an increase in the total amount of
labor used. Increases in labor productivity and reductions in material consumption indicate a reduction in labor used per unit of
output. Increasing the total amount of labor used and economizing
on labor used per unit of output are the two basic ways of increasing industrial output. It should be pointed out that the various factors contributing to increased production do not play their roles independently; they are mutually dependent and mutually reinforcing.
For example, to increase industrial production and fixed assets and
circulating assets, the amount of labor used or the level of labor
productivity must be correspondingly increased. Economies in material consumption are often the result of an increase in labor productivity. Therefore, the specification of the rate of growth of industry cannot be based one-sidedly on the potential for growth of
only some factors, but must be based on all-round research of each
factor, taking into account the mutual interaction among all factors.
Only in this way can the specified plan be realistic and reliable.

As for the whole of China's industry, the basic method of increasing industrial production is to enlarge the industrial base and to
carry out industrial capital construction; in other words, to increase the stock of embodied labor. Only by increasing fixed assets and circulating assets can more labor be absorbed into industrial production. Only new technology can rapidly increase labor

productivity and economize on material consumption. However, for individual industrial branches or for certain time periods, the main way to increase production probably does not lie in building new plants and mines, but in increasing the utilization rate of existing facilities, economizing on raw materials, or raising workers' skill levels. In sum, the central problem in guaranteeing a high rate of growth of industrial production is to discover and eliminate contradictions among various factors and to enable a perfect combination of the various factors.

In industrial production planning, different rates of growth should be specified for different industrial branches according to need and feasibility. In general, the growth of type A industry must be faster than that of type B industry. This is in accordance with the principle that producer goods must be given priority in growth. Only in this way can the accumulation of producer goods be guaranteed and output be expanded. If we look at it from the perspective of need, the rate of growth of the machine-building industry should generally be the highest of the type A industries. The iron and steel industry, electric power, fuel, and chemical industries should also have a relatively high rate of growth. However, from the perspective of resource feasibility rather than simply that of need, the above conditions may not be applicable. In this case, the existing production facilities, the number of workers that can be absorbed, and the supply of raw materials become the determining factors. As far as need is concerned, most products of type B industries still do not fully satisfy the people's needs. However, because of limited resources, the priority of various needs must be carefully weighed in the development of type B industry. Based on the level of reserves of resources, branches that produce industrial goods urgently needed for daily living by the broad laboring masses should be developed first. For example, if resources are available, branches such as food, textiles, medicine, and paper should be developed faster than others.

The rates of growth of all industry and of the individual industrial branches are unequal in different periods. As far as the whole of industry is concerned, the rate of growth of industry in the construction period is lower than that in the recovery period. In the recovery stage, the average annual growth rate of China's industry (excluding the handicraft industry) was about 36.9 percent. But the estimated growth of 1954 compared with 1953 was only 17 to 18 percent. Why was the rate of growth of industrial output faster in the recovery period than in the construction period?

First of all, during the recovery period, the potential of industrial enterprises was immense. Labor productivity and industrial production could be rapidly increased through production reform and democratic reform. Second, it was easier to restore old enterprises ravaged by war than to build new enterprises. Particularly where the production capacity was unbalanced and uncoordinated, after adjustment, renovation, and expansion, the utilization rate of equipment could be rapidly raised. Furthermore, in the recovery period, the share of light industry in industry as a whole was comparatively large, and it was easy to increase production in light industry. But in the construction period, the potential of various branches is relatively less (naturally, the potential is not exhausted). At the same time, we cannot begin to satisfy the daily increasing needs by merely relying on tapping the potential of existing enterprises to increase production. Therefore, the further growth of industrial production must primarily depend on building new enterprises which will have the most advanced technology and renovating or expanding existing enterprises with advanced technology. But this is extremely difficult and complex, requiring a relatively long period to achieve. Consequently, the rate of growth of industry in the construction period is different from the rate of growth of industry in the recovery period.

On this point of differential rates of growth of industry in different time periods, we must distinguish the difference and the relationship between temporary reductions in the rate of growth of industry and the average rate of growth of industrial output over the long run. We say that China's industrial production is rising in a straight line and that the absolute quantity of industrial production is growing in a straight line. But this is not to say that the rate of growth of industry is also rising year after year. Unequal rates of growth in different time periods show that the rate of growth of industry sometimes rises and sometimes falls. It neither rises continuously nor falls continuously. Therefore, in analyzing the rate of growth of industry, we should not only consider the percentage rate of growth of industry, but should also consider the absolute value implied by every percentage point increase in industrial output.

III. The Proportional Relation between the Output of Producer Goods and the Output of Consumer Goods and the Relative Shares of Socialist Industry and Nonsocialist Industry in the Gross Value of Industrial Output

Industry is composed of many branches. Industry includes the machine-building industry, the metallurgical industry, the electric power industry, the fuel industry, the textile industry, the food industry, and other branches. These branches can be broadly classified into producer goods industries and consumer goods industries according to their different roles in social production. The former is generally referred to as type A, and the latter is generally referred to as type B.

The proportional relation between the production of type A and type B industries is the most important proportional relation in our economy's industrial production plan. It is also one of the most important proportional relations in the national economy. Industry is the leading sector of the national economy. The development of other sectors of the national economy is determined by the development of industry. Therefore, any change in the proportional relation between type A and type B industries also directly affects changes in many major targets of the national economic plan. The larger the share of industry in the national economy, the more evident this effect will be. For example, if the relative share of type A industry is increased when both type A and type B industries grow, because the products from type A industry cannot be used directly for people's consumption and can only be used to expand output, the proportional relation between accumulation and consumption in the national economy will change as a result of a change in the proportional relation of type A and type B industrial output. To develop type A industry rapidly, the number of workers must be appropriately increased. At the same time, because the average wage is higher in type A industry than in type B industry, the wage fund for type A industry is thus increased. On the other hand, when the relative share of type A industry is increased, the relative share of type B industry is reduced (although its absolute value is increased). Consequently, a contradiction between the people's purchasing power and the available supply of consumer goods arises, thus affecting the proportional relation between the total amount of wages and the total quantity of commodities in circulation. Everyone knows that agriculture produces raw materials for type B industry. The growth of type B industry must be geared to the growth of agriculture. Therefore, the proportional relation between type A and type B industries also greatly affects the proportional relation between industry and agriculture. It must be pointed out that although the proportional relation between type A and type B industries has an immense effect on the other proportional relations, there exists no direct quantitative dependence among them.

To sum up, the proportional relation between type A and type B industrial production has a bearing on the correct combination of social production needs and personal consumption needs as well as on the correct combination of long-term interests and short-term interests. Therefore, in national economic planning, the correct specification of the proportional relation between type A and type B industrial production is an extremely important and complex task.

The determination of the proportional relation between type A and type B industries is different from the determination of the material proportional relation among material production branches. There is not a fixed quantitative proportional relation. This proportional relation changes according to political and economic conditions at home and abroad. And it reflects the inner connections of those political and economic relations. Therefore, the general principle for the determination of the proportional relation between type A and type B industries is to guarantee the smooth realization of the political and economic tasks in the plan period.

The general direction of change in the proportional relation between type A and type B industrial production is to specify a higher rate of growth of type A industry than type B industry under the premise that both type A and type B industrial production will be raised at the same time. Thus, the relative share of type A industry in industry as a whole is gradually increased and the relative share of type B industry is correspondingly reduced. However, the extent to which the rate of growth of type A industry exceeds that of type B industry differs at different time periods. Analyzing from concrete economic processes, the major factors that determine the extent of change in the proportional relation between type A and type B industries are:

1. The proportional relation between type A and type B industrial production existing in the base period, namely, the structure of industrial production in the base period.

2. The proportional relation between the growth rate of capital construction investment and the growth rate of gross social production in the plan period.

3. National defense needs in the plan period.

If the difference between the proportion of type A and type B industries in the base period and the required proportion in the plan period is not too large, then the differential between the rate of growth of type A and type B industries is reduced somewhat. Otherwise, it is increased somewhat. The more the rate of growth of capital construction investment exceeds the rate of growth of gross social output, the more the growth rate of type A industry exceeds the growth rate of type B industry. This is because products from type A industry — machinery, equipment, and construction materials — are all essential materials for capital construction. The value of these products is gradually transferred to consumer goods over a long period of time. However, in the plan period, not all of these products will be directly used for increasing the production of consumer goods. Therefore, the larger the relative share of such products in the gross social output, the more the rate of growth of type A industry will exceed that of type B industry. Most of the national defense requirements consist of type A industrial products. After these products are produced, they always leave the circulating process of production forever and never again play a direct role in expanding social output. They do not become a factor in increasing type B industrial production either. Thus, the larger the national defense needs, the more the rate of growth of type A industry will exceed the rate of growth of type B industry.

The general direction of change in the proportional relation between type A and type B industries by no means excludes the possibility that the rate of growth of type B industry could exceed the rate of growth of type A industry in order to eliminate the backward condition of consumer goods production at particular times. However, the following conditions must be fulfilled for such situations: (1) the proportion of type A industry must already far exceed that of type B industry; (2) the machine-building industry must have already built a strong base; (3) the growth of agricultural output must guarantee the agricultural raw materials necessary for a rapid increase in the output of consumer goods. It must be explained that a faster rate of growth of type B industry than of type A industry at a particular time in no way implies a negation of the principle that producer goods should grow more rapidly, but is instead a result of the growth priority which has long been given to producer goods.

At present, China is in the industrialization period. The development of heavy industry is the central link for realizing national socialist industrialization. Therefore, the faster rate of growth of type A industry compared with that of type B industry must be guaranteed. Major manpower, material, and financial resources must be concentrated on the development of heavy industry and capital construction. When the rapid growth of type A industry is guaranteed, type B industrial production should be correspondingly developed.

As far as method is concerned, the principle to be followed in specifying the proportional relation between type A and type B industries is: the growth of type A industrial production should match the needs generated by the growth of social production; the growth of type B industrial production should match the increase in people's purchasing power.

In the transition period, China's industry has several economic components, namely: state-managed industry, cooperatively managed industry, public-private jointly managed industry, and privately managed industry. In addition, there is the large individual handicraft industry. Each economic component of Chinese industry has a certain function in China's present national economy. Therefore, in formulating the industrial production plan of the national economy, not only must we correctly specify the proportional relation between type A and type B industries, we must also make all-round arrangements for each economic component of industry in accordance with the policy of "overall planning and individual consideration." On this basis, the share of each economic component of industry is correctly determined. The continuous steady growth of socialist industry must be guaranteed and nonsocialist industry must be gradually transformed into socialist industry.

IV. Specify the Production Quotas for Major Industrial Products

In industrial production planning, all rates of growth and proportional relations among industries are determined by specifying the level of output for each major industrial product. The output levels for major industrial products are the basic targets of industrial production planning. They are the basis for the target of gross value of output in money terms. The formulation of the industrial production plan starts with suggested production quotas for major industrial products and ends with their final determination.

The task of correctly specifying in physical terms the output levels of major industrial products has immense significance for guaranteeing the realization of the political and economic task in the plan period. This is because the satisfaction of the various needs of the national economy and the solution of all kinds of economic tasks all require definite industrial products. Only by specifying the level of output of major industrial products can the economic links among various branches be concretely determined, enabling coordinated development among them.

20

There are many kinds of industrial products. It is not possible for the state to specify all their production quotas. Only when one of the following requisite conditions is fulfilled is the output level specified by the state: (1) products that play major roles in the national economy; (2) products that are closely related to the development of many sectors; and (3) products which are widely consumed and which need to be appropriately distributed. The number of products whose output is planned by the state should not be too large; nor should it be too small. If it is too large, the strength of the state planning organs will be so diluted as to affect the correct formulation of the output plan for major industrial products and restrict the initiative of localities and various branches' planning organs. If it is too small, the role of the state plan will be limited, leading easily to a lack of coordination. Thus, in every plan period, the state must reexamine and amend the catalog of planned products. With the development of China's industry and the successful trial manufacture and large-scale production of new products, the catalog of products must be suitably expanded every year according to needs.

The general procedure to determine the level of output of various major industrial products is: (1) understand how much the product is needed in the national economy; (2) calculate the material resources needed to produce the product; and (3) determine the level of output by balancing needs with resources.

To specify the level of output of major industrial products, we must first understand the amounts of various products which are needed by the national economy. This is because the goals of socialist production are determined by its commitment to satisfy social needs. Since each product has many consumers and the method of calculating the needs of each consumer is distinct, it is an extremely complex job to understand the amounts of various types of products needed by the national economy — particularly for products with many specifications and models. For example, it is especially difficult to determine precisely the amount of machinery needed. But an accurate determination of needs is a prerequisite for formulating plans. Therefore, we must do a good job in this.

The general procedure for understanding the needs for type A industrial products is: (1) Find out who the users of the product are, that is, list the units that need the product. (2) Calculate the amounts needed by each user, that is, determine the amount of the product used in connection with production flow on the basis of the unit's level of output and its fixed quota of consumption per unit of output.

21

[That is, determine the unit's input-output coefficient.] Thus, the amount of required stock of the product is computed according to the level of output, the fixed quota of consumption, and the reserves the user has. (3) Understand the market requirements. This is necessary because a very large part of China's type A industrial products is sold through the market. (4) Determine the reserve requirements of the state. (5) Decide the export requirements. Among units that need type A industrial products, the requirements of the users mentioned in item 2 above generally represent the largest share. Consequently, whether the calculation of their requirements is accurate or not is the key to whether the total requirements are accurately calculated or not. And the key to accurately calculating the needs under item 2 above is to determine correctly the input-output coefficient of the user. Therefore, in formulating the plan, the state must calculate amounts needed according to an average quota among advanced units.

The determination of requirements for type B industrial products is based on people's purchasing power and the structure of purchasing demand. This is because in formulating the production plan for type B industry at the present time, what is of practical importance is not the natural level of people's requirements but their present level of requirements under the constraint of purchasing power. Only when the highest stage of communism is reached can the requirements for consumer goods be fully satisfied.

After the requirements are determined, the material resources needed to produce the product must be taken into account. They are: (1) production capacity and its utilization rate; (2) circulating assets such as raw materials, processed materials, fuels, and electric power; and (3) labor.

The level of output of various industrial products is determined mainly by calculating the production capacity of industries and their utilization rates. However, in the case of type B industry which depends on agricultural products as raw materials, the problem of raw material supply must also be taken into account. In newly established enterprises, attention must be paid to the problem of training skilled workers. In sum, although production capacity and its utilization rate must be considered as major resources in determining the level of output of industrial products, other resources must also be fully considered. Tapping the potential for increasing output, raising the utilization rate of facilities, economizing on raw materials, using substitutes, and raising labor productivity are all important ways of accelerating the growth of industrial production on the basis of currently existing resources. Therefore, correctly determining the utilization rate of facilities and the rates of consumption of raw materials and labor in the advanced units has immense significance for fully tapping resources and developing industrial production.

After needs and resources are separately determined, they are coordinated through the formulation of material balance tables. A separate material balance table must be formulated for each product whose output is planned. Therefore, in the production plan for the whole industry, hundreds, or even thousands, of material balance tables must be formulated. Among these balance tables, those for equipment, steel products, fuels, electric power, and cement in type A industry and for textiles, food, and granulated sugar in type B industry have a decisive significance for the formulation of the whole national economic plan. Therefore, the problem of balance in these balance tables must be solved first.

The initial formulation of material balance tables is invariably out of balance. Also, requirements generally exceed resources. This is because under the socialist system, requirements always lead production and provide impetus to output. This is a very good phenomenon. However, it is necessary to tap resources, calculate needs, and carry out systematic balancing in order to achieve a balance of requirements with resources in each balance table. Only on the basis of balance can the output of each industrial product be correctly determined.

Note

1. Stalin, "On the Tasks of Economic Administrators," Jen-min ch'u-pan-she, 1953 edition, p. 13. [Speech to the First All-Union Conference of Leading Personnel of Socialist Industry, February 4, 1931, published in Pravda, February 5, 1931. — N. R. L.]

LECTURE 6: AGRICULTURAL PRODUCTION PLANNING

Yen Shao-ch'un*

I. The Basic Task of Agricultural Production Planning

Like industry, agriculture is one of society's most important material production sectors. Agriculture is the source of food. It is also a source of raw materials for light industry and a major market for industrial products. At present, China's agricultural products are also one of its major exports. Without rapid growth of agricultural output, rapid industrial growth will be hampered, and it will be very hard to raise the people's standard of living.

The important role of agriculture in the growth of the national economy determines the basic tasks of agricultural production planning. These tasks are: rapidly increase agricultural output, guarantee the satisfaction of the people's need for food and light industry's need for raw materials, and establish reserves of food and raw materials in order to guarantee the smooth progress of socialist industrialization.

To guarantee the fulfillment of the above tasks, when formulating the agricultural production plan, we must correctly work out the rate of growth of agricultural output (including that of marketed output) and the proportions of growth among the various agricultural branches.

II. The Proportional Relation between the Rate of Growth of Agricultural Production and the Growth of the Branches of Agriculture

Correctly determining the rate of growth of agricultural output and the proportionate growth of various agricultural branches and

*Yen Shao-ch'un, "Nung-yeh sheng-ch'an chi-hua." CHCC, 1955, No. 6, pp. 27-31.

continuously struggling to increase agricultural output, especially marketed agricultural output, are the central issues in formulating the agricultural production plan. Because of the growth of industry and other sectors of the national economy, the rapid increase of the urban population, and the continuous improvement in the people's standard of living, the need for agricultural products such as food grains, vegetables, and meat increases daily. At the same time, the rapid growth of industry also steadily increases the need for agricultural raw materials such as cotton, oil-bearing crops, and wool. If agriculture cannot increase its production in the proper proportion, it will not be able to satisfy the national economy's need for agricultural products. In today's China, fulfilling this need is also a necessary condition for guaranteeing the smooth progress of industrialization.

As a general rule, the rate of growth of agriculture is lower than that of industry. Because industry is the sector that provides technical equipment to the national economy, giving priority to the growth of industry is a fundamental condition for the continuous growth of agriculture. The so-called proper proportionate growth of agriculture really is not setting the growth rate of agriculture equal to that of industry; it means that the marketed output supplied by agriculture can satisfy the needs of industrial growth. The growth rates of marketed agricultural output and gross agricultural output are not equal. Their general pattern is: When gross agricultural output grows rapidly, the share of agricultural products consumed within the agricultural sector itself is reduced and the rate of marketing of agricultural products increases. Therefore, the rate of growth of marketed output is higher than that of gross output.

To increase agricultural production rapidly and to make the growth of marketed output be in the proper proportion to the growth of industry, agricultural production equipment must be based on a technology and an economic foundation that correspond to the socialist industry, that is, socialist agriculture with equipment embodying new technology. This is because agricultural production based on a loosely organized, small peasant economy cannot accommodate the growth of socialist industry. A loosely organized, small peasant economy cannot fully utilize agricultural technology, agricultural machinery, and the achievement of agricultural science. Consequently, the rate of marketing of agricultural products is very low. This contradiction is inevitable in the early stages of industrialization. Only with the growth of cooperativization in heavy industry and agriculture can it be gradually overcome.

In each plan period, the rate of growth of agricultural output is determined by the possibility of increasing the area of land under cultivation, the producer goods, and manpower and of raising the level of agricultural technology. At the same time, in specifying the rate of growth of agricultural output, we must also consider the effects of natural calamities. The effects of natural calamities cause a certain element of instability in agricultural output. This element of instability is especially pronounced under the conditions of the small peasant economy.

The fact that the growth of agricultural output is not steady enough makes it somewhat difficult to coordinate overall national economic planning. To prevent possible dislocations, we must establish large reserves of agricultural products, especially of food grains.

At any given level of output and consumption, a definite proportion exists among the national economy's needs for various types of agricultural products. There is also a definite proportion enabling further output that exists among various agricultural branches (for example, the proportion between animal husbandry and the production of fodder). Only by correctly specifying the proportional relations for the growth of various agricultural branches can the people's needs for various types of agricultural products be satisfied. This is also a fundamental condition for ensuring coordination between the output and the sales of agricultural products and for an upsurge in the whole of agricultural output. Correctly specifying the proportional relations of the growth of the various agricultural branches has even greater significance for formulating long-term plans for the growth of agricultural output.

When formulating agricultural production plans, we should pay attention to the following major proportional relations.

1. The proportion between crop production and animal husbandry.

The general pattern governing change in this proportion is: When the rate of growth of gross agricultural output increases, the rate of growth of animal husbandry will be faster than that of crop production. Consequently, the share of animal husbandry in gross agricultural output will gradually increase. This change is determined by a change in the composition of people's consumption. The higher the people's standard of living, the higher the proportion of consumer goods such as meat, milk, oil, and woolen fabrics in people's consumption. Consequently, the output of animal husbandry must be increased correspondingly.

The above pattern should be the basis for arranging the proportions of growth between crop production and animal husbandry. The extent to which the rate of growth of animal husbandry exceeds that of crop production primarily depends on the feasible conditions, above all, on the level of output of staple foods.

2. The proportions of the output of various types of crops within crop production itself.

The general pattern is: With the rapid growth of crop production, the growth rate of the output of staple food crops will be lower than those of industrial crops, fodder crops, and horticultural crops. Consequently, the relative share of staple food crops in the output of crop production will gradually decrease. This change is also determined by a change in the composition of people's consumption. With the increasing satisfaction of people's staple food requirements, the needs for light industrial products, vegetables, and fruits will steadily increase. Therefore, in specifying the growth rates of various types of crops, the growth rates for industrial, fodder and horticultural crops should generally be set comparatively high. If the output level of staple food is very high, the growth rates of the above crops can be set even higher.

3. The proportions in the reproduction of various types of animals.

The general development pattern of this proportion is: The growth rate for small domestic animals (pigs, sheep, and so forth) must be higher than the growth rate of large domestic animals (cattle, horses, donkeys, mules, and so forth). Among small domestic animals, the growth rate of pigs should be higher than that of sheep. Among large domestic animals, the growth rate of cattle should be the fastest. This trend is determined by the following three factors combined: (1) the national economy's need for various types of animals and their products, (2) the breeding rate of various types of animals, and (3) the breeding value of various types of animals.

From the above trends of growth in the proportions among various agricultural branches, we can see that the growth rate of staple food production should be relatively slower, but this is not to say that staple food production is not essential. On the contrary, the growth of various agricultural branches is based on the growth of staple food output. And the rates of growth of other agricultural branches primarily depend on the level of staple food output.

It was only because the output level of food in the Soviet Union was high that she could propose a rapid growth in animal husbandry and the production of industrial crops. The measures that were adopted to achieve this involved rapidly developing staple food production. This is because if the problem of staple food is not solved first, the supply of staple food and fodder to the industrial crop regions and pastoral areas cannot be guaranteed. Consequently, the output of industrial crops and animal husbandry cannot be developed rapidly. At present, because of China's backwardness in staple food output, the growth of other agricultural branches is also restricted. Therefore, in order to have all agricultural branches grow rapidly and to specify correctly the proportions of growth among various agricultural branches according to the national economy's needs, we must first rapidly increase the output of staple foods.

Rapidly increasing the output of staple foods and guaranteeing the supply of staple foods is also a precondition for achieving a proper distribution of agricultural output according to the economic conditions and natural characteristics of various regions.

To sum up, the guiding principles for arranging the proportions of growth among the various agricultural branches are: The development of output in the various agricultural branches must be in proper proportion with the national economy's needs for various types of agricultural products, and the output of the various agricultural branches must be in proper proportion with the expansion of output within agriculture itself.

III. Specify the Output for Major Agricultural Products

The growth rate of agriculture and its proportional relations are realized through specifying the output for agricultural products. To formulate the agricultural production plan, we must start with the formulation of the output plans for various major agricultural products.

The first step in formulating such plans is to do research and calculate the national economy's need for the particular agricultural products.

In agricultural planning, it is extremely important to calculate the amount of need for various types of agricultural products. If there are discrepancies between the calculated and the actual need, the agricultural production plan thus formulated will not be accurate, and dislocations in the form of either surpluses or shortages of certain products will be inevitable.

To calculate accurately the amount of need is a complex job. Because every product must satisfy a whole range of needs at once and because the same needs are often satisfied by more than one product, the calculation of needs must be based on complex economic analyses which draws on much statistical data.

For example, in order to calculate the national economy's need for staple foods, it is necessary to analyze and determine the following needs: (1) the increasing need for staple foods resulting from an improvement in people's standard of living; (2) the need resulting from population increases; (3) the need resulting from the expansion of area sown to industrial crops; (4) the need resulting from growth of animal husbandry; (5) the increase of staple food inventories and reserves; (6) the need for seeds; and (7) the export needs. The increase of each of the above requirements depends in turn on the relation between the increase in production and consumption. To accurately calculate each of these needs, it is necessary to conduct a series of complex economic analyses. For example, to estimate the increase in the need for staple foods resulting from an improvement in people's standards of living, it is necessary to analyze the degree to which these needs were satisfied in the base period and the extent to which people's standards of living can be expected to rise in the plan period. This analysis must also be conducted separately by urban and rural areas, by region, and by types of staple foods respectively. The complexity of this analysis lies in the fact that every factor is in turn affected by many conditions. For example, the extent to which people's standards of living can be expected to increase in the plan period is influenced by the degree of increase in people's income in the urban and rural areas, price changes, and so forth.

The calculation of need is made through the compilation of requirements tables. Accurately determining consumption quotas (such as the average per capita staple food consumption quota, the average per animal fodder quota, and so forth) is the most important and complex job in compiling requirements tables. Whether or not these quotas are correct greatly affects the accuracy of the requirements tables. Consequently, regularly accumulating data and carrying out economic analysis and research is necessary for accurately formulating quotas.

In addition, the output of each type of agricultural product must be determined not only according to need but also according to feasibility. Therefore, the second step in planning agricultural output is to calculate resources and tap potentials for increasing output.

As far as crop production is concerned, the feasibility of increasing the output of various types of agricultural products in the plan period depends on increasing the yield per unit of area of the particular crop and expanding its sown area, the former being the most important of the two.

The level of yield per unit of area depends directly on the following technical conditions in agricultural production: (1) the power and agricultural implements used; (2) the introduction of superior seed and seed selection; (3) irrigation, water and soil conservation, and soil improvement; (4) the quality of farming techniques; (5) the prevention and control of floods, drought, and pests; and (6) the quality of harvesting. In addition, soil, climate, and other natural conditions also greatly affect the level of yield per unit of area. To increase yields per unit of area continuously and rapidly, we must improve the above technical conditions for agricultural production by formulating a plan of technical measures for agricultural production.

The plan for agricultural technical measures must be formulated on the basis of the technical policies of the Party and the state for developing agricultural output in the plan period and in relation to the concrete conditions in each locality.

Deciding targets for yields per unit of area according to agricultural technical measures is a complex problem in agricultural planning. Because an increase in the yield per unit of area is a result of the combined effects of all technical measures it is not possible to prepare a plan of yields per unit of area by a simple sum of the effects produced by each type of measure.

There are many ways to plan yields per unit of area. Of them, the most scientific method is to plan yields per unit of area after investigating the yields per unit of area in advanced production units. This method is especially suitable for the formulation of long-term plans. The content of this method is: (1) group advanced units by the degree to which their yields per unit of area repeatedly exceeded the stable yields per unit of area in the past few years; (2) study the conditions under which they achieved these yields; (3) decide whether it would be feasible for other production units to create similar conditions in the plan period; and (4) if it is possible for other production units to produce similar conditions, then it is all right to specify the same yields per unit of area. The major difficulty in applying this method lies in how the models are selected.

In formulating annual plans, since the conditions determining yields per unit of area are unlikely to change a great deal, a reverse procedure is adopted in the application of this method. It is: (1) first determine the probability that the conditions determining yields per unit of area will improve in the plan period; and (2) then find out the yields per unit of area already achieved in the base period by some advanced production units under similar conditions. These yields can then be used as the planned yields per unit of area.

To make the planned yields per unit of area better correspond with reality, it is necessary to grasp and analyze regularly the past variations in yields per unit of area and the functional relation between an increase in the yield per unit of area and various conditions (soil, climate, agricultural technology, production organizations, and so forth). These analyses must be conducted by region, crop, type of economy, and production units with differing yields.

The yield per unit of area of a given crop can be initially calculated by pooling the data on yields per unit of area obtained by the above method.

After the yields per unit of area of various types of crops have been initially determined, the sown area for each type of crop can then be determined. The procedure is as follows:

First, the initially determined yield per unit of area of each type of crop is multiplied by its respective sown area in the base period to obtain initial estimates of the gross output of each crop. Then, the initial estimate of the gross output of each crop is compared with the national economy's need for it to see whether the area sown to the crop should be expanded or contracted. By calculating the expansion or contraction of the area sown to each type of crop, the gross sown area in the plan period can be determined.

Expanding the sown area depends on expanding the area under cultivation and increasing the multiple crop index, the former being the more important.

Expanding the cultivated area itself depends on many things. The first is the amount of cultivable land. This in turn is related to the land area of the country, the composition of the land, and the degree of utilization of the cultivable land in the base period. The second is the amount of effort to be devoted to land reclamation during the plan period. This is mainly reflected in the amount of capital construction investment in agriculture.

The multiple crop index depends primarily on climatic conditions. For instance, the longer the frost-free period is, the higher the multiple crop index can be. Secondarily, it depends on the extent to which the cultivated land is used. This is related to agricultural technology and farming practice. If the extent to which the cultivated land is utilized is low, then the multiple crop index can be increased.

Based on variations in the multiple crop index during the plan period, the amount of expansion in the total sown area can be determined.

Usually, the extent to which the total sown area can be expanded is less than what is required. Consequently, it is necessary to rationally distribute this limited total sown area among each crop.

Changes in the proportional distribution of the sown area are more or less in proportion to changes in the output proportions of crops. From the long-term data on Soviet practice, the trend of proportional changes in the distribution of the sown area is as follows: the area sown to industrial crops, horticultural crops, and fodder crops increased, while the area sown to staple food crops decreased. Among the staple food crops, the area sown to refined grain increased. The question of which crops' sown area should be increased and which crops' sown area should be decreased must be decided on the basis of concrete conditions in the plan period.

After we determine the extent of increase or decrease in the sown area to the various types of crops, we must still allocate them by region. This distribution must be made according to the principle of gradually realizing rational procurement of agricultural production.

If the sown area allocated to some crops is inadequate to satisfy the needs, further steps have to be taken to tap production potentials, and the initial proposals for increasing the yields per unit of area of those crops have to be amended.

The policy governing output increases in China's agriculture in the present stage emphasizes raising the yields per unit of area and where conditions permit, expanding cultivated area. According to estimates, there are more than 100 million hectares of cultivable land in China that has not been cultivated. But, because China is at present concentrating her major efforts on developing heavy industry, conditions do not yet exist for the large-scale use of machines for land reclamation. Only in regions where favorable conditions are present can land reclamation be conducted on any significant scale. Therefore, there is a limit to how much the cultivated area can be expanded. But on the other hand, the potential for increasing yields per unit of area is still great. Only if we energetically develop agricultural production cooperatives and popularize new farm tools and other measures, will it be entirely feasible to further increase agricultural output.

As for animal husbandry, the feasibility of increasing the production of each type of animal product during the plan period depends on the number of animals producing the particular product and the product yield from each animal, increasing the number of animals being the major factor.

Increasing the number of each type of animal depends directly on the following conditions: (1) The original composition of the herds and flocks. The larger the share of female animals, the greater the rate of multiplication. From the angle of a long-term plan, the larger the share of young female animals, the faster the animals will multiply. (2) The natural reproduction of animals. This is related to the utilization rate of female animals. If artificial insemination is done well, the natural multiplication of animals will also be greater. (3) The survival rate of young animals and the death rate of animals. This is related to the control of animal diseases and wolves and to general care. (4) The slaughter rate of animals and the composition of the slaughtered animals. The higher the slaughter rate, the smaller the number of animals left for reproduction. If those which are slaughtered are mostly old, male animals, the effect on the multiplication of the herds and flocks is relatively small.

The method for planning the number of the various types of animals is the method of herd or flock turnover, that is, the compilation of balance tables for animal group turnover. The characteristic of this method is that it can comprehensively reflect the variations in the composition of particular animal groups and the equilibrium between animal group resources and the needs for them.

Increasing the output of each type of animal product also depends on increasing the output per animal. The rate at which the animals produce depends on three things: the breed of animal, the quality and quantity of fodder, and the quality of the animal's care.

If the needs are still not satisfied by raising the rate of output per animal, measures must then be taken to increase the number of animals.

Whether in the formulation of plans for yields per unit of area and the sown area of crops or for the number of animals and the rate of output per animal, it must be in proper proportion with the producer goods and production technology which can be supplied and the organization of labor in the plan period. Therefore, in order to formulate plans for increased output of each type of crop, we must at the same time compile a series of related plans and balance tables. Examples are plans for technical measures for agriculture, supply plans for major producer goods, and balance tables for cultivated area, draft animals, agricultural machines and tractors, fodder, and so forth. Without calculating these comprehensive balances of material resources and guaranteeing of these planned measures, it would be impossible to formulate and realize various plans for increasing output.

Not only that, but under the present conditions in China, the output increase plans of various types of crops must also be formulated with reference to the plan for agricultural cooperativization. This is because many measures to increase agricultural output and to advance agricultural technology are conditional on the development of cooperativization.

Targets for increasing the output of each crop are determined by a process of repeated balancing between resources and needs. This process of repeated balancing is also the process for establishing correct proportions between the output of agricultural products and relevant aspects of the national economy. For example, suppose that in specifying the cotton output target, after the initial balancing, it is discovered that the resources cannot meet the needs. We should first consider increasing output to achieve a balance. If we solve the problem by increasing the share of the area sown to cotton, the proportion between cotton and the output of other crops will be affected. If we solve the problem through land reclamation, the proportion between investment in agricultural construction and in industrial construction will be affected. If we do not increase cotton output enough, it will influence the proportions of the output of the textile industry. In addition, other proportions related to the above proportions will also be affected. The process for balancing cotton output is simply the process for establishing the above proportional relations.

The balancing of the various agricultural products is conducted through the compilation of material balance tables for those agricultural products. Examples are the staple food balance table, the cotton balance table, the oils balance table, the animal food-products balance table, and the balance table for animal products for industrial use.

In addition to compiling the balance tables for gross output to determine gross output targets, balance tables for marketed output must also be compiled to determine marketed output targets.

This is because the coordination and balance among the plan targets for agriculture, industry, commerce, and transportation are based on marketed output targets.

IV. The Characteristics of Agricultural Production Planning

The following major characteristics are present in formulating and implementing the agricultural production plan.

First of all, the agricultural production plan formulated in China at the present stage is only an estimate. This feature of the agricultural plan results from the predominance of the small peasant economy in China's agriculture at present.

In the small peasant economy, producer goods are privately owned. Production is backward and scattered. Therefore, these factors determine that:

1. The agricultural production plan formulated by the state, unlike the agricultural production plan in a socialist state, which is based on scientific statistics and plans of collective farms, can only be formulated on the basis of surveys and estimates. As a result, its accuracy is comparatively low.

2. The agricultural production plan formulated by the state can only serve as a set of control figures for the planning agency to balance and manipulate. It is not to be conveyed directly to the peasants in the form of targets. Plan implementation depends primarily on a series of political mobilizations and economic measures. Of these, the primary ones are unified purchasing and marketing policy, price policy, and the system of advance purchase contracts. The strengthening of the above measures is in turn closely related to the development of the cooperativization movement. The better these measures are carried out, the more assured the realization of the state agricultural production plan will be. Even so, the implementation of the plan can at best be approximate.

Second, the formulation of the agricultural production plan is scattered and regional in nature. This feature is a result of the natural conditions of agricultural production. Agricultural production is heavily dependent on climate, soil, and other natural conditions. And different regions have very different natural conditions. In order that the formulation of the agricultural production plan can more closely match the actual conditions of various regions and to achieve the goal of arranging for agricultural production according to those conditions, the formultion of the agricultural production plan must rely primarily on the basic planning units. The planning agencies at the top simply check and balance on a comprehensive basis. When arranging agricultural production and specifying the quotas for marketed output, consideration must be given to the climate and soil conditions of each region. It is especially important to consider each region's natural conditions in formulating the plan for agricultural technical measures in order to prevent the tendency of "uncritical approbation."

Explanations of Some Terms Used in This Lecture

Cultivated Area: Cultivated area refers to the irrigated and unirrigated land area sown to various crops. It includes the land which has been cultivated for a long time, newly reclaimed land, land reclaimed within three years, and land left fallow for the year. Land devoted primarily to crops but which has some fruit trees and mulberry trees is still regarded as cultivated land. However, specialized orchards, mulberry tree farms, natural steppes, and grazing land are not regarded as cultivated land.

Sown Area: Sown area refers to the land area having standing crops. It is the area from which agricultural products are expected to be obtained at the end of each crop season. However, in calculating the sown area, land area which can produce two or three crops a year is counted twice or three times respectively.

Sown area and crop area are synonyms. Now we uniformly use the term sown area.

Staple Food Crops: This is a collective term for rice (paddy rice and unirrigated rice), wheat, soybeans (yellow beans, black beans, and green beans), miscellaneous grain (maize, sorghum, millet, barley, Tibetan wheat, buckwheat, glutinous millet, [another] sorghum, polished rice, broad beans, garden peas, and so forth). In addition, tuber crops (sweet potatoes, potatoes, and other tuber crops) are also included because they are often used as staple foods in China. In the Soviet Union, soybeans are classified as industrial crops, and potatoes are classified in a separate category called root tuber crops.

Industrial Crops: Industrial crops included in China's plans are primarily cotton, jute, ramie, baked tobacco, sugarcane, sugar beets, and oil-bearing crops (peanuts, sesame seeds, rape seeds, linseed, hemp, sunflower, castor oil seeds, and perilla ocymoides).

In the Soviet Union, industrial crops include fiber crops, oil-bearing crops, spices, medicinal herbs, rubber, Malay gum trees, sugar-bearing crops, other industrial root crops (lettuce, sweet potatoes, and others), tobacco, tea, hops (yeast), and other industrial crops (rushes, loofah gourds).

36

LECTURE 7: TRANSPORT PLANNING

Kuo Tzu-ch'eng*

I. The Basic Tasks of Transport Planning

The transport industry is a special material production branch. Transport is a direct continuation of the production process in the circulation process. The transport industry is different from other material production branches. Its special characteristic is that on the one hand it reflects the production process while on the other hand it belongs to the realm of circulation. Consequently, transport planning reflects not only the production process but also the circulation process.

There are many modes of transport in the national economy, such as railroad transport, motor vehicle transport, river transport, ocean transport, air transport, and so forth. The transport plan of the national economy is a plan that includes all kinds of transport. But in countries with huge land masses, such as China and the Soviet Union, the volume of transport carried by the railroad is the largest. Consequently, the railroad transport plans of these countries occupy the most important position in their overall transport plans.

The transport requirements of the national economy and the people are freight and passenger carriage. Therefore, transport can be classified into freight transport and passenger transport. And the basic tasks in formulating the transport plan are to satisfy fully the national economy's increasing demand for freight transport and the people's increasing demand for passenger transport.

To formulate the transport plan correctly, it is first necessary to accurately determine the following important proportions:

First, the proportion between the transport demand of the national economy and the people and the distribution of these

---

*Kuo Tzu-ch'eng, "Yun-shu chi-hua." <u>CHCC</u>, 1955, No. 8, pp. 30-33.

demands among various modes of transport.

Second, the proportion between the demand of each mode of transport for capital goods and the output of these capital goods.

II. Determine the National Economy's Demand for Freight Transport

The national economy's demand for freight transport is expressed by the volume of freight turnover. The volume of freight turnover is the volume of work of the transport industry. Its cost is determined by the freight rates.

To determine the volume of freight turnover, it is first necessary to determine the volume of freight transport (tonnage) and the transport distance (kilometers). This is because the volume of freight turnover is the product of the volume of freight transport and the distance of transport. The volume of freight turnover is expressed in "ton-kilometers."

The volume of freight transport is primarily determined by the scale of material production, that is, the volume of material output. Since transport is a continuation of the production process, changes in the scale of material production are necessarily reflected in the transport process.

Unlike capitalist production, socialist production grows at steady and high rates. Therefore, regular growth in the volume of freight transport is the general pattern of socialist transport development. This pattern is the basis for our calculation of the volume of freight transport and the rate of growth of freight transport. But because the rate of growth of output varies from year to year, the rate of growth of the volume of freight transport also varies from year to year. For instance, the annual growth rates of the volume of freight transport in the First Five-Year Plan of the Soviet Union were: 14 percent in 1928, 21 percent in 1929, 18 percent in 1930, 14 percent in 1931, and 11 percent in 1932. Therefore, in planning the growth rates of the volume of freight transport, it is not enough merely to know the general pattern. It is also necessary to concretely analyze the annual rate of growth of output. In the national economic plan, the higher the specified rate of growth of industrial and agricultural output, the higher must be the planned rate of growth of the volume of freight transport. But the growth rates of the two are not the same. The reason is that the composition of material output and the share of the output of various goods that do not have to be transported are subject to frequent changes.

Changes in the composition of material output themselves do not directly affect the growth rate of the volume of freight transport. They are worth studying primarily because the transport coefficients of various types of products are different. A product's so-called transport coefficient refers to the ratio of the transport volume to the volume of output of the product. For instance, if the output of coal is 100 tons and the transport volume is 80 tons, then its transport coefficient is 0.8. The transport coefficients of various products differ. Transport coefficients of products transported by railroad in the Soviet Union in 1940 are as follows:

Product	Coefficient
Coal	0.87
Petroleum products	0.95
Iron ore	0.87
Sugar beets	0.46
Potatoes	0.04
Cement	0.90
Peat	0.32

Because the transport coefficients of various products are different, the rate of growth of the volume of freight transport is affected by changes in the composition of material output. In the plan period, if the share of output of products with high transport coefficients is increased, the planned rate of growth of the volume of freight transport should be higher than the rate of growth of output, and vice versa. To make this easily understood, we give the following simple examples:

Example 1

	Output			Transport volume	
	Base period	Plan period	Transport coefficient	Base period	Plan period
Mineral-type construction materials	50	100	0.4	20	40
Coal	50	200	0.8	40	160
	100	300		60	200

+ 200 percent (Rate of output)

+ 233 percent (Rate of transport volume)

39

Example 2

	Output			Transport volume	
	Base period	Plan period	Transport coefficient	Base period	Plan period
Mineral-type construction materials	50	200	0.4	20	80
Coal	50	100	0.8	40	80
	100	300		60	160

+ 200 percent (Rate of output)

+ 166 percent (Rate of transport volume)

The above examples show that because the transport coefficients of the two products are different (low for mineral-type construction materials and high for coal), the rate of growth of the volume of freight transport should be planned higher than the growth rate of output if the composition of output changes as in Example 1 (the relative share of coal in the total output increasing). The opposite applies if Example 2 holds.

Changes in the proportion of nontransported products among all the products depend primarily on variations in the amount of these products which are consumed locally. Suppose that in the plan period the local consumption of a certain product increases. Then the amount of this product that has to be transported will be reduced. This also implies that the transport coefficient of this product will be reduced. In these circumstances, the planned rate of growth of the volume of freight transport should be lower than the growth rate of output, and vice versa. From this, we can see that in order to determine the volume of freight transport and its rate of growth, it is necessary to study: (1) the rate of growth of output; (2) the transport coefficients of each kind of product; and (3) changes in the composition of output and changes in the proportion of nontransported products among all the various products.

We mentioned earlier that the volume of freight turnover is the product of the volume of freight transport and the transport distance. Therefore, to plan the volume of freight turnover, it is also necessary to determine the distance of freight transport. The transport distance depends on four factors: (1) the regional distribution of the state's productive forces; (2) the relations between the producing areas and the consuming areas; (3) changes in the composition of freight; and (4) the transport share of each mode of transport.

The principle governing the regional distribution of socialist productive forces is to locate the producing areas near the sources of raw materials and fuels and the consuming areas. This will shorten the distance of transport. However, at some periods of time, we may well have the opposite situation. For instance, in the early stages of socialist construction, the establishment of some new industrial areas requires a large amount of material assistance from the old industrial areas, and the new industrial areas are generally quite far from the old industrial areas. This not only makes it impossible to reduce the distance of transport, but instead lengthens it. We can see this tendency in the data related to the Soviet Union's economic recovery period and her First and Second Five-Year Plans.

Average Transport Distance of Material Resources
Carried by the Railroad of the Soviet Union
(in kilometers)

Year	1913	1928	1932	1939
All material resources	496	598	632	686

In China, with the growth of state-operated industries and the establishment of many new industrial areas, the transport distance is bound to lengthen for some time. But we must point out that this lengthening of transport distances is only a temporary phenomenon. It is inevitable in the process of national economic development and is beneficial to the national economy. After the establishment of new industrial areas is completed the old economic ties among regions will change and this phenomenon will gradually fade away.

With a given regional distribution of productive forces, the transport distance will vary if the mutual relations between the producing and the consuming areas are different. Because a single producing area can have ties with many consuming areas but the distance between the producing area and each consuming area differs, if the producing area has ties to the closest consuming areas, the transport distance will be reduced. Otherwise, it will be lengthened. For example, before 1954 the anthracite coal needed in Peking was transported from the Chao-tso Coal Mine but the anthracite coal of Men-t'ou-kou near Peking was transported southward. This method of linking with the far and ignoring the near obviously lengthened the transport distance.

The effects on the transport distance owing to changes in the composition of freight transported result mainly from changes in the proportions between long-distance freight and short-distance freight in the total freight transported. If in the plan period the proportion of long-distance freight increases while that of short-distance freight decreases, the average distance of freight transport will lengthen. But if the proportion of short-distance freight increases, then the average distance of freight transport will be reduced.

Various modes of transport can be used to transport goods from one area to another. But within the same area the length of the routes of different modes of transport will vary. For instance, the routes of river transport are constrained by the natural distribution of rivers. In general, river routes are longer than railroad routes within a given area. Therefore, if in the plan period the proportion of freight transported by modes of transport with long routes increases, then the average transport distance will lengthen. Otherwise, it will be reduced.

Thus, we can see that the determination of the transport distance is dependent on changes in the above four factors. Of these, the regional distribution of the whole country's productive forces is of primary importance.

Above, we have studied how to determine the volume of freight transport and the transport distance from the analysis of various factors. Below, we will talk further about the methods of determining the volume of freight transport and the transport distance.

The primary method of determining the volume of freight transport is that of balancing. Specifically, it is the compilation of the economic balance table for transport. There are both national and regional economic balance tables for transport. Through the national economic balance table for transport, we can determine the transport volumes of bulk freight, such as raw coal, charcoal, mineral ores, iron and steel, timber, petroleum, mineral-type construction materials, and staple foods. With regard to other commodities, because there are a great many varieties whose transport volume is small, it is not necessary to compile individual balance tables. Their transport volumes can be determined from their proportion in the gross transport volume.

To determine accurately the volume of freight transport, it is necessary to compile regional economic balance tables for transport. This is because national economic balance tables for transport can only indicate the transport volume of major goods on a nationwide basis. But the process of freight transport is a concrete one. We must know the types and quantities of goods which are to be transported into and out of each region. Therefore, it is necessary to investigate the material resources which must be transported for the exporting and importing areas and to establish inter-relationships among the areas in the matter of freight transport. We determine these interrelationships by means of regional economic balance tables for transport.

Although the method of balancing is the primary method of determining the volume of freight transport, it requires complete statistical data and a good deal of time. Therefore, when statistical data are incomplete and the volume of freight transport must be submitted in a relatively short time, another, simpler, method, called the method of coefficients, can also be used. To use this method, we must first calculate the output of products and their transport coefficients. Suppose the output of coal is 4,000 tons and the transport coefficient is 0.9, then the transport volume is 3,600 tons. This calculation is approximate because the transport coefficient is frequently affected by changes in local consumption, inventory, and by imports. Therefore, the accuracy of the volume of freight transport determined by this method is lower. It is only a supplementary method.

There are two major methods of determining the distance of transport. One is the method of shortest transport distance. This method is the simplest. It involves linking the producing area to the closest consuming area. But the shortest transport distance is not necessarily the most economical. For instance, area A is 400 kilometers from area B and 500 kilometers from area C. The freight rate between area A and area B is 6 yuan per ton-kilometer, but it is only 4 yuan between area A and area C. Under these conditions, the total freight cost between area A and area B is 2,400 yuan, but it is only 2,000 yuan between area A and area C. From this, we can see that the method of shortest transport distance has its drawbacks. The second method is based on the lowest transport cost. This method involves choosing from among several transport distances with varying transport costs, the transport distance with the lowest overall transport cost. Generally speaking, this is economically beneficial. Needless to say, when we decide which of the two above methods to adopt, we must still start from the political and economic tasks of the country at the present stage and the transport needs of the whole country.

III. How to Allocate the Volume of Freight Transport among Various Modes of Transport

After the volume of freight transport needed by the national economy has been determined, the next step in the planning work is to allocate the volume of freight transport among various modes of transport.

Correctly allocating freight transport has immense significance for the national economy. If freight transport is not correctly allocated, the transport capacities of some modes of transport may be overloaded while the transport capacities of other modes are lying idle. This not only would affect the balanced growth of different modes of transport, but would also lengthen the delivery time for freight, thereby obstructing the normal progress of production. This would not be at all beneficial to the growth of the national economy.

The allocation of the volume of freight transport among various modes of transport depends on the qualitative demands placed on transport by the national economy. These qualitative demands are: (1) low transport expenditures; (2) fast transport; (3) wide geographical coverage; and (4) high continuity. Each mode of transport satisfies these demands in varying degrees, but none of them can fully satisfy these demands. For example, although ocean and river transport are the cheapest, they are slow, and their continuity and geographical coverage are also low. On the other hand, air and truck transport have the opposite characteristics. Although their freight rates are high, their speed and coverage are also high.

How then should we allocate freight transport according to these demands? We must consider this from the perspective of the whole national economy. As far as the needs of national economic development are concerned, the most important factors are low transport costs and high speed. This is because low transport costs reflect economy of labor consumption in the transport process, and rapid transport can accelerate the circulation process of social production and promote the growth of the national economy. Consequently, we should determine the relative loads of freight transport assigned to each mode of transport according to how well they can satisfy these two requirements. In this respect, because the freight rates of railroad transport are relatively low and its speed is relatively high with high continuity and wide coverage, the relative load of freight transport assigned to the railroad is the largest. In the Soviet Union, it represented about 80 percent of the total volume of freight transport. The same is generally true for China.

When considering the transport cost, we should also consider the influence of the transport cost on the output price of the product. This is because each different product has a different output price. And the same transport cost will affect the output price of products to varying degrees. In general, products with a low output price, such as timber, staple foods, and mineral-type construction materials, should be allocated to those modes of transport with low transport cost. The freight rate has little effect on the value of products with high output prices, such as scarce medicines, precision instruments, and so forth, so they should be allocated to those modes of transport with high transport value because the transport expense has a small influence on the price. To sum up, the allocation of freight transport among various modes of transport depends primarily on the cost and speed of transport.

However, the total value of transport and the total time required for freight transport also depend on the distance of transport. Therefore, when we plan the allocation of the volume of freight transport among the various modes of transport, we must keep the distance in mind.

Based on the transport volume and distance of each good thus determined, we can obtain the volume of freight turnover for each type of good. And the sum of the volume of freight transport for each type of good carried by a given mode of transport is the gross volume of freight carried by that mode of transport. Because the volume of transport and the transport distance for each mode of transport are different, the volume of freight transport carried by various modes of transport also differs greatly.

The proportional allocation of the volume of freight transport among various modes of transport is by no means fixed. In the Soviet Union, the following tasks were required in every plan period: reduce as much as possible the load on railroad transport, fully use water and truck transport, and specify high growth rates in the volume of freight transport by river, ocean, and truck.

In China, based on the principle of rationally using transport means, we should fully utilize water transport and promote combined water-land transport in allocating freight transport in order to reduce the present overloading of railroad transport.

In addition, the many forms of traditional transport which exist everywhere, such as wooden boats, rubber-tired vehicles, and iron-wheeled vehicles, as well as private modern transport means should also be fully and rationally used according to the principle of "overall planning, all-round consideration, and comprehensive arrangement." Under the present condition of inadequate transport capacities, their role in supplementing the nation's transport capacities is of vital importance.

In the transport plan, there is passenger transport as well as freight transport. The planned demand for passenger transport does not fall into the production sphere, but rather into the consumption of services. Even so, its position in the transport plan should be investigated. This is because passenger transport and freight transport are a unified process in many respects. Examples are the routes covered and the workers who serve the transport process. Consequently, it is not possible to exclude passenger transport from the transport plan.

The major target in the passenger transport plan is the volume of passenger transport turnover. It is the product of the number of passengers and the distance of passenger transport and is represented by "person-kilometers."

IV. How to Determine the Material and Technical Resources Required by the Transport Industry

After the transport needs of the national economy are determined, the next step is to coordinate transport capacity with these needs. In other words, the transport plan is drawn up according to the transport means (locomotives, vehicles, boats, and so forth), fuels, and labor required by the transport industry. Of these, determining the transport means and the fuel requirements of various transport modes are the most important. These needs are then balanced with the output plans of relevant branches.

Although each mode of transport has different characteristics, the need for additional transport equipment can be determined by the following points: (1) the specified volume of freight transport; (2) the degree of utilization of transport equipment; (3) the quantity of existing transport equipment in the base period; (4) the quantity of transport equipment to be retired in the plan period; and (5) the inventory of transport equipment and changes in that inventory.

We will explain below using the example of cars required for railroad transport:

The freight train in railroad transport is composed of the freight cars and the locomotive. The gross need for freight cars depends on: the volume of freight transported, the average net carrying capacity per car, and the turnover time of the freight cars. Of these, the most important factor is the volume of freight transported. But given the volume of freight transported, the need for freight cars depends on their quality of utilization. In other words, on the average net carrying capacity per car and the turnover time of freight cars.

The average net carrying capacity per car is the average volume of freight it can carry. Therefore, increasing the net carrying capacity can increase the volume of freight carried and thereby reduce the need for freight cars. To increase the net carrying capacity, we must adopt various effective measures, such as increasing the manufacture of large cars, using cars rationally according to the type of goods (light goods or heavy goods), and improving loading and packing techniques.

The turnover time of freight cars refers to the period of time between the start of the first loading and the completion of the second loading. The length of this period indicates the speed at which the freight cars turn over. Therefore, if we reduce this time, we can speed up the turnover time of freight cars and reduce the need for freight cars.

The turnover time of freight cars includes: the time in motion, the waiting time at intermediate stops, the waiting time at intermediate transfer stops, and the loading and unloading time. However, the proportions of these times are different. The proportion of waiting time at stops is the highest (in China, this was about 70 percent in 1954). Therefore, to speed up the turnover time of freight cars, we must not only reduce the time in motion, but must also pay special attention to reducing the waiting time of freight cars at intermediate transfer stops and working stops. To do this, we must continuously improve labor organization and raise technical standards.

Once we have the figures on the volume of freight to be carried, the average net carrying capacity per car, and the turnover time of freight cars, we can determine the gross need for freight cars. Subtracting the number of freight cars existing in the base period from the gross need for freight cars and adding the number of replacements for cars to be retired in the plan period, we arrive at the number of cars that must be added in the plan period.

After the number of freight cars is determined, we must determine the gross need for locomotives and the need for new ones. The gross need for locomotives depends on the following points: (1) the number of trains on fully loaded and empty trips; (2) the average capacity of locomotives; (3) the average gross weight of each train; (4) the average distance each train goes; and (5) the average turnover time of locomotives. Sometimes two locomotives are required for one trip. We must also anticipate this situation in calculating the need for locomotives. Subtracting from the gross need for locomotives the existing number of locomotives in the base period and adding the number of locomotives that cannot be used in the plan period, we arrive at the actual number of locomotives that must be added.

To ensure the smooth progress of transport work, it is necessary to have sufficient fuel as well as transport means. The need for fuel depends on the gross long-ton-kilometers and the fuel consumption quotas. Therefore, once we have the data on the gross long-ton-kilometers and the fuel consumption quotas, we can calculate the need for fuel.

After the need for additional cars, fuel, and other transport materials is determined, the next step is to finalize the transport plan in accordance with the output plans of the various branches that supply the transport industry with its needed material and technical resources. From this, we can see that in the initial stages of formulating the transport plan, the production branches appear to be customers for transport. But in the final stages of formulating the transport plan, the production branches in turn serve as suppliers of the means of transport required by the transport industry.

LECTURE 9: THE MATERIAL-TECHNICAL SUPPLY PLAN

Chou Shu-chün*

I. The Basic Tasks of the Material-Technical Supply Plan

The material-technical supply in the national economy is the supply of producer goods to the various sectors of the national economy, which is a necessary condition for achieving expanded output. Here material refers to raw materials, processed materials, fuels, and electric power. Technical refers to machinery and equipment. Regardless of the type of economy, the expansion of output requires the consumption of a certain amount of means of labor (namely, machines and equipment) and objects of labor (namely, raw and processed materials, fuels, and electric power). Marx said, "The act of production itself, in all its factors, is also an act of consumption." [1]   Therefore, in order to expand output, we must supply a corresponding amount of producer goods. However, in capitalist society, because producer goods are privately owned by the capitalists, production is chaotic. The producer goods needed by enterprises are supplied through market transactions in an unplanned way. Only in socialist society and in the transition period, when all or the major producer goods are publicly owned, can the state systematically plan the material-technical supply and thereby overcome the overstocking and waste of materials and use all material resources in a rational way, thus guaranteeing the fulfillment and overfulfillment of the production plan, the capital construction plan, and the sustained growth of the national economy.

The national economy's material-technical supply plan is the plan by which producer goods are allocated and supplied to each sector of the national economy in the transition period and in socialist society. It is a link between production and consumption

---

*Chou Shu-chün, "Wu-tzu chi-shu kung-ying chi-hua." CHCC, 1955, No. 10, pp. 30-33.

(mainly the consumption connected with production). At the same time, it is also an important means for determining the proportional relations of expanded output. Therefore, it is a very important and integral part of the whole national economic plan.

The most basic task of the material-technical supply plan in the national economy is: to supply continuously, punctually and completely each sector of the national economy with producer goods — equipment, raw materials, processed materials, fuels, and electric power. Priority should be given to supplying the production and capital construction requirements of the machine-building industry, the iron and steel industry, the nonferrous metal industry, the electric power industry, the fuel industry, and the chemical industry, and other leading branches of the national economy in order to guarantee the smooth realization of China's socialist industrialization.

Based on the above fundamental tasks, we must correctly solve the following problems when formulating the national economy's material-technical supply plan: (1) correctly determine the national economy's material-technical need; (2) tap all material resources in the national economy and balance them against the needs; (3) determine the plan for distribution on the basis of balancing and urge the supply and marketing units at each level to sign economic contracts so that the allocation plan can be correctly and thoroughly implemented.

II. Determine the National Economy's Material-Technical Needs

The national economy's material-technical needs are many and varied. However, according to the major economic uses of the various materials, they can be classified into production and operational needs, capital construction needs, market needs, export needs, needs for increasing state reserves, and reserve needs for the year and for surpluses at the end of the year. When the state formulates the material-technical supply plan it must strictly check the material-technical request forms and calculation tables of the central ministries and the provinces (municipalities) to determine separately each of the needs listed above.

Production and operational needs are the most important item among all the needs. The materials required for this purpose include the following: materials (1) for production; (2) to increase production reserves; (3) to increase products-in-process; (4) for routine maintenance and major repairs. These are explained individually below.

Materials for production refer to those that are consumed in the production process. Their amount is determined by the level of output or work load and the consumption quota per unit of output or per unit of work load. Other things being equal, the increase in these needs is directly proportional to the level of output or work load. Since the level of output or work load continues to increase in each plan period, these needs also increase continuously. Consumption quotas for materials are the scientific basis for calculating needs. The more accurate the consumption quotas are, the more accurate the estimated needs will be. This also contributes to overcoming waste and using materials effectively. Therefore, it is necessary to ensure that the quotas are both advanced and realistic and to set scientific consumption quotas for material resources. This has immense significance in formulating the material-technical supply plan. In each plan period, consumption quotas for materials generally decrease due to the adoption of new scientific and technological achievements and the extension of available advanced experience. As a result, needs decrease correspondingly. However, since the rate of growth of the level of output or of the work load always far exceeds the rate at which the consumption quotas for materials are reduced, the absolute level of needs still increases continuously.

Production reserves also require a certain amount of materials. Production reserves are the reserves of materials of the consumption unit. They consist of regular reserves and emergency reserves. Regular reserves are rotating reserves that are required to ensure the continuous operation of the enterprise between supply deliveries. The average amount of regular reserves depends on the daily material needs and one half of the time interval between supply deliveries. Emergency reserves are reserves required to avoid work stoppages due to accidental delays or shortages in supply. Their amount depends on the needs for materials in twenty-four hours and the number of days for which emergency reserves are required. And the number of days for which emergency reserves are required is generally determined by a weighted average of the actual frequency at which, and number of days for which, normal supplies failed during the base period. It must also be adjusted with reference to the improvement of supply conditions in the plan period. In general, owing to the rapid growth rate of production, the production reserves at the end of each plan period will be larger than those at the beginning of the plan period. Therefore, this increase must be included in the needs.

In certain branches in which the production period is relatively long, products-in-process also require a certain amount of materials. From the time when raw and processed materials are put into production until the time when the finished products are inspected, all products in the production process which are not yet fully finished are regarded as products-in-process. The amount of products-in-process can generally be calculated on the basis of the daily output and the length of the production period. After we know the amount of products-in-process, and with the help of the consumption quotas for materials, we can determine the amount of materials needed by products-in-process. When formulating the material-technical supply plan, we should not list all the materials needed by products-in-process. We should only calculate the amount of materials needed for additional products-in-process in the plan period.

The production and operational needs include the needs for material resources connected with routine maintenance and major repairs. Material resources required for routine maintenance are those consumed in the course of carrying out medium and small repairs so that fixed assets can be used properly (to maintain normal working conditions of fixed assets) and those required for the operation and management of the production enterprise. It is a very complex and difficult job to calculate accurately the needs for material resources under this heading. This is because there are many types of repairs, and their needs for material resources are all different. Consequently, with the exception of some branches (for example, routine maintenance of railroads) in which conditions enable such calculations, the needs are generally determined by the method of dynamic comparison which takes into account changes in the base period and economy measures to be taken in the plan period. Because the materials required for major repairs are the materials used to carry out repairs of fixed assets in a given period according to the major repair plan, they should be calculated based on the actual amount of work to be done or the costs of major repairs.

Second are the needs of capital construction. They also constitute the major items among the total needs. Not only are machines and equipment required for capital construction, various types of buildings and other structures are also required. As a result, the material-technical needs of capital construction are twofold, one being machines and equipment and the other, construction materials.

The needs of capital construction for machines and equipment are generally based on the technical design reports. This is because in the technical design reports, the types, specifications, and quantity of machines and equipment are already described. However, because many important capital construction projects span more than one year, the machines and equipment stipulated in the technical design reports cannot all be used in one plan year. Therefore for any construction project lasting more than a year the determination of the needed quantity of machinery and equipment in the plan year must be based not only on the technical design report, but also on the progress of the construction project and the quantity remaining unused on the construction site.

To determine the needs of capital construction for construction materials, the planning units under China's management departments use fixed consumption quotas of materials per project unit. The planning units above the management departments use the consumption quotas of material resources per expense unit to calculate these needs.

The so-called expense unit refers to the unit of measurement used for construction and installation expenses. The Soviet Union uses one million rubles as the unit. Based on the construction and installation expenses and the consumption quotas of materials per expense unit, we can calculate the needs for various types of construction materials.

The project unit refers to the unit of measurement used for construction and installation projects. For example, certain buildings use cubic meters as the unit, and electric power lines use kilometers as the unit. If we want to calculate the needs of buildings for construction materials, we should base our calculation on the structure of the buildings (steel, reinforced concrete, brick and timber, and so forth) and the type of buildings (such as plants, warehouses, offices, and so forth). This is because buildings of different structures and types have different consumption quotas of construction materials per cubic meter. On the basis of the number of buildings of each structure and type and the consumption quotas of construction materials per cubic meter, we can calculate the needs for each type of construction material relatively accurately.

Third are the market needs. At present, the needs for producer goods in China's market are not only many and varied in terms of specifications, but are also huge in volume. This is a result of the following reasons: (1) in the transition period, there still exist nonsocialist economic elements, especially privately managed industries which possess definite productive capacities, and to engage in production, these privately managed industries must buy producer goods in the market; (2) many producer goods (such as charcoal and pure carbon) can be used both for production and for people's consumption, so a certain portion must be sold to the people through the market; (3) some local, state-operated enterprises and business units under the jurisdiction of special districts, counties, and municipalities must temporarily buy some of their producer goods through the market because the supply agencies of the provinces and municipalities are still not fully established and because the conditions within enterprises themselves are still not prepared. Market needs are difficult to calculate accurately. They are generally determined by the method of dynamic comparison.

Fourth are export needs. At present, China already has trade relations with many countries. The variety and quantity of exported producer goods are bound to increase with the growth of China's national economy. The quantity of exported materials is based on trade agreements signed with each country.

Fifth are needs to increase state reserves. The primary functions of state reserves are to guarantee national security, prevent imperialist aggression, and satisfy national defense needs in case of war. Their secondary function is to make up for imbalances created by natural calamities. Finally, they can be used in case of serious imbalances in the national economy. Therefore, state reserves consist only of reserves of a few strategic resources and major materials that are vital to the national economy and the people's livelihood. Certainly not all materials are included in state reserves. The amount of state reserves is determined with reference to the international environment, internal conditions, and the characteristics of the materials concerned. Since state reserves have immense significance for the national economy, the plan for state reserves in China is now formulated by the State Planning Commission. The material-technical supply plan includes only any increase or decrease in state reserves.

Sixth are reserve needs for the year. They are government reserves. In the Soviet Union, they are known as reserves of the Council of Ministers. Their function is to accommodate within the annual plan temporary increases or decreases in various sectors of the national economy, for example, to avoid changes in the plan and to make up for inadequacies in the original plan and other possible dislocations. The amount of government reserves is generally based on the experience of past base periods and also takes into account conditions in the plan period.

Last is the surplus at the end of the year. These are the reserves of finished products at the end of the plan period which are kept by the supply branches. Their function is to guarantee a steady supply of finished products to consuming units in order to prevent production stoppages. Year-end surpluses include the following three parts. (1) Reserves of finished products in the supplying factories. These are determined on the basis of the factories' output in twenty-four hours and the number of days for which reserves are required. (2) Reserves in the warehouses of the marketing offices. Their amount depends, on the one hand, on the amount of finished products sent to the marketing offices by the supplying factories and the supply intervals and, on the other, on the amount of raw and processed materials and the frequency at which they are received by the consuming factories from the marketing offices. (3) Finished products in transit, namely, finished products on their way from the supplying factories to the marketing offices. Their amount depends on the amount of finished products shipped and the transit time.

III. Tap All Material Resources in the National Economy and Balance Them with the Needs

After the needs are determined, it is necessary to tap actively all material resources in the national economy to satisfy these needs. The material resources of the national economy consist of surpluses at the beginning of a given year and that year's annual output, imports, internal resources, and allocations from state reserves. They are explained below.

The surplus at the beginning of the plan period is simply the surplus at the end of the base period. However, when the material-technical supply plan is formulated, the base period is not yet over. Therefore, we can only determine the estimated surplus at the beginning of the plan period on the basis of the actual results of the past nine months and our estimate of the situation at year's end. In the Soviet Union, inventory in the warehouse is taken twice a year (on January 1 and October 1). The estimated surplus at the beginning of the plan period is therefore based on the results of the inventory taken on October 1.

The annual output is the most important source of material

resources. In the Soviet Union, the annual output is the source of more than 90 or 95 percent of the total amount of material resources. At the same time, other resources, with the exception of imports, such as surplus at the beginning of the year and internal resources, are merely past output which is put to good use. From this, we can see that the annual output plays a decisive role in determining the size of the gross amount of material resources. Although the figures for the annual output can be obtained from the production plans of relevant sectors, the branches in charge of allocating material resources must also calculate output with reference to the productive capacities and their rate of utilization so they can better grasp the output volume and tap resource potential to the maximum.

Imported materials are also an important means of increasing material resources. At present, machines, equipment, and other producer goods are the most important imported materials. Since China's modern industry has a weak foundation and heavy industry is incomplete, with a particularly backward machine-building industry, some important producer goods, especially machines and equipment, will give impetus to establishing China's heavy industry and rapidly realizing China's socialist industrialization.

Mobilizing internal resources plays a significant role in augmenting the total volume of material resources. Examples are using the reserves that exceed the fixed quotas in various branches and recycling scrap iron and steel and the timber used in mining. This not only economizes on materials but also helps expand output.

Finally there are allocations from state reserves which are conditional. Since state reserves have been established for special needs (such as military attacks on China by imperialist nations and natural calamities in agriculture), they cannot be lightly used without state approval. In addition, state reserves do not include reserves of all kinds of materials but include only strategic materials and the materials which are most important for the economy and the people's livelihood. Thus, not all materials can be allocated from state reserves.

This then is the general picture of material resources in the national economy.

After the needs and material resources are determined, they should be coordinated through the compilation of material balance tables. Therefore, when the state formulates the material-technical supply plan, a separate balance table must be compiled for each material that is subject to unified distribution by the state.

The balancing between material resources and needs through a material balance table is not a simple process of numerical computation because these figures have an extremely rich economic meaning. They can affect the development of the whole national economy. Therefore, in order to achieve a correct balance between material resources and needs, when repeated balancing calculations are carried out, we must take account of the following points: (1) We do not balance for the sake of balancing, but for a definite goal. That is to say, we must base our balancing on the basic economic laws of socialism and the long-term political and economic tasks and on the concrete economic policies of the Party and the state. (2) It should not be a passive balancing, but rather an active balancing. That is, we should not allocate whatever material resources that happen to be available, but should instead actively adopt the measures necessary to tap potential and prevent waste in order to increase the amount of material resources and satisfy the needs. (3) We should attain not only a balance within the state-operated economy, but also a balance for the whole society according to the policy of overall planning with all-round consideration and comprehensive arrangement. (4) We should attain not only annual balance, but also quarterly balance. If we only balance the annual figures and neglect quarterly balances, the inevitable result will be the piling up of materials in some quarters while in other quarters there are shortages, causing work stoppages in production and capital construction due to insufficient materials. (5) We should attain not only a national balance, but also regional balances. That is to say, we have to balance production and marketing on a regional basis to prevent waste due to cross-haul transport, long-distance transport, and circuitous transport.

When the material balance tables are initially compiled they almost never balance; the needs generally exceed the resources. This is because in countries with planned economies, needs always run ahead of output, continuously stimulating the growth of production. This is naturally a good phenomenon. In this situation, we must further increase the productive capacities for certain products, thus increasing output. At the same time, we must adopt economy measures, reduce consumption quotas, eliminate reserves that exceed the fixed quotas, use substitutes, and increase imports. If, after this kind of overall tapping of resources, the needs can still not be satisfied, then we must reduce the needs. However, the reduction in needs must be in line with the Party's economic policies and the concrete conditions of the country at the moment and must dialectically take into account the following three points. (1) Between the current production needs and capital construction needs, some secondary basic construction needs should be reduced after key-point construction projects (such as the 156 construction projects on which the Soviet Union is assisting China) have been guaranteed. This is because the material resources required for basic construction are all currently produced products. If we do not first ensure the needs of current production, then we will not be able to produce enough products, and consequently, no capital construction will be possible. (2) Between the production of producer goods and the production of consumer goods, we should first reduce the needs of consumer goods production. This is because producer goods are the material basis for expanding output and should therefore be given growth priority. (3) Among the various sectors of the national economy, we should first reduce the needs of nonleading sectors. This is because the growth of the leading sectors influences the growth of the whole national economy. However, we must emphatically point out that the above three points are related and cannot be dealt with independently and mechanically. Only when they are in line with the Party's economic policies and the concrete conditions of the country at the moment and are applied dialectically can mistakes involving principles be avoided and excess needs be correctly reduced in order to attain a balance between needs and the available resources.

When material balance tables are initially compiled, material resources may sometimes exceed needs for individual products. This is primarily a result of the following two things: first, excess material resources may be caused by comparatively large productive capacities; and second, they may be due to imbalances in productive capacities such that the varieties and specifications of products are not complete. Products with certain specifications which are individually produced can also form false material resources surpluses. For example, two years ago we had a surplus of some small metal-cutting lathes but a shortage of large, precision lathes. This was a result of an imbalance in productive capacities due to backward technological standards. In this situation, consumption and export of such surplus resources should be appropriately increased. Moreover, we should do everything possible to trial manufacture new products which are in short domestic supply in order to attain a balance with the needs.

IV. The Material Distribution Plan and Economic Contracts

The material distribution plan is formulated on the basis of a balance between resources and needs achieved through the compilation of material balance tables. The material distribution plan is a concrete manifestation of the material balance tables. It concretely specifies what material resources are to be distributed to what branches, the quantity to be distributed, and the quarterly allocations. The quantities of materials distributed are identical with those of the balance tables.

After government approval, the material balance tables and the material distribution plan of the national economy are passed down level by level. The supply bureaus (divisions) of the central ministries and those of the provinces and municipalities should compile detailed order forms (that is, concrete distribution plans) based on the allocations within the specified time. They should list the resources required by the various direct-user units (or supply offices) according to variety, specification, quantity, time, and region. These are then separately submitted to the general marketing bureaus of the central ministries in charge. After the general marketing bureaus of the central ministries in charge receive the detailed order forms, they should coordinate production and marketing according to variety, specification, quantity, time, and region on the basis of the state's material distribution plan and in the light of the detailed order forms. They should also formulate supply plans within the specified time after receiving the detailed order forms, assigning direct-supplying factories and mines (or marketing offices) to the direct-user units (or supply offices), determining the variety, specifications, quantity, and time of supply, and notifying the supply bureaus (divisions) of the various ministries and those of the provinces and municipalities to send in orders. This will ensure the realization of the state allocation plan for materials.

When ordering, each supply and marketing unit must sign various types of economic contracts. Economic contracts are the legal expression of the economic relations among various branches and enterprises. They strengthen the responsible attitude of enterprises toward implementing the plans and are forceful weapons for ensuring plan fulfillment. In the economic contracts, not only are the variety, specifications, quantity, delivery time and place, price, and method of settling accounts explicitly and precisely specified, at the same time, penalty provisions are also specified in case of contract violations. At present, there are three kinds of economic contracts in China, namely, general contracts, concrete contracts, and direct contracts. General contracts are signed between the general marketing bureaus of the central ministries in charge and the supply bureaus (divisions) of various central ministries and those of the provinces and municipalities. Concrete contracts are signed between various direct-user units (or supply offices) and direct-supplying factories and mines (or marketing offices) and are based on the stipulations of the general contracts. Direct contracts are still signed centrally by the marketing bureaus of the central ministries in charge because their local branch agencies are not properly established. In the past few years, this type of direct contract has been widely adopted.

Note

1. Marx, Critique of Political Economy, Jen-min ch'u-pan-she, p. 153.

LECTURE 10: LABOR PLANNING

Li Yu-heng*

I. The Basic Tasks of Labor Planning

There are two basic tasks in formulating the labor plan.

The first is to determine the rate of increase of labor productivity in each sector of the national economy during the plan period.

The second is to correctly allocate the various types of labor required by the various sectors of the national economy and to establish labor reserves to satisfy the basic needs of the national economy for skilled workers and cadres.

The rate of increase of labor productivity to a large extent determines the growth rates of other important targets in the national economic plan. This is because an increase in labor productivity implies growth of the social product. And the larger the social product is, the larger will be the accumulation fund for expanding output and the consumption fund for further increasing the people's material standard of living. Moreover, since the rate of increase of labor productivity usually exceeds the average rate of growth of wages, the growth rate of output is higher than the rate of increase of production expenses. Therefore the cost of production per unit of output can be reduced. Because of the reduction in the cost of production, we can increase the profit rate and reduce prices, thus expanding both production and consumption. From this we can see that some important targets in the national economic plan — such as reducing the cost of production, reducing prices, increasing production, expanding accumulation, and raising consumption — largely depend on the level of increase in labor productivity. If this target is not correctly determined, it will adversely affect the accuracy of a series of other targets.

*Li Yu-heng, "Lao-tung chi-hua." CHCC, 1955, No. 11, pp. 28-33.

To increase output in each plan year, we must add a certain amount of labor in addition to increasing labor productivity. There-fore, allocating labor in a planned way according to the needs of the various sectors of the national economy becomes an important problem to be solved in our formulation of the labor plan.

II. The Targets of the Labor Productivity Plan and How They Are Calculated

Labor productivity is the value of the output produced by one worker in a given period of time, or the number of labor hours used to produce one unit of output. The targets of labor produc-tivity set in the national economic plan are primarily the follow-ing four:

1. The gross output per worker in physical terms. For example, the number of tons of coal mined per worker in the mining industry.

2. The number of labor hours used per unit of output. For ex-ample, the number of labor hours used to produce one machine.

3. The gross value of output per worker calculated at constant prices.

4. The value of net output per worker calculated at constant prices (net output is the difference between gross output and pro-duction expenses).

In sectors with simple products, targets expressed in physical terms are widely used in planning labor productivity. The method for calculating such targets is as follows.

First, calculate the gross output of various products in physical terms by sector in the plan period.

Second, find out the number of workers in those sectors in the plan period.

Third, divide the gross output by the number of workers to ar-rive at the physical output per worker in the plan period.

Fourth, comparing the physical output per worker in the plan period with that in the base period, we can calculate the rate of increase of labor productivity in the plan period.

However, targets of labor productivity expressed in physical terms cannot be converted into composite targets. That is, these targets cannot express in a composite form the labor productivi-ties of every different sector. This is because it is impossible to add the output of all the different products in physical terms. For example, we cannot simply add up so many tons of steel products, so many tons of cement, and so many rolls of printed fabrics.

Labor productivity targets expressed in numbers of labor hours are basically similar to those expressed in physical terms. The only difference between them is the form of expression. The basic formula for calculating labor productivity in labor hours is as follows:

$$\text{Labor productivity} = \frac{\text{Total hours worked}}{\text{Output}}.$$

Such targets can be calculated only by type of product.

To calculate labor productivity in labor hours, we must know the consumption of labor in each of the operations in a product's manufacture. The sum of these labor hour quotas (amount of labor consumption) for the various operations equals the number of labor hours needed to produce this product. The rate of increase of labor productivity in the plan period can be calculated by comparing the number of labor hours spent on this product in the plan period with the number of labor hours spent on the same product in the base period. This shows that these targets can only be applied in sectors where labor quotas are set fairly accurately (such as the machine-building sectors).

The target for the gross value of output per worker calculated at constant prices is determined by dividing the total number of workers into the gross value of industrial output calculated at constant prices. This target can express a composite labor productivity of different production sectors because the quantities of different products can be added together in money terms.

However, the shortcoming of this target is that the accuracy of labor productivity is easily affected by changes in the composition of output in the plan period. For example, if in the plan period the proportion of production in sectors originally having comparatively high labor productivity were increases, then this method of calculation would create an upward bias in the average labor productivity. In the opposite case, there would be a downward bias.

To avoid influences due to changes in the composition of production, we must also calculate average labor productivity by the index method. The calculation procedure for the index method is to first calculate the index of growth of labor productivity in each sector. Then, multiply these indices by the number of workers in each sector and add the products. Finally, divide the sum by the total number of workers. The result is the average growth index of labor productivity.

Another composite target of labor productivity is the net value of output per worker expressed in constant prices. Labor productivity in terms of net output value reflects not only changes in the consumption of live labor, but also changes in the consumption of embodied labor. Owing to economy on material consumption in each plan period, the growth index of labor productivity in terms of the net value of output is generally larger than the growth index of labor productivity in terms of the gross value of output.

III. Factors Which Increase Labor Productivity

To set correctly the growth rate of labor productivity in the plan period, we must first know the various factors which determine increases in labor productivity. These factors are: the organization of social production, the material and cultural standard of living of the working people, the level of scientific development, the level of production technology, the utilization rate of the labor force, the skill levels of the labor force, the wage system, and the natural conditions.

The planned nature of social production based on the system of public ownership of the means of production and the socialist labor attitude produced by this system are the basic factors which increase labor productivity. When the workers realize that they no longer work for the capitalists but are working for themselves and their country, their enthusiasm and creativity are greatly mobilized. There is a new upsurge in labor competition, resulting in substantial increases in labor productivity.

Increases in people's material standard of living in turn promote the growth of social production. Before liberation, the majority of the laboring people in China were living from hand to mouth. Since liberation, the livelihood of the laboring people has been guaranteed. They can now wholeheartedly engage in production and improve technology, thereby raising labor productivity. With increases in their cultural levels, the people's potential for inventiveness and innovation in production and construction has also increased.

The increase in the level of production technology is a major factor in raising labor productivity. It is obvious that the output of a given worker will vary tremendously with varying production tools. The output of a textile worker using a spinning machine will be several hundred times that of a textile worker using a spinning wheel. However, the increase of our level of production technology is built on the increase in the level of scientific development. Therefore, the country's level of scientific development directly or indirectly affects the rate of growth of labor productivity. Only with a high level of scientific development is it really possible to rapidly increase the level of production technology.

The increase in the level of production technology requires a corresponding increase in the level of the workers' labor skills. Only when skilled labor is combined with the most advanced technical equipment can labor productivity be increased substantially.

From the point of view of the labor productivity of the whole society, reducing unemployment, lengthening the average work year, strengthening labor discipline, and reducing absenteeism and work stoppages all increase production time proportionately and consequently increase the average labor productivity of the whole society.

The adoption of an advanced wage system can also stimulate the worker to increase labor productivity. For example, the replacement of the hourly rate wage system by the piece-rate wage system can usually increase the worker's average labor productivity.

Fully exploiting natural conditions and rationally locating production and consumption areas can also increase the labor productivity of the whole society. For example, by making the location of production and consumption increasingly rational, labor consumption involved in transportation can be relatively reduced so that the same number of employees can handle more freight transport tasks, thus increasing the average labor productivity of the whole society.

IV. The Method of Formulating the Plan to Increase Labor Productivity on the Basis of the Factors Which Increase Labor Productivity

As for the effects of the above factors on labor productivity, some can be accurately calculated, but others can only be approximately estimated by means of the dynamic relation method.

The effect of natural conditions on labor productivity can be directly calculated. For example, in the base period, due to varying natural conditions, a coal miner in some mines could extract only 500 tons of coal per year while at other mines the corresponding figure was 900 tons. Suppose in the plan period the regional composition of coal production changed so that the proportion of the gross output of coal represented by the first kind of coal mine was reduced from 60 percent to 40 percent and the share represented by the second kind of mine was increased from 40 percent to 60 percent. With each kind of mine maintaining its original level of labor productivity, labor productivity in the plan period would increase by 12 percent because of the change in the regional composition of output:

$$\frac{\text{Plan period} = (0.4 \times 500) + (0.6 \times 900) = 740}{\text{Base period} = (0.6 \times 500) + (0.4 \times 900) = 660} = 1.12.$$

Increases in labor productivity due to improvements in the utilization of labor time can be calculated according to the same principle. Suppose that in the base period the average total number of labor days per worker in the coal-extracting industry was 270 and the actual utilization was 265, but that in the plan period absenteeism was to be eliminated so that the total number of labor days was fully utilized. As a result, the annual labor productivity would be increased by 1.9 percent ($270/265 = 101.9$ percent).

From data on the improved utilization of equipment, it is also possible to calculate concretely how raising the equipment utilization rate affects the rate of growth of labor productivity. For example, if in the plan period the utilization coefficient of the effective capacity of blast furnaces is to be reduced from 1.0 to 0.8, then the labor productivity of blast furnace workers will be increased by 25 percent.

Studying advanced methods of work is particularly important for correctly planning the level of labor productivity. By analyzing and summing up advanced methods of work, we can determine the prerequisites for a certain increase in labor productivity. By analyzing the trend of labor productivity in the advanced enterprises, we can tell what measures and methods to adopt and under what conditions labor productivity reaches its highest level. However, at the same time that we analyze the labor productivity of the advanced enterprises, we must also study the reasons for the comparatively low level of labor productivity in other (average and backward) enterprises. Only by comprehensively studying the relevant data concerning the various enterprises mentioned above can the growth potential of labor productivity be fully tapped.

Analyzing the trend of growth of labor productivity in past years is also very significant for the formulation of the plan to increase labor productivity in the plan period. In conducting this kind of analysis, the following three kinds of data must be made available.

1. The growth rate of labor productivity in each year.
2. The average annual growth rate of labor productivity.
3. The conditions required to reach the highest growth rate of labor productivity.

The conclusions obtained from this analysis provide a definite standard for solving the problem of growth rates of labor productivity in the plan period.

V. Planning the Size of the Labor Force

After the labor productivity for the plan period is calculated, we can determine the number of workers required to complete the production tasks in the plan period, because the number of workers is simply the gross output divided by labor productivity. For example, if the production task set for a certain enterprise in the plan period is 100 million yuan and the labor productivity per worker is 10,000 yuan (that is, the average value of the production of each worker in the plan period is 10,000 yuan), then in order to complete the production tasks which have been set (100 million yuan), that enterprise needs 10,000 workers.

After the number of workers is determined, we can calculate the need for engineering and technical personnel, because the need for them is determined by the number of workers and the quotas of technical personnel assigned to each branch by the State Planning Commission. In the Soviet Union, the quotas of technicians (per thousand workers) for various major branches in the Second Five-Year Plan were as follows: metallurgical industry, 115; machine-building industry, 155; chemical industry, 140; electric power industry, 185; petroleum industry, 150; coal industry, 105; construction materials industry, 90; textile industry, 80; and food industry, 110. These quotas are determined according to the following conditions.

1. The level of production technology. The proportion of engineering and technical personnel is larger in branches in which the level of production technology is higher and production is more mechanized and automated.

2. The nature of production. Whenever there is integrated production, especially in departments with large-scale production, the proportion of engineering and technical personnel in the labor force can be reduced.

3. The complexity of the products. The proportion of engineering

and technical personnel must be relatively high in branches in which the products are complex; for instance, in the branches which manufacture precision instruments.

4. The production organization. This quota can be proportionately reduced if production organization is improved and the technical operation procedure is rationally organized.

5. The quality of engineering and technical personnel themselves. The required number of engineers and technicians can also be proportionately reduced if their quality is improved and their ability is well matched with their jobs.

The quota of engineering and technical personnel should be formulated according to occupational specialties in similar types of enterprises. The formulation procedure is as follows.

First, similar types of enterprises are grouped by their most important characteristic, such as their level of technology.

Second, a model enterprise is selected from each group. This enterprise must have excellent production organization and be good at the rational utilization of engineers and technicians.

Third, analyze the feasibility of extending the conditions of this model enterprise to other enterprises.

Fourth, determine the quota of engineering and technical personnel for that type of enterprise with reference to the number of engineering and technical personnel already set for the model enterprise.

In the Soviet Union, the number of engineering and technical personnel for some branches is calculated according to the "standard employment quotas table." This employment quotas table stipulates the quotas of engineering and technical personnel for each type of enterprise in each branch. For example, it specifies the number of engineering and technical personnel including the numbers of various kinds of specialists required for coal mines with a daily output of 1,000 tons of coal. In the Soviet Union, the number of engineering and technical personnel needed by certain branches is also calculated by the "method of factory employment quotas." By this method, the number of engineering and technical personnel including the numbers of various kinds of specialists, are calculated for every million rubles of output. Then the gross value of the production of factories of the same type is added up, divided by a million rubles, and multiplied by the number of persons in the employment quotas table to arrive at the number of engineering and technical personnel required by this type of factory.

In the Soviet Union, the ratio of engineers and technicians to all the engineering and technical personnel is 1 to 2. If the engineers and technicians in the scientific research organizations are included, the ratio becomes 2 to 3.

Among the productive personnel of an enterprise, in addition to the workers and the engineering and technical personnel, there are also some apprentices. The plan for apprenticeships should be formulated according to the number of replacements for skilled workers the enterprise requires and the training assignment.

The number of staff and janitorial personnel can be determined according to the state staffing quotas table. Their growth rate should be lower than that for the workers.

The number of security policemen and firemen can be determined, in accordance with the principle of ensuring the security of the enterprise, on the basis of the number of sentry posts and the method of changing.

After the needs for the above six categories of personnel are determined, we can determine the number of other personnel in the industrial branches by using the ratio of the personnel [described above] to other personnel. In the Soviet Union, this ratio is 10 to 1.

The number of workers required by the capital construction branches can be determined according to the proportions of the various kinds of structures and the labor quotas for them. The total number of workers required by the capital construction branches in the plan period is calculated by dividing the average amount of work per construction worker in a year's effective construction period into the project volume of various structures in the plan period.

The number of workers and staff in the transport and commercial sectors can be obtained by dividing the average labor productivity of these branches into the gross transport volume or the gross turnover volume. However, in determining these numbers, we must also take into account the transport volume and staff quotas for the different routes as well as the staff quotas for various systems in the commercial network.

The manpower plan for the cultural, educational, and health departments can be determined according to the planned staff quota and the proportions of staff for these organs.

The manpower plan for state administrative organs and financial organs should be formulated according to the state staff quotas under the principle of reducing staffing, simplifying personnel, reducing duplication, and increasing work efficiency.

The needs for various types of labor force should be balanced with the labor resources. Labor resources consist of all able-bodied residents of working age. The working age in the Soviet Union is set at fourteen to fifty-four for men and fourteen to forty-nine for women in the urban areas. In the rural areas, it is fourteen to fifty-nine for men and fourteen to fifty-four for women who are engaged in agricultural activities. The working age for the nonagricultural population in the rural areas is the same as that in the urban areas.

When calculating the number of able-bodied residents of working age for the annual plan, we should use the "method of age flows." The procedure is: First, from the total number of able-bodied residents, subtract the number of those who will become of non-working age during the year, and then add the number of residents who will become of working age during the plan period. Finally, from this subtract the number of deaths among able-bodied residents in the plan period. The number of deaths can be estimated from the general death rate.

In order to express the labor resources which are over and under the working age as a portion of the regular labor force, it is necessary to know the following:

First, the number of this type of residents in the plan period.

Second, the number of working days per person among those who reached this age in the base period.

Third, the number of working days of the regular labor force during the plan period.

The labor resources which are over and under the working age as a portion of the regular labor force is the product of the first and second numbers divided by the third.

However, the labor for which the national economy needs replacements is not entirely general labor; it is a certain number of skilled workers. Because socialist production is built on the basis of a high level of technology, we must strive to train skilled workers who can grasp modern technology.

In the Soviet Union, the training of skilled workers is carried on through two major systems. One is the system of technical schools under the Ministry of Labor Reserves. The other is the system of technical schools under the various specialized branches. The system of technical schools under the Ministry of Labor Reserves primarily train skilled workers for six major branches of the national economy (metallurgy, coal mining, electric power, machine building, petroleum, and construction). Skilled workers required by other branches, such as the light industry branches, are trained by the various administrative branches themselves.

In the Soviet Union, the plan for training and allocating each kind of specialized skilled worker is specified by a training and alloca- tion balance table for each kind of specialized skilled worker. The major targets of this balance table include the titles of the various skilled workers such as fitters, lathe turners, cutters, and so forth. The secondary targets in the balance table include the following items:

1. the number of persons at the beginning of the plan period;

2. the number of persons at the end of the plan period;

3. the number of persons added or subtracted during the plan period;

4. the number of skilled workers needed to replace those leav- ing their jobs (these include those who have to leave their jobs be- cause of old age, schooling, military draft, or other reasons and those who transfer to work in other specialty branches);

5. the number of skilled workers to be trained in the plan pe- riod (these include those who are trained in the state labor re- serve system and those trained on the job).

Through the compilation of this balance table, we can establish a balance in the national economy between the replacement needs for various specialized skilled workers and the number of these workers to be trained.

When formulating the plan for training the various specialized cadres, we must take into account not only the needs of the na- tional economy, but also the feasibility of satisfying these needs. That is to say, the state's establishment of higher-level schools and middle-level specialized schools, and its allocation of the teaching staff, buildings and equipment, teaching materials, and education funds to these schools must also be coordinated with the number of the various specialized cadres to be trained.

Because it generally takes four to five years to train a special- ized cadre, the quota of students to be admitted in the plan period by the middle-level specialized schools and higher-level schools must be based on the national economy's expected needs for spe- cialized cadres in four to five years' time. That is to say, the proportional relation between the needs for the various specialized cadres and the number of trainees can only be correctly established through long-term planning. If there is no long-term planning, the training of specialized cadres will not be in line with the national economy's needs for them. Therefore, we must establish a labor force balance through long-term planning. This is an important characteristic of the method of formulating the cadre-training plan.

The formulation of plans to train the various specialized cadres must be carried out through a balance table for specialized cadres. The major targets of this balance table include such sectors as industry, agriculture, commerce, transportation, construction, and culture, education, and health. The secondary targets of this balance table include the following items.

1. The number of cadres at the beginning of the plan period. Of these, there are separate listings for the number of graduates of higher-level schools, middle-level specialized schools, and specialized-training classes and the number of people trained on the job.

2. The number of cadres at the end of the plan period. Of these, the number of graduates from higher-level schools, middle-level specialized schools, and specialized-training classes and the number of people trained on the job are also listed separately.

3. The proportion of each type of cadre at the end of the plan period compared to the beginning.

4. The proportion of the total number of each type of cadre for both the beginning and the end of the plan period graduating from higher-level schools and middle-level specialized schools.

Through the compilation of this balance table, we can establish a balance between the national economy's replacement needs for the various types of specialized cadres and the number of trainees.

VI. The Proportionate Distribution of the Labor Force and Its Pattern

After an overall balance has been attained between the requirements for labor force and the labor resources, we can begin to carry out distribution. Correctly distributing the labor force has tremendous significance for the rational utilization of labor resources. At present, strengthening our work on the planned distribution of the labor force is the major step in overcoming labor waste.

The proportionate distribution of the labor force differs in each plan period. There are two direct factors which determine the changes in these proportions.

The first is that the rate of growth of output in each sector of the national economy is different.

The second is that the rate of growth of labor productivity in each sector of the national economy is also different.

The growth rates of production and of labor productivity affect the proportionate distribution of the labor force in opposite directions. The growth of production increases the need for labor, while the growth of labor productivity reduces the need for labor. Therefore, different combinations of these two factors result in different proportionate relations in the distribution of the labor force. However, in general the differences in growth rates of production among the various sectors are greater than the differences in increases of labor productivity among the various sectors. Therefore, different rates of growth of output among various sectors have a greater influence on the proportionate distribution of the labor force.

The most important proportions in the distribution of the labor force are those between the productive and nonproductive spheres of the national economy, between the production of producer goods and consumer goods, between industry and agriculture, between the transportation industry and the whole national economy, and so forth. There are definite rules governing changes in these proportionate relations.

The general pattern governing the allocation of labor force between the productive and nonproductive spheres of the national economy is to use most of the labor force in the material production sphere and relatively little in the nonproductive sphere. However, the labor force in the nonproductive sphere can be divided into two parts. One is the labor force in the management organs of the national economy, such as the cadres in the State Planning Commission and each of the central industrial ministries. The other is the labor in the organs for health, education, and the arts and the public utilities. These types are distinguished by the fact that the former primarily serve production and construction and the latter primarily serve the people's consumption.

Owing to the rapid growth of output and the increasing complexity of economic relations, the labor force required by the management organs of the national economy steadily increases. But its rate of growth is lower than that of the labor force in the productive sphere. For example, if the number of production workers in the First Machine-Building Ministry increased by 50 percent because of the construction of new machine-building plants, generally, the number of cadres in the First Machine-Building Ministry would not necessarily have to increase by 50 percent. Therefore, when setting the labor force quantity plan in the Soviet Union, the rate of growth for management personnel is usually set lower than that for production workers.

The second component determining the proportionate distribution of the labor force between the productive and the nonproductive spheres is just the reverse of that explained above. Owing to continuous improvements in the people's material and cultural standard of living, the needs for education, health, the arts, and public utilities steadily increase. Therefore, the labor force serving these needs should be increased not only absolutely, but also proportionally. Another reason for this is the low rates of growth of labor productivity in these branches. The professional levels of doctors, teachers, and literary experts cannot increase as fast as the technical skills of production workers.

The above patterns can be discovered in the relevant data of the Soviet Union. Between 1928 and 1937, the number of workers and staff in the productive sphere increased by 246 percent, while the number of workers and staff in the nonproductive sphere increased by only 223 percent. The first part of the nonproductive sphere increased by 153 percent. The second part increased by 298 percent (Summary of the Implementation of the Second Five-Year Plan for the Economic Development of the Soviet Union).

In the material production sphere, a particularly significant proportion in the distribution of the labor force is the one between the first and second categories of social production. Its general rule is that comparatively large amounts of labor are used to produce producer goods and relatively little is used in branches which produce consumer goods. This is because the growth of production of producer goods must have priority. However, this proportionate distribution of the labor force is not permanent. When socialist industrialization accelerates, as in the First Five-Year Plan of the Soviet Union, the proportion of labor in type A industries increases very rapidly (in the Soviet Union, it increased from 56 percent to 70 percent). After socialist industrialization is basically completed, the proportion of labor in type B industries increases correspondingly. For example, in the Soviet Union's Second Five-Year Plan, the task of doubling or tripling the people's consumption level was proposed. Corresponding with this, the proportion of labor in the branches producing consumer goods was to be increased from 36 to 41 percent.

In the first type of social production, industry and agriculture are the two decisive sectors. Therefore, the correct distribution of the labor force between industry and agriculture has tremendous significance for ensuring the smooth progress of expanding social output. The general rule for allocating labor between industry and

agriculture is that in each plan period, the proportion of labor in
industry increases, while that in agriculture decreases. Furthermore, after agricultural collectivization is completed, the quantity
of labor in the agricultural sector can decrease, not only relatively,
but also absolutely. The Soviet Union's population census data for
1926 and 1939 supports this point. In 1926, the rural population of
the Soviet Union was about 120 million, representing 82.1 percent
of the total population. In 1936, the rural population of the Soviet
Union had decreased to 104 million, representing only 67.2 percent of the total population. This shift in residence from the rural
to the urban areas reflects in general terms the change in labor
allocation between industry and agriculture.

The above patterns are the result of two things.

The first is necessity. The rapid development of socialist industrialization requires a substantial increase of workers in a
short period.

The second is feasibility. Agricultural collectivization and mechanization rapidly increase labor productivity in the agricultural
sector so that a large quantity of labor can be released to participate in industrial production.

The consumption of labor in the transport sector as a share of
the whole material production sphere depends, on the one hand, on
the proportion between transport and industrial and agricultural
production and, on the other hand, on the growth of labor productivity in the transport sector compared with its growth in the whole
material production sphere. The general rule for change in this
proportionate distribution of the labor force is that in the whole
material production sphere, the proportion of labor consumption
in transport decreases. For example, in the First Five-Year Plan
of the Soviet Union, the number of staff and workers in the national
economy increased by 97 percent, in the industrial sector by 92
percent, and in the transport sector only by 75 percent. This is
primarily because the growth rate of output is generally higher
than the growth rate of the transport volume. The higher rate of
growth of production workers over transport workers results in a
relative decrease in the proportion of labor consumption of the
transport sector in the whole material production sphere.

The proportionate distribution of the labor force among each
sector of the national economy is closely related to the proportionate distribution of the labor force among each region of the national economy. Because the enterprises of each sector are all located in a certain region, the distribution of the labor force

according to the national economy's regions is simply a more concrete expression of the distribution of the labor force by sector.

The calculation of the needs for labor and labor resources by region is roughly the same as the calculation by sector described above. After comparing the total need for labor in one region with its total labor resources, we can discover whether that region has a labor shortage or surplus. This work must be done by means of a regional labor balance table. The central planning organs can then distribute labor on an overall basis according to the labor surplus or shortage represented in each regional labor balance table. This kind of distribution is carried out according to regional labor distribution plans. Correctly formulating regional labor distribution plans is the basic key to strengthening China's labor distribution work at present. The redistribution of labor on a regional basis will establish new proportions of labor quantity among the regions. These new proportions can ensure the realization of the national economy's new production structure in the plan period.

(The major content of this paper is based on relevant materials about the Soviet Union in M. V. Belayev, Lecture Notes on the Process of National Economic Planning.)

LECTURE 11: WAGE PLANNING

Wu Ching-ch'ao*

I. The Basic Tasks of Wage Planning
in the National Economy

In a socialist society, wages are the monetary expression of the share of the social product obtained by each laborer according to the quantity and quality of his own labor. This is fundamentally different under the capitalist system where wages are the price of labor. Under the capitalist system, wages reflect the relationship between the exploiter and the exploited. Because of increasing capitalist exploitation, the worker's real wages decline continuously. Under the socialist system, wages reflect the relationship between the whole society as represented by the socialist state and individual laborers who work for themselves and their society. The wages of the workers and staff increase continuously with the uninterrupted growth of production and labor productivity.

The basic economic law of socialism suggests the general direction for formulating the wage plan. This is: the wage plan should guarantee continuous growth of the wages of the workers and staff on the basis of continuous growth of production and labor productivity. However, the basic economic law of socialism does not suggest a principle on which the share of output which is to be consumed by individuals should be distributed among the workers. Only the socialist principle of distribution according to labor can suggest that the wage fund and average wage of each sector of the national economy should be set according to the quantity and quality of labor consumed. Under the socialist system, the productive forces have still not reached a level at which they can provide as high a consumption level as under communism. At present labor is still not the primary need in the livelihood of the members of

---

*Wu Ching-ch'ao, "Kung-ssu chi-hua." CHCC, 1955, No. 12, pp. 27-31.

society. Therefore, the only feasible and necessary form of distribution of the consumption fund is distribution according to labor. Only in this way can we use material incentives to induce workers to pay attention to increasing their labor productivity and social production. Equal distribution of the consumption fund is not consistent with socialism. If petty bourgeois egalitarianism exists in the wage plan, labor turnover will worsen, labor productivity decrease, and costs of production increase, thus causing losses to socialism and socialist construction.

There are five basic tasks in wage planning:

First, we must guarantee the continuous increase of wages to satisfy the requirements of the basic socialist economic law.

Second, we must establish a correct proportional relation between wages and labor consumption in the national economy based on the socialist law of distribution according to labor.

Third, we must establish a correct proportional relation between the rate of growth of wages and the rate of growth of labor productivity in the material production realm.

Fourth, we must adopt advanced wage systems to encourage labor productivity growth, material consumption economy, and product quality improvement.

Fifth, within the realm of exchange we must establish an appropriate relationship between the wages and other money income of the people on the one hand and the volume of marketed commodities and their prices on the other.

II. The Procedures for Formulating the Wage Fund and the Average Wage in the National Economy

In socialist society, the wage fund and average wage of workers and staff are continuously rising. In the plan period, these two targets are always set somewhat higher than those in the base period. This point can be illustrated by the relevant targets in the several five-year-plan periods of the Soviet Union and by the growth of wages in China. The average wage in the Soviet Union in 1932 (the end of the First Five-Year Plan) increased by 100 percent (actual figures) over 1928 (the beginning of the First Five-Year Plan). The increase was more than 110 percent (actual figures) between 1932 (the beginning of the Second Five-Year Plan) and 1937 (the end of the Second Five-Year Plan). According to statistics from five of China's central industrial ministries (the Ministry of Heavy Industry, the Ministry of Fuel Industries, the Ministry of First Machine-

Building Industry, the Ministry of Textile Industry, and the Ministry of Light Industry), the average money wage increased by 84 percent between 1950 and 1953. China's First Five-Year Plan for developing the national economy specifies an increase of about 33 percent in the average wage of the workers and staff in five years.

The size of the wage fund in the national economy depends on two factors, the number of workers and staff and the average wage. The wage fund of each sector also depends on these two factors. Owing to differences in the average quality of labor consumed (degree of experience) in each sector, the wage fund of each sector as a share of the wage fund of the national economy is not the same as the labor force as a share of the total labor force of the national economy. In general, in industry, construction, and transportation the share of the wage fund is higher than the share of the labor force because the quality of labor consumed in these sectors is relatively high. In agriculture and commerce, the share of the wage fund is lower than the share of the labor force because the quality of labor consumed in these two sectors is relatively low. In addition, the average wage in agriculture is lower because costs of living in rural areas are less.

The whole process of formulating the wage fund and the average wage of the national economy can be divided into the following steps.

First, we must accurately estimate the average wage of each type of worker and staff (for example, workers: apprentices, engineers and technicians; staff: janitorial staff, security police, firemen, and so forth), each ministry, and each sector of the national economy in the base period.

Second, on the basis of the general tasks of the state, especially the proportional relationship between production and consumption as determined by the general tasks and taking into consideration the quantity of labor consumed, the increase in the workers' experience, the wage increases that should be given to those workers whose wages were too low in the base period, and the even higher wages which the various decisive sectors of the national economy must have, we must specify an approximate rate of growth for the average wage.

Third, we must determine the average wage of each type of worker and staff, each ministry, and each sector of the national economy on the basis of the average wage in the base period and the approximate percentage increase in the wage in the plan period.

Fourth, we must determine the wage fund for each type of worker and staff, each ministry, and each sector of the national economy on the basis of the average wage and the number of workers and staff.

Fifth, we obtain the wage fund for the whole national economy by adding the wage fund of each sector of the national economy.

Sixth, we obtain the average wage of the whole national economy by dividing the total number of workers and staff into the wage fund of the national economy.

Seventh, we then decide on the final plan for the national economy by comparing and balancing the wage fund and other money income of the people with the total volume of marketed commodities during the plan period calculated at base period prices.

III. Determine the Average Wage according to the Quantity and Quality of Labor Consumed

As has been pointed out above, the wage fund depends on the number of workers and staff and the average wage. The number of workers and staff in each sector is determined by the labor-force quantity plan. The average wage, on the other hand, is determined by the wage plan.

The average wage of each type of worker and staff should correspond with the quantity and quality of labor consumed. Therefore, to determine the average wage we must first determine the average quantity of labor consumed and then determine the average quality of labor consumed.

To determine the quantity of labor consumed, we must consider the following four factors. First, the length of the working day. The longer the working time, the greater the amount of labor consumed. Second, the intensity of labor. In a given unit of time, the higher the labor intensity, the more the labor consumed, and vice versa. Third, the difficulty of the labor. In the same period of time, the body energy used is higher for heavy labor than for light labor. Fourth, the working conditions. More energy is used in workshops where the air is bad and the temperature is high.

The most complicated step in planning the average wage is to deal with the quality of labor consumed, that is, solving the problem of converting complex labor into simple labor for the purpose of making calculations. In socialist society, the solution for this problem depends on the system of wage grades. It should be pointed out that the system of wage grades solves not only the problem of labor quality, but also the problem of labor quantity. A correct system of wage grades must be able to deal with the problems of the quantity and quality of labor consumed.

The system of wage grades has three components, namely, the skill standards of the grades, the table of wage grades, and the wage standard.

The skill standards of the grades include detailed production characteristics for all types of jobs in all sectors and what they require from the workers. For example, they include what a worker should know and be able to do for a certain job and concrete examples of how much of certain kinds of work should be completed.

The table of wage grades is composed of a certain number of grades and their corresponding grade coefficients. The compilation of the table of wage grades and the specification of the grade coefficients are based on the following two points. One is the production characteristics, such as the multiple aspects and complexity of the work and the worker's degree of experience. The other is that the grade coefficients should increase steadily from the lower to the higher grades to provide material incentives to the worker to work hard to increase his experience level. After undergoing tests, each industrial worker is assigned to a certain wage grade corresponding to his level of skill. The higher the skill level, the higher the wage grade assigned. The worker's labor remuneration is based on his wage grade.

The wage standard specifies the labor remuneration for a worker of the first grade in each type of enterprise in a given labor hour or labor day. The first-grade wage standard is the starting point for determining the wage standard of every other grade. The product of the first-grade wage standard and the grade coefficient of each grade is the absolute level of wages of the grade. For example, if the daily first-grade wage standard is 1.5 yuan and the grade coefficient for a worker of the eighth grade is 2.6, we can calculate the daily wages of the eighth-grade worker to be 3.9 yuan.

With the table of wage grades and the wage standard, we can calculate the average wages for a given enterprise. The method of calculation is: sum the products obtained by multiplying the number of workers in each grade by their respective wage coefficients and divide the sum by the total number of workers to obtain the average wage coefficient of all the workers. The average wage is obtained by multiplying the average wage coefficient by the wage standard of the first-grade worker.

IV. The Proportional Relationship between the Rate of Growth of the Average Wage and the Rate of Growth of Labor Productivity

In socialist society and the people's democratic state, the average wage and labor productivity increase continuously due to the superiority of the social system. The growth of labor productivity causes growth of the social product. The increase of the average wage is thus built upon a solid material basis. However, we must note that the growth rates of labor productivity and the average wage should not be the same. The growth rate of the average wage should be lower than that of labor productivity. This is one of the most important principles in the planning work because it is necessary for increasing accumulation and expanding output.

China's First Five-Year Plan for developing the national economy strictly follows this principle. In the five years, labor productivity in state-owned industry increases by 64 percent, and the average wage of the workers and staff increases by about 27 percent. The rate of growth of labor productivity far exceeds that of the average wage.

It is not only necessary, but also rational, to set the growth rate of labor productivity higher than that of the average wage. The rate of growth of the average wage depends primarily on improvements in the level of labor skill. But the rate of growth of labor productivity depends not only on improvements in the level of labor skill, but also on many other factors, such as improvements in the level of production technology, the mechanization of labor intensive processes on a broader scale, and the development of electrification in the national economy, and so forth. We had one coal mine whose coal output per man per day increased from 1.6 tons to 8 tons after coal-cutting machines were used. That is to say, labor productivity increased by five times. At the same time, it is obviously irrational to increase the average wage by five times.

To ensure the realization of this principle, we must concentrate on correctly specifying technical quotas. All plants, mines, and construction projects must specify output quotas and labor-time quotas based on technology. With continuous technical innovations, we must amend already outdated technical quotas after a certain period of time. Technical quotas are indispensable for correctly specifying wages and are extremely important in improving labor productivity. They are also a powerful lever in regulating the proportional relationship between the growth rate of wages and that of labor productivity.

V. Wages Are an Economic Lever in Production Management

The fact that the wage plan is formulated on the basis of the principle of distribution according to labor does not imply that it only passively reflects objective laws. Instead, it exercises effective management over production by means of wages such that the wage system becomes an economic lever to manage and develop production.

An advanced wage system must fulfill two important tasks. First, it must ensure a correct allocation of the labor force among the various regions and sectors. Second, it must make the wage system a powerful weapon for raising the level of skill and labor productivity, economizing on material consumption, and improving product quality.

The correct allocation of the labor force among the various regions and sectors of the national economy is of decisive significance in specifying both the production proportions among the various sectors and regions and the composition of the national economy. To make the workers and staff feel at ease in their jobs and locations, it is not enough simply to mobilize and redistribute. Through a rational wage system we must make them content to serve in the posts to which they are assigned. Therefore, in specifying and planning wages, we must take into account the contributions which certain sectors make to the whole national economy, the intensity of labor, and the working conditions, as well as the geographical distribution of the enterprises. For example, the wages for those workers who work in regions with cold climates can be set somewhat higher. The wages in major industrial branches, such as coal mines, petroleum, metallurgy, and other heavy industries can be set comparatively high because these branches not only occupy very important positions in the whole national economy, but their working conditions are also poorer than those in light industry. With the help of a rational wage system, we should encourage the labor force to flow regularly into the most important sectors of the national economy and should ensure the rational allocation of the labor force among the various regions. Setting differential wage standards in the various sectors and regions is an important means for carrying out this task. Appropriate regional subsidies for the workers and staff who are sent to remote areas are set according to the needs of national construction and the differing regional circumstances. These are also an effective means of encouraging workers and staff to feel satisfied with their jobs in remote regions.

Next, we must also establish a wage system that will encourage unskilled workers to strive voluntarily to become more skilled, encourage the workers to unfold labor competition willingly so that they learn from the advanced producers in the course of production, and encourage the workers to be concerned about raising labor productivity so that they further economize on the consumption of raw and other materials, increase the utilization of production facilities, and improve product quality.

The piece-wage system is an advanced wage system that can achieve the above goals. Therefore, we should actively and systematically extend the piece-wage system on the basis of scientifically determined production norms and fixed working hours.

The piece-wage system can be divided into the individual piece-system and the collective piece-system. The individual piece-system is the basic form of piece-wages. In the individual piece-system, the size of the worker's income depends on the quantity and quality of his output. The worker knows the piece unit value of each product in advance. Thus, he will try his best to increase his labor productivity, adopting advanced operating methods in order to raise the quantity and quality of his output. The collective piece-system is usually adopted by those production sectors in which the output of individual workers cannot be calculated. Under this wage system, the wages of each worker do not depend directly on his own personal production; they are determined indirectly on the basis of the output of the whole group (such as a squad). Therefore, the collective piece-system is less effective in stimulating the growth of labor productivity than the individual piece-system.

Both the individual piece-system and the collective piece-system can be divided into the direct piece-system and the progressive piece-system depending on the piece unit values used. Under the direct piece-system, the payment for every piece of product is based on the same piece unit value regardless of the output level. Under the progressive piece-system, wages are paid according to several piece unit values. These piece unit values increase progressively according to the extent to which the output norm is exceeded. Before the progressive piece-system is implemented, we must establish norms which are truly based on technology and must accurately calculate the economic effectiveness of this system. If we suddenly implement this system without adequate preparation, it will not only be impossible to raise labor productivity and reduce costs, but balanced production will also be somewhat adversely affected.

At the same time that the direct piece-system or the progressive piece-system is used, we can also adopt the piece- and bonus-system. The purpose of the bonus system is to encourage the workers to economize on raw materials, processed materials, fuels, and electric power in order to exceed the planned reductions in production costs, to raise the utilization of production facilities, and to improve product quality. The adoption of rational bonus wages can reduce costs and overfulfill the accumulation targets. Part of the excess accumulation can be used to expand output. The rest can be used as a bonus to the workers to encourage their creativity and activism in the struggle to economize on resources and to help the enterprises strive to overfulfill their accumulation tasks.

In our enterprises, in addition to piece-wages, we also have time-wages. The level of time-wages depends primarily on the actual working hours and the skill level. This type of wage cannot bring about a direct relationship between labor output and wages. That is to say, time-wages provide only weak stimulation to the workers to improve the quantity and quality of their work. Therefore, time-wages should only be used when it is not possible to implement work quotas and statistical work and where it is not economically suitable to adopt piece-wages because of the nature of production. There are two kinds of time-wages, namely the simple time-wage system and the time-bonus wage system. Simple time-wages are calculated according to the worker's wage grade and working hours. Time-bonus wages enable the worker who overfulfills the quantity and quality targets of the output plan within the specified time to receive a bonus over and above the wage specified in the wage standard. Therefore, these are more effective incentives than simple time-wages.

The leadership personnel, engineers, technicians, and staff of each enterprise cannot be paid by the piece-wage system since there are no targets that directly express their labor quantity and quality. In addition to their salaries, they may receive bonuses according to the quality and quantity of the work done in their own work sections, workshops, enterprises, or branches. The planned targets and the plan to reduce production costs must both be fulfilled if they are to receive bonuses. Only in this way, by giving them individual material incentives, can we make the engineers and technicians pay attention to the fulfillment and overfulfillment of the whole plan.

VI. Certain Characteristics of the Wage Plan in the Nonproductive Sphere

The principle of distribution according to labor is the basis of the wage plan in the material productive sphere. This principle is also entirely suitable for planning the wages of workers and staff in the nonproductive sphere. However, there are also special characteristics of the wage plan in the nonproductive sphere. First, the wage fund in the productive sphere is obtained from the sale of the enterprises' own products. It is the result of a first-round distribution of the national income within the productive sphere. The wage fund in the nonproductive sphere comes mainly from state budget allocations. It is the result of a second-round distribution or redistribution of the national income. Second, in the productive sphere, there is an extremely close relationship between wages and labor productivity. In the nonproductive sphere, however, the problem of the proportional relationship between the rate of growth of labor productivity and the rate of growth of wages never arises because the working personnel there do not produce physical goods and strict fixed labor productivity targets are difficult to set. Third, with a few exceptions, the wages of the working personnel in the nonproductive sphere are set by the government-approved standardized salary scale. The standardized salary scale takes into account the working personnel's education level, years of service, degree of experience, scope of work, degree of responsibility, and so forth.

Before July 1955, part of the personnel working for the state in China was paid by the pao-kan system.* In order to unify and improve the remuneration system for personnel working for the state and to carry through the principle of distribution according to labor and equal pay for equal work, the state converted the pao-kan

---

*Under the pao-kan or supply system many government administrative employees, particularly at the hsien (county) and ch'ü (district) levels, were paid in kind rather than in money wages. In a directive issued in August 1955 the State Council abolished this system because its lack of uniformity violated the principles of distribution according to labor and equal pay for equal work. State Council, "Kuan-yü kuo-chia chi-kuan kung-tso jen-yuan ch'üan-pu shih-hsing kung-tzu-chih he kai-hsing hua-pi kung-tzu-chih ti ming-ling " (Order concerning the full implementation of the wage system and the reform of the money wage system for employees of state organs) in Chung-hua jen-min kung-ho-kuo fa-kuei hui-pien (Compendium of Laws and Regulations of the People's Republic of China) Volume 2 (Peking: Legal Publishing House, 1956), pp. 684-686. — N.R.L.

system for these working personnel into a wage system starting in July 1955. This was an important measure adopted in China's First Five-Year Plan to improve the wage system so that it could promote the building of socialism.

VII. The Determination of the Wage Fund Plan of the National Economy

The wage fund is the product of the average wage and the number of workers and staff. Therefore, with the labor quantity plan and the average wage plan, there is a basis for the formulation of the wage fund plan. But the wage fund plan based on the above two types of data is only a preliminary plan.

After the preliminary wage fund plan is formulated, we must further analyze the relationship between the wage fund and the total volume of marketed commodities. The correct solution of this relationship must rely on the balance table of the people's money income and expenditure. The money income of the people naturally does not all come from wages, and their expenditures do not exhaust all their purchasing power. However, most of their wages are used to purchase marketed commodities. Therefore, we must specify a correct proportional relationship between the rate of growth of the wage fund and the rate of growth of the total volume of marketed commodities.

If the rate of growth of the volume of marketed commodities is higher than that of the wage fund, then we can plan to lower prices to coordinate the volume of marketed commodities with the people's purchasing power. In the Fourth and Fifth Five-Year Plans in the Soviet Union, prices were lowered to coordinate the people's purchasing power with the volume of marketed commodities. However, it is also possible to raise wages appropriately to coordinate the people's purchasing power with the total volume of marketed commodities.

However, at the beginning of socialist industrialization, because the rate of growth of the production of producer goods far exceeds that of consumer goods, the rate of growth of the volume of marketed commodities is generally lower than that of wages. This proportional relationship can lead to shortages in the market. To solve this problem, savings and public debt can be used to absorb part of the people's purchasing power. When necessary, rationing can also be adopted so that a given quantity of consumer goods can be distributed to the broad masses of laboring people on a fair and rational basis. In addition to these methods, we can also suitably lower the planned rate of growth of the wage fund or adjust the prices of marketed commodities to coordinate the wage fund with the total volume of marketed commodities.

The final wage fund plan can be correctly specified after the above balancing calculations have been made. After the wage fund is set, we must strengthen management so that deficits will not occur. We must gradually establish and strengthen the State Bank's supervision over the wage fund and prevent wage-fund deficits and waste.

VIII. The Real Wage Plan

Wages paid in money are called money wages or nominal wages. Therefore, when prices rise or fall, the same amount of money wages does not purchase the same amount of consumer goods. Real wages are wages expressed in terms of the worker's means of livelihood. They indicate the quantity of consumer goods and services that can be bought with the worker's money wages. Real wages deviate from money wages as prices rise or fall.

In capitalist countries, the rate at which prices rise usually exceeds the rate of growth of money wages. Therefore, real wages often fall. In the socialist and people's democratic countries, because prices are stable and the state often lowers prices, the worker's real wages usually increase continuously. The rate of growth of real wages is usually higher than that of money wages. The increase of real wages in the socialist and people's democratic countries indicates first that the money wages of the workers and staff continuously increase. Second, because the state continuously lowers the prices of commodities for daily use, the same amount of money enables the workers and staff to buy even more consumer goods. In addition, the increasing amount of free cultural and welfare services provided by the state and other sources to the workers and staff also increases their real wages. Such cultural and welfare benefits had to be paid for by the workers and staff from their own money wages before they were provided free by the state and other sources.

(The major content of this lecture is based on relevant materials about the Soviet Union in M. V. Belayev, Lecture Notes on the Process of National Economic Planning.)

LECTURE 15: PRICE PLANNING

Ch'en Hsi-jun*

I. The Roles and Tasks of Price Planning

Product prices are the monetary expression of product values. They are composed of production costs, profits, taxes, and other elements.

Under the capitalist system, product prices are formed through blind competition under the spontaneous effects of the law of value. Under the socialist system, due to the effects of the law of planned and proportional development of the national economy, prices are determined by the state according to the requirements of economic laws.

The major roles of price planning in the national economy are as follows.

First, we correctly determine the factory prices of products so that they can stimulate the state-owned enterprises to improve operation and management and to fulfill and overfulfill production plans.

We all know that the production tasks of the state-owned enterprises are specified by the state. The enterprises must organize production according to the state plan with respect to the production level, variety, specifications, and quality of their products. They cannot oppose the requirements of the state plan. However, correctly specifying factory prices of products is still very important in encouraging the enterprises to better carry out the state plan.

The state-owned enterprises use the economic accounting system. The economic accounting system in the enterprises is an important factor in ensuring that they fulfill or overfulfill their

---

*Ch'en Hsi-jun, "Chia-ko chi-hua." <u>CHCC</u>, 1956, No. 7, pp. 30-33.

production plans. And correctly specifying prices is very significant for the enterprises' implementation of the economic accounting system. To implement the economic accounting system, the
enterprises must rely on their own revenues to pay their production expenses. At the same time, they must also have a certain
amount of profit in order to expand output and to establish an enterprise reward fund for improving worker and staff welfare. If
the factory prices of products are not set rationally and production
costs cannot be covered, it will be hard for the enterprises to continue production. If the factory prices are not high enough to guarantee a certain amount of profit to most of the enterprises, they
will not be able to expand output or use the enterprise reward fund
to provide material incentives to stimulate the workers and staff
to actively fulfill and overfulfill the output plan.

By specifying rational factory prices, we can encourage the enterprises to improve operation and management and strengthen the
economic accounting system. Prices are determined according to
values. In this situation, those enterprises with poor management
and high production costs are very likely to suffer losses. To turn
losses into profits, these enterprises have to improve labor organization, practice economy, adopt careful budgeting, and reduce
waste to lower costs.

Specifying rational prices so that the prices of the various types
of products are in proper proportion to one another is an important
lever for encouraging the enterprise to fulfill the variety plan. If
the prices of some types of the enterprise's products are too high,
resulting in large profits, and the prices of some products are too
low, resulting in small or no profits, then the workers and staff of
the enterprise will pay too much attention to the production of products with high prices and large profits, thus adversely affecting
the fulfillment of the variety plan.

Specifying rational prices is very significant for improving
product quality. If the prices for high-quality and low-quality
products are the same, it will weaken the enthusiasm of the enterprise for improving product quality; product quality may even de-
teriorate, resulting in huge waste for the state.

Second, with rational planning of prices, we can consciously distribute the income of the national economy's various sectors.

A rational distribution of the income of the various sectors is
an important condition for ensuring their proportional development.
There are two major levers for rationally distributing income: the
first is the state budget, and the second is prices. For example, if

the prices of machines and equipment are constant and we reduce the factory price of steel, part of the income of the steel branch will be transferred to the machine-building industry.

Third, correctly specifying the factory prices for producer goods can promote their rational allocation. Among state-owned enterprises, the allocation of producer goods is determined by the material-technical supply plan. However, the level of prices still has a definite effect on the allocation of interchangeable products. When there is a shortage of certain products, their factory prices can be suitably raised and the factory prices of their substitutes can be suitably lowered to encourage the enterprises to use substitutes wherever possible so that the policy of key-point use can be carried out.

Correctly specifying the retail prices of industrial goods is highly significant for adjusting the supply-demand relationship of individual consumer goods. When certain consumer goods are in short supply, we can raise their prices suitably to limit consumption. And when certain consumer goods are in surplus, we can lower their prices suitably to stimulate consumers to buy these goods.

Fourth, price planning also has great influence on improving the people's standard of living. If the increase in the retail prices of consumer goods is very large, then even if the money wages of workers and staff are increased, the people's livelihood still will not be appropriately increased or it can even be lowered. Therefore, a gradual reduction of the retail prices of consumer goods through price planning is important for improving the people's standard of living.

From these points we can see that product prices are closely related to the various aspects of the socialist process of expanding output. The level of prices and the relative prices of products directly affect production, exchange, and distribution. Therefore, it is necessary to formulate the price plan according to the law of socialist production and distribution. The basic economic law of socialism requires that prices be continuously lowered, because lower prices are an important condition for improving the people's material standard of living. The law of planned and proportional development requires that there be correct proportional relations among the prices of the various types of products. The law of value requires that prices be set on the basis of the values of marketed commodities. The basic task of price planning is to correctly specify the price level and the relative prices of each product

according to the requirements of the above laws so that the socialist process of expanding output can be actively influenced.

II. The Economic Bases for Formulating the Plan
for Factory Prices of Industrial Products

There are many types of prices. In industry, there are factory
prices, wholesale prices, and retail prices. In agriculture, there
are procurement prices, wholesale prices, and retail prices. In
transport, there are various freight rates, and so forth. In this
lecture, we will only talk about the problems related to formulating the plan for factory prices of industrial products.

The major economic bases on which to formulate the plan for
factory prices of industrial products are: (1) the price policy of
the state; (2) the product values; (3) the balance between the output
and the sales of products; and (4) the proportional relationship
among the prices of various types of products.

1. The price policy of the state. In a given period of time, the
state adopts different price policies for different products according to the production requirements and consumption needs of the
people as well as the products' production costs and the accumulation requirements of the state. The prices of some products have
to be lowered, while the prices of other products have to be sta-
bilized.

The Party and state's policy of low prices for producer goods
is at present the most important basis for the formulation of the
price plan for producer goods. When the prices of producer goods
are low, the various branches willingly replace manual labor with
machines, thus raising their technical levels. And higher technical
levels are the key to ensuring a high rate of growth of output, reducing the amount of heavy labor which the workers must do, raising labor productivity, and lowering production costs. At the same
time, a policy of low prices for producer goods is also very significant in the priority development of heavy industry. Low prices for
producer goods increase sales so that the development of the heavy
industrial branches will not be adversely affected by poor sales of
their output.

The policy of stable retail and factory prices for consumer
goods is the basis on which China's present price plan for consumer goods is formulated. At present, because China is still
undergoing socialist industrialization, the growth of consumer
goods production has definite limits. Demand exceeds supply for

many consumer goods, so we cannot vigorously lower the retail prices of consumer goods. However, in order to guarantee the people's standard of living, we must stabilize the retail prices of consumer goods. Since retail prices cannot be lowered, factory prices should not be lowered either. Otherwise, the profit of the commercial sector will be too large, thus affecting the consolidation of the commercial sector's economic accounting system.

2. The product values. Since the prices of products are expressions of their values, to determine prices, we must calculate the values of products. At present, we have still not undertaken research on simple methods for calculating values. In practical work, prices are determined with respect to costs, profits, taxes, and so forth.

The production cost of a product is the monetary expression of the majority of that product's value. It includes material consumption and wages. Determining prices on the basis of costs enables us to make prices approach values in general.

The planned price of a product is determined according to the average production cost of the branch in the plan period. Because the level of technology and the level of operation and management are not the same in different enterprises, the production costs of individual enterprises cannot reflect the value of a product. The value varies as labor productivity is raised or lowered. The average cost of the branch in the base period also cannot reflect the value of the product in the plan period. Therefore, only the average production cost of the branch in the plan period can reflect the value of the product in the plan period.

For some products, which are produced in different regions, the natural conditions vary a great deal. Thus, the material and labor consumption for the production of the same types of products is not uniform. Under these conditions, we should not determine the factory prices according to the average costs in the plan period of all enterprises in the country which produce these products. Instead, we should specify different factory prices according to the average costs of the enterprises producing these products in different regions in the plan period.

Determining prices according to the average production costs of the branch is important for ensuring uniform prices for the same types of products. If prices are determined according to the costs of the various enterprises, the prices for the same types of products will not be uniform because the costs of the various enterprises differ. Without uniform factory prices for the same types of products, backward enterprises cannot be stimulated to catch up with advanced enterprises.

Determining prices according to the average costs of the branch imposes certain difficulties on the mining branch because it is greatly affected by natural conditions. Owing to different natural conditions, the difference in the costs of products from various mines is often substantial. The level of operation and management for some mines is very high, but due to extremely poor natural conditions, their costs may be higher than the average costs of the branch. The level of operation and management for some mines is very poor, but due to excellent natural conditions, their costs may be lower than the average costs of the branch. Under these circumstances, if we set prices according to the average costs of the branch without appropriate adjustments, some irrational situations will result, thus undermining the economic accounting system of the enterprise. In the Soviet Union, the system of accounting prices has been adopted for individual industrial branches. The enterprise sells its products to the marketing organ of its branch at accounting prices. The marketing organ of the branch then sells the products to other branches at uniform wholesale prices. The accounting prices are determined according to the planned production costs of the enterprise. The uniform wholesale prices of the branch are determined according to the average costs of the branch. However, there are certain shortcomings in the system of accounting prices. Because accounting prices are determined according to the costs of the enterprises and not according to the average costs of the branch, the accounting prices have lost their function of providing a standard measure of enterprises' production and consumption. Therefore, only some branches in the Soviet Union (petroleum-industry branches) use the system of accounting prices.

Profits and taxes are part of the product values. Therefore, in order to make prices approximate values, we must consider the amount of profit and taxes in addition to calculating the product cost.

It is essential to include a certain amount of profit in product prices if we are to consolidate the economic accounting system of the enterprise.

In the Soviet Union, part of the profit included in the product price is remitted to the state. The rest is retained by the enterprise for its own use. This latter part of the profit is mainly used for the following two things: the welfare fund for the workers and

staff and the fund for expanding the enterprise's output. The welfare fund for the workers and staff is wholly financed by enterprise
profit. The increase in working capital required by the enterprise
to expand output is mainly financed by enterprise profit, but the
enterprise is mainly dependent on state budget allocations for capital investment funds. Only part of it is financed by enterprise
profit.

Therefore, when determining the amount of profit to be included
in product prices, we cannot decide entirely on the basis of what
the enterprise needs; we must also consider the amount of state
investment for expanding the enterprise's output.

Taxes (in the Soviet Union, they are mainly turnover taxes) are
one of the major sources of state financial revenue. In the Soviet
Union, due to the policy of low prices for producer goods, no turnover taxes are included in the factory prices of producer goods.
The state exacts turnover taxes only on consumer goods.

Because there are no turnover taxes on producer goods, the
prices of producer goods are generally lower than their values.

3. The balance between the output and the sales of products.
Product prices depend not only on values, but are also affected by
the product's supply and demand conditions. However, the supply
and demand conditions require that the retail prices of consumer
goods be regulated to a certain extent. This is manifested as follows: prices for consumer goods in short supply should obviously
not be increased indiscriminately; nor should they be lowered.
Otherwise, the shortage would become more serious, leading to
market chaos. Prices for products in surplus should be lowered.
Otherwise undesired inventory buildups will result, adversely affecting production. It should be pointed out that prices and the
supply-demand relationship are interdependent. On the one hand,
we must set retail prices of consumer goods with reference to the
supply and demand conditions. On the other hand, prices can also
affect the supply-demand relationship.

As for the factory prices of producer goods, since the production
tasks of the enterprise are determined by the state, the quantity of
producer goods needed by the enterprise is allocated by the state
according to the plan. Therefore, the level of prices for producer
goods does not regulate the quantity of producer goods required by
the enterprise. However, when determining the factory prices of
producer goods, we must still consider to a certain extent the influence of the supply-demand relationship.

4. The proportional relationship among the prices of each type

of product. In the national economy, the production of each type of product is interrelated. Therefore, the rise or fall of the price of a particular product will lead to changes in the prices of other products. For example, the level of prices for steel affects the level of prices for machines, the level of prices for machines affects the level of prices for various types of products, and so on and so forth. Therefore, in setting the prices of certain products, we must consider the proportional relationship between the prices of these products and those of other products. In the price plan for industrial products, the main price relationships to be considered are as follows:

1. The price relationship between the retail prices of industrial products and the procurement prices of agricultural products. The factory prices of industrial products are the basis of their retail prices. Therefore, in determining the factory prices of industrial products, we must consider maintaining a suitable proportion between the retail prices of industrial products and the procurement prices of agricultural products. On the one hand, it must enable a rational exchange between agricultural products and industrial products, which in turn helps consolidate the worker-peasant alliance. On the other hand, it must be able to ensure the growth of agricultural production on the basis of new technology and to absorb part of the accumulation of the agricultural sector to finance industrialization.

2. The proportion between the factory prices of producer goods and the factory prices of consumer goods. This proportion should carry out a policy of low prices for producer goods on the basis of consolidating the economic accounting system of the sectors which produce producer goods in order to facilitate the extension of new technology in the national economy. The factory prices of consumer goods must basically correspond to their values.

3. The proportion between the factory prices of products from the extracting industry and the factory prices of products from the processing industry. This proportion must promote a rational use of products from the extracting industry and the growth of the processing industry.

4. The proportions among the factory prices of products which can be used interchangeably. For example, the price relationships between concrete and lime and among coal, firewood, petroleum, and so forth. These price relationships should benefit the enterprises which substitute more abundant products for scarcer products. The direction of these price relationships should be to

raise proportionately the prices of scarcer products to encourage enterprises to economize on them and use substitutes.

5. The price relationships between domestic products and imports. The function of these price relationships is to substitute domestic products for imports in order to save foreign exchange and protect the growth of domestic industry.

6. The proportions among prices of products of varying quality. The basic principle to follow in determining these proportions is to encourage the enterprises to improve product quality by setting high prices for excellent quality.

III. The Major Targets and the Formulation Procedure for the Plan for Factory Prices of Industrial Products

There are two major targets for the factory prices of industrial products: one is the level of prices, and the other is the rate of price reduction. The level of prices refers to the prices of certain products in the plan period. The rate of price reduction refers to the percentage by which the planned prices are lower than the actual prices were in the base period. The formula to calculate the rate of price reduction is:

$$\frac{(\text{Prices in the base period} - \text{prices in the plan period}) \times 100}{\text{Prices in the base period}}.$$

There are many kinds of industrial products, each having a different price. Therefore price planning is extremely complicated. At the same time, the factory prices must be based on production, sales, and cost conditions. But the output, sales, and cost conditions of different products are all different. It is impossible for the state to determine the prices of all products. Therefore, the state, the various branches, and the various regions must share the job of separately determining the prices of different kinds of products.

In the Soviet Union, the factory prices of all mass-produced or batch-produced products are approved by the Soviet government. The price formulation for other kinds of products is carried out according to the following principles:

1. The prices of products produced by the whole industry of the Soviet Union and its various republics are negotiated and set by the branches which supply and use them.

2. The factory prices of products produced by the industry of a

republic are set by the Republic's Council of Ministers.

3. The factory prices of products produced by local industry and cooperative industry are decided by the executive committees of the provinces or the frontier regions.

The principles governing the division of labor in formulating China's present factory prices for industrial products are:

a. The prices of products whose production and sales are balanced by the state are centrally determined by the state. For some products, though their production and sales are balanced by the state, their prices can be determined for the state by the relevant ministries or the People's Councils of the provinces (municipalities) and autonomous regions due to the absence of favorable conditions for their central determination by the state.

b. The prices of products whose production and sales are balanced by the central industrial ministries are determined by them.

c. The prices of products from local industry whose output and sales are balanced by provinces (municipalities) and autonomous regions are determined by their People's Councils.

d. The prices of products marketed by the enterprises themselves are negotiated directly between the enterprises and the user branches.

In the national economy, new products are often trial manufactured by many enterprises. In the Soviet Union, the prices of new products are determined according to the following principles:

1. Those products whose prices are already set in the state price list will be priced according to the list.

2. Those products whose prices are not currently included in the state price list but which were once determined by the state will be priced according to past prices. The branches that trial manufacture these new products must submit, within six months after producing the first batch of products, price proposals to be approved by the government of the Soviet Union.

3. For products that are trial manufactured for the first time and for which mass production or batch production is planned, temporary wholesale prices should be negotiated between the supplying branches and the major ordering branches according to the planned costs of the products. The supplying branches should submit, within six months after producing the first batch of products, price proposals to be approved by the Council of Ministers of the Soviet Union.

4. For products that are trial manufactured for the first time and for which small-batch production according to individual orders

is planned, the factory prices should be negotiated between the supplying branches and the ordering branches on the basis of production costs.

The price plan is expressed in the form of a price list. The price list is a legal document. In addition to the specified prices of the various products, the price list must also contain the technical specifications for the products (including the names of the products, their measurements, weights, and brand names or short names, instructions for use, and so forth), and the method of delivery.

LECTURE 16: FINANCIAL PLANNING

Feng Li-t'ien*

I. The Basic Tasks of Financial Planning

In China's transition period and under the socialist system, owing to the continued existence of commodity production and exchange, in national economic planning we must formulate plan targets not only in material terms but also in money (value) terms.
Financial planning serves exactly this purpose.

What is financial planning? Financial planning seeks to guarantee the socialist expansion of output and the satisfaction of the people's consumption needs by accumulating, allocating, and using
money capital according to the national economic plan.

The financial plan is closely related to the economic plan for the
nation as a whole. Neither production nor consumption can be divorced from the relationship with money. Whether it is the productive sector, the capital construction sector, the transport sector,
or the education and health sectors, their plans will be in vain if
they are not guaranteed an adequate amount of money capital. It is
obvious that financial balancing is a very important link in the balancing work of national economic planning. The various targets of
the financial plan must correspond to the requirements of the various development tasks specified by the economic plan for the nation
as a whole.

The basic tasks in formulating and implementing the financial
plan are:

First, we must mobilize all the money capital of society that can
possibly be mobilized and correctly allocate this capital fund among
the various sectors of the national economy according to the requirements of the law of planned and proportional growth of the national economy and the Party's policies, in order to ensure a bal-

*Feng Li-t'ien, "Ts'ai-cheng chi-hua." CHCC, 1956, No. 8, pp. 29-33, 4.

ance between financial revenue and expenditure and the stability of commodity prices.

Second, we must actively promote the growth of the national economy through financial control.

To fulfill these two tasks in all respects and to fully exploit the enormous role of finance in the national economy, we must correctly formulate the following five financial plans:

1. The financial revenue and expenditure plans of each of the productive sectors.

2. The state budget.

3. The credit plan and the cash plan of the State Bank.[1]

4. The comprehensive financial revenue and expenditure plan of the national economy.

II. The Financial Revenue and Expenditures Plans of the Various Productive Sectors [2]

In the system of financial plans, the financial revenues and expenditures plan of each productive sector is the base of all the other financial plans.

The financial plan of a sector is expressed in the form of a revenues and expenditures balance table. It is the comprehensive financial reflection of the output, capital construction, materials supply, labor, production, costs, prices, and marketing plans for that sector, and it is formulated with reference to these plans. The financial plan of the sector reflects sources and uses of money capital of that sector in the plan period. To correctly formulate this plan, we must carry out the system of economic accounting and economy. By improving the organization of production and labor as well as by raising the quantity and quality of output, and satisfying financial revenue targets, we can correctly calculate the amount of money capital needed to fulfill the various plan targets. To correctly formulate this plan, we must also establish a correct financial relationship between the enterprise or the higher administrative organ and the state to ensure the punctuality and stability of state financial revenues.

The format of the financial plans of the various responsible organs in China is briefly outlined on the following page.

The financial revenue and expenditure plan of each sector is compiled with reference to the financial revenue and expenditure plans of the various state-owned enterprises and organizations in the sectors concerned.

Chinese Economic Planning

Financial Revenue and Expenditure Plan of the XX Sector

Income Items	Expenditure Items
1. Profits in the current period	1. Capital construction expenditure
2. Taxes payable	2. Major repairs expenditure
3. Capital depreciation fund	3. Surplus from current period major repair fund
4. Major repair fund	4. Increase in the quota of owned working capital
5. Major repair fund carried over from the previous period	5. Planned losses
6. Income from the sale of fixed assets	6. Deduction for the enterprise reward fund
7. Surplus working capital	7. Other expenditure
8. Increase in the fund for fixed obligations	8. —
9. Other income	9. —
10. Total income	10. Total expenditure
Budgetary allocation when total expenditure exceeds total income	Budgetary remittances when total income exceeds total expenditure
11. Allocation for capital construction	11. Profit remitted
12. Allocation for increased working capital	12. Capital depreciation fund remitted
13. Allocation to subsidize planned losses	13. Taxes remitted
14. Other allocations	14. Surplus working capital remitted
15. —	15. Income from the sale of fixed assets remitted
16. —	16. Other remittances
Grand total income	Grand total expenditure

From the above table, we can see that the financial revenues and expenditure plan of each sector can be divided into two parts: one reflects the enterprises' own revenues and expenditures in the plan year; the other reflects the relation between the enterprises' financial remittances to end allocations from state budget. Below, we will briefly explain the content of the table.

Profits in the current period refers to the total planned profit obtained from the sale of products in the plan period. It is calculated with reference to three elements: the sales volume at wholesale prices, and profit rates for the products of state-owned enterprises. Given constant wholesale prices and profit rates, the lower the production costs, the greater the profit. Therefore, to increase the capital accumulation of the enterprises and the state, we must require the enterprises to reduce costs and increase profits as much as possible, provided that the production plans and marketing plans determined by the state are fulfilled and product quality is guaranteed.

The amount of taxes payable depends on the quantity of the product sold, price, and the tax rate.

The capital depreciation fund is calculated with reference to two factors: the total value of fixed assets and the major repair depreciation rate. It is used to put the fixed assets back in working order. This fund is controlled by the enterprise. Deposits to this special account are made monthly to the State Bank and payments are made according to the plan for major repair of fixed capital.

Major repairs are made at definite intervals. In general, major repairs are made once in somewhat over a year. But deductions for this fund are made every year. Hence the item of major repairs fund carried over from the previous period.

The sixth item refers to net income from the sale of scrapped fixed assets.

Working assets (such as raw materials) are indispensable for the production process. The monetary expression of working assets is working capital. Usually when output increases, the need for working capital increases commensurately. However, because of reductions in the material consumption quotas and the acceleration of capital turnover, the need for working capital does not generally increase as fast as production. To accelerate the turnover of working capital, we must prevent excessive inventory, shorten production cycles, strengthen coordination among enterprises, fulfill the output plan, and guarantee product quality.

Working capital can be divided according to its origin into owned working capital and borrowed working capital. The former is allocated by the state financial department to ensure the minimum normal requirements of the enterprise. The enterprise may require large amounts of working capital in individual seasons and months. At that time, the enterprise can apply for a short-term loan from the bank to make up temporarily for the lack of working capital. This is classified as borrowed. In the financial revenue and expenditure plan, only the owned part is listed.

The seventh item, surplus working capital, refers to the amount by which the actual amount of working capital left at the end of the previous year exceeded the working capital quota for the previous year and the amount by which the quota of owned working capital in the plan year is less than the quota of the previous year. This must be indicated in order to discover why the actual amount of the previous year exceeded the quota of the previous year and at the same time to facilitate comparison with the plan year.

Fixed obligations refers to the enterprise payments that should be but have not yet been made, for items such as wages, water and electricity fees, taxes, and so forth. Since these payments are made at fixed intervals, the fund from which these payments are made can be regarded and used as owned working capital before the payments are made. As enterprise production increases year after year, the various production expenses increase correspondingly, and hence the portion of payments that should be but have not yet been made also increase.

The following discussion relates to financial expenditure.

Capital construction expenditure refers to capital funds required for capital construction in the plan year. Increases or decreases of working capital in the capital construction sector should be included in this. This item also includes expenses for improvements of technical processes and production systems, expenses for the trial manufacture of new products, and miscellaneous capital construction expenses which are related to the increase in fixed assets.

Capital construction expenditure should be determined strictly on the basis of the construction and engineering budget, the capital construction plan, the enterprise's plan for improvements of technical processes and production systems and the plan for the trial manufacture of new products.

Major repair expenditures in the plan year are usually less than the sum of the deduction for the major repair fund in the plan year and the surplus of the previous period. Hence, the item of surplus from the current period major repair fund. This is a balancing item and is therefore listed under the expenditure column.

An increase in the quota for working capital indicates that the working capital quota of the plan year exceeds the working capital quota of the previous year.

Planned losses result when the enterprise income after taxes cannot cover production costs.

The enterprise reward fund is mainly used for various welfare facilities for the staff and workers of the enterprise, prizes for suggestions concerning rationalizing enterprise operation, special relief payments to selected staff and workers, and so forth. It is deducted from profits according to a fixed rate of deduction. The rate of deduction is higher for unplanned profit than for planned profit in accordance with the principle of material incentives.

The second part of the table concerns the relationship between the sectors' finances and the state budget. This relationship is manifested as remittances and allocations.

The capital depreciation fund, taxes, and income from the sale of fixed assets are wholly remitted to the state budget. Profit remitted is the balance after the deductions for planned losses and the enterprise reward fund have been made from current period profit. Therefore, in a given sector, if there is profit remitted, there will be no allocation to make up for planned losses.

In general, the allocation for capital construction is equal to the capital construction expenditure. If, in the plan period, the enterprise has sources of investment for capital construction that do not require budgetary allocations (such as the value of local civilian voluntary labor, capital funds arranged by the enterprise, and so forth), they should be subtracted and listed under income.

The problem of required increases in the enterprises' owned working capital quota should in the first instance be solved by internal adjustments within their own sector. Therefore, the allocation for this item should be equal to item 4 of expenditure minus items 8 and 9 [7 and 8? — N. R. L.] of income. Hence, a single sector cannot have both the items of surplus working capital remitted and the item of allocation for increased working capital.

Since there must be financial relationships between each sector and the state budget, differences between the budgetary allocations and the budgetary remittances for various sectors at various times will not be completely identical. In general, three conditions are possible: the first occurs when remittances exceed allocations, the second, when allocations exceed remittances, and the third, when remittances equal allocations. If we look at it by sector, the first condition is the most common and in conformity with the law. This is because only under this condition can the state have the money capital to develop and maintain the activities of the nonproductive sectors of culture and education, administration, and national defense. The second condition occurs at various times and in various sectors. For example, the general condition in China in the past few years has been that remittances exceeded allocations in light industry, the textile industry, the food industry, and so forth, whereas allocations exceeded remittances in heavy industry. This is in conformity with the policy of giving priority to the development of heavy industry. The condition in which remittances equal allocations only occurs by chance for individual cases.

If we look at it according to the various systems within a given sector, then the first condition applies to the production enterprises, supply and marketing units, and the construction-contracting enterprises, and the second condition applies to the capital construction units, whose allocations often far exceed their remittances.

III. The State Budget

A socialist-type state budget is a systematically established financial plan for the allocation of accumulated money capital to satisfy the demands of expanding socialist reproduction and social consumption.

The state budget occupies an important place in the financial planning system and is a basic financial plan. The state budget is the focal point for the allocation and redistribution of money capital, and the greater part of money capital is accumulated and allocated through the medium of the budget.

The first reason we must distribute and redistribute concentrated money capital is the imbalance in the various departments of the national economy between the amounts of money capital which they can themselves produce or accumulate and their requirements in the way of money capital, some departments having too much and some too little. Because of this the state must carry out a unified and concentrated adjustment; only in this way can we guarantee in a financial sense the proportional expansion of all departments of the national economy. For example, heavy industry must be expanded, but in promoting large-scale industrial construction, the money capital produced by the departments of heavy industry is as a rule insufficient to meet their expansion requirements. The task of financial departments is through the medium of financial plans, the primary one being the national budget, to redistribute to the departments of heavy industry the money capital produced by light industry, agriculture, and other production departments.

Second, there are within the national economy productive and nonproductive departments. For example, there are culture and education, health, administration, defense, and nonproductive service departments. The money capital requirements of these departments are satisfied from the redistribution of money capital that is produced either directly or indirectly by the material producing departments. This redistribution process is carried out chiefly through the medium of the state budget.

Last, the state budget fulfills an important function in effecting the allocation and redistribution of money capital between economic sectors and in guaranteeing the priority development of the socialist sector of the economy. The income of the state budget comes from all economic sectors (income from the state-operated sector occupying the chief position), but expenditures go for the most part to expanding the socialist state-operated sector.

The state budget is composed of two parts, the central government budget and local budgets. Most of the funds of the state budget (70-80 percent) are concentrated in the central government budget, which provides for expenditures of a national nature and state economic construction. For example, construction of a national nature and all defense expenditures are provided for in the central government budget. Local budgets provide for the actual functioning of local administrative organs. The expansion of local economic affairs and local cultural and educational affairs, as well as local administrative expenses, are provided through the local budget.

The central government budget and local budgets are closely connected. To maintain an adequate balance between income and expenditures in budgets at all levels, the state stipulates that in local budgets (i.e., those for provinces, autonomous regions, municipalities directly under the control of the central government, and hsien), income in excess of expenditures should be remitted to the central government budget, and expenditures in excess of income should be subsidized from the central government budget. For example, 70-80 percent of annual expenditures in the local budget of Tibet from 1952 to 1955 were subsidized by allocations from the central government budget.[3] From this it can be seen that the central government budget performs an important function in regard to balancing receipts and expenditures of local budgets.

The important items of revenue and expenditures in the national budget are as follows:

Budgetary Revenue	Budgetary Expenditure
All income from taxes	Expenditure for economic construction
Revenue from state-operated enterprises	Expenditure for social culture and education
Revenue from credits, and insurance, and other revenue	Expenditure for government administration
Total revenue this year	Expenditure for credits and other expenditures
Surplus revenue carried over from last year	General reserve
Gross revenue	Total expenditure this year
	Gross expenditure
	Budgetary surplus for this year

Income from taxes is in the form of industrial and commercial taxes and an agricultural tax. All economic sectors are liable to taxation. For example, industrial and commercial taxes are paid by state-operated, cooperative, jointly operated, and privately operated enterprises,[4] and an agricultural tax is paid by peasants. Income from taxes is an effective method whereby the state mobilizes all economic sectors for payment of a portion of the money capital required to satisfy the needs of the nation and society.

Income from state-operated enterprises is in the form of funds remitted not as taxes into the state budget by state-operated industry, communications, commercial, and agricultural enterprises, and some operational units. For example, profits, capital depreciation funds, surplus working capital, income from the sale of fixed assets, and other sums are remitted to the state. Profits remitted to the state account form the greatest proportion of these remittances. The present financial system requires that all profits of state-operated enterprises, after deductions for bonus funds and planned losses, be remitted to the state.

Income from state-operated enterprises also includes operational income. This includes income from designs of inspection and design organs, income from the sale of products of experimental research organs, income from water conservation and irrigation operations, income from cultural, educational, and health operations and news broadcasting and other such income. These operations generally do not carry out economic accounting. All revenues and expenditures are handled by the method of remittance to the state and allocation by the state through the medium of the state budget.

The third item of income is divided into two parts. One is income from credits, and insurance, such as income from the sale of bonds, income from foreign loans, and surplus income remitted to the state by the People's Insurance Company of China. The other is other income, for example income from fees,[5] income from fines, and income from public property.

The last item of budgetary income is surplus income carried over from last year. Strictly speaking, last year's surplus cannot be considered budgetary income for the current plan year because the State Bank will have considered this surplus as credit and loan capital and will have already loaned it to enterprises. Therefore, only when the amount of last year's budgetary surplus that has been used by the State Bank to extend credit is less than the total budgetary surplus for last year can the difference be included in the budget for the current plan year as one of the components of budget income.

The first item of expenditure is expenditure for economic construction. These are funds allocated for capital construction investment, working capital, and planned losses in state-operated enterprises and some operational units concerned with industry, agriculture, animal husbandry, forestry, water conservation, meteorology, transportation, communication, and telecommunications, commerce, the purchase of grain and agricultural products, foreign trade, culture, education, and health, and municipal construction. Expenditure for economic construction also include expenditure for state stockpiling. The great bulk of economic construction expenditure is used for capital construction, chief among which is socialist industrial construction.

Social, cultural, and educational expenditures are more specifically expenditures for current expenses in culture, higher-level education, general education, cadre training, physical culture, science, news reporting and broadcasting, health, pensions, and social relief and welfare.

Defense expenditures go for the various expenses of all branches of the armed forces.

Expenditure for government administration are various items of expenses to guarantee the organization and necessary leadership of economic and cultural construction. These include expenses for government administration, expenses for political affairs,[6] foreign affairs, and aid to democratic parties and people's organizations. In addition, there are expenditures for the general expenses of public security, judicial, and investigative organs.

Credits and other expenditures are payments on the principal and interest on state bonds and foreign loans, payments for foreign aid, and other such expenditures.

The last item of budgetary expenditure is the general reserve. The general reserve is set aside to insure that socialist construction is successfully carried out and to avert unforeseen errors. The amount set aside for the general reserve is calculated as a fixed proportion (generally 3-5 percent) of gross budgetary expenditures. At present financial reserves include both the capital required for the stockpiling of materials by the state and the general reserve. The former is included in expenditures for economic construction. Because of this, the general reserve is only a part of the total financial reserves. This reserve is generally used, with the approval of the State Council, when the need for further capital arises as a result of the addition of new items of capital construction, natural calamities, or the overfulfillment of production quotas by certain departments.

Under ordinary circumstances, gross expenditures should be smaller than gross revenues, thereby making possible a budget surplus for the plan year. This surplus has two important uses — the first is as a credit fund for the State Bank, and the second is as a financial revolving fund.

The State Bank must during the course of the plan year issue various loans to enterprises of all departments of the national economy. The principal source of capital for these loans is the surplus in the national budget.

The financial revolving fund is for the temporary use of local financial organs when their cash expenditures are in excess of cash revenues. These funds must be repaid when revenues are in excess of expenditures. Because in the long run this is a continuously circulating process, it is generally impossible to deplete this fund.

The preceding has been an explanation of the important components of the revenue and expenditure items of the state budget. Of all revenues, income in 1956 from state-operated enterprises will account for almost one half of the budgetary income, and second in importance will be income from taxes. Along with the expansion of the state-operated sector of the economy, the relative proportion of income from state-operated enterprises will continuously increase while that of income from taxes will decrease. Of total expenditures, expenditures for economic construction in 1956 accounted for more than one half of budgetary expenditures.

From the above discussion of the revenue and expenditure items of the national budget it can be seen that departmental financial revenue and expenditure plans are the basis for the state budget. Because the principal source of income in the state budget is from production departments, the prime source is state-operated enterprises. Also, by far the greatest portion of expenditures in the state budget go to satisfy the demands of socialist economic construction.

IV. Comprehensive Financial Revenue and Expenditure Plan of the National Economy

All financial plans indicate separately the sources of money capital and their allocation, and in addition each one in different ways fulfills the two basic tasks of a financial plan. Inasmuch as departmental financial plans are the basis for the state budget, the state budget is a basic financial plan. Financial revenues and expendi-

tures, as well as the needs of departments for capital, are inseparable from the credit and loan plan and cash plan of the State Bank.
It is obvious therefore that there exists an internal connection between these financial plans. So that all financial plans may be com-
plementary, it is necessary to compile a national economic comprehensive financial revenue and expenditure plan.

Another reason for the necessity of compiling a comprehensive
financial revenue and expenditure plan is that it is the basis upon
which the national economic plan is compiled and investigated.
When the national economic plan is drawn up, not only must attention be paid to balancing materials but capital must be calculated
so as to balance. As the state budget is the basic financial reflection of the national economic plan, it follows that the comprehensive financial revenue and expenditure plan is a complete financial
reflection of the national economic plan. Also, as the state budget
is only compiled annually, it can only basically reflect the annual
national economic plan. The comprehensive financial revenue and
expenditure plan is compiled not only annually but also for long
periods and can therefore reflect whether or not long period plans
are financially in balance.

Of the uses to which a comprehensive revenue and expenditure
plan can be put, an important one arises from the fact that this
plan not only reflects the sources and distribution of the money
capital concentrated in the state, but also reflects the sources
and distribution of that money capital directly controlled by state-
operated enterprises. In other words, this plan can completely reflect the financial balance of the national economy.

There are many similarities between the components of the national economic comprehensive financial revenues and expenditure
plan and those of the state budget. Items in the state budget are
also reflected in the comprehensive financial revenue and expenditure plan. However, separated into individual items, there are
many differences between these two plans, as evidenced by the
following:

First, the comprehensive financial revenue and expenditure plan
includes certain financial items dispersed among the individual
state-operated economic departments, items which do not appear
in the state budget. For example, the comprehensive plan includes
amongs its revenues all income from profits of state-operated enterprises, whereas the state budget includes only those profits remitted to the state. Two other items of income found in the comprehensive revenue and expenditure plan but not in the state budget

are mobilization of internal capital and funds for major repairs in state-operated enterprises. The mobilization of internal resources means chiefly last year's surplus capital construction materials, reserve funds of public-private jointly operated enterprises, civilian voluntary labor, overseas Chinese investments, and other such items.

As with revenue items, there are differences in regard to expenditures. For example, the comprehensive financial revenue and expenditure plan includes, among expenditures for capital construction, expenditures for major repairs and for the mobilization of internal resources. Among expenditures for cultural and educational affairs, this plan includes expenditures for workers' welfare from enterprise bonus funds. Neither of these items is included in the state budget.

From this it can be seen that the national economic comprehensive financial revenue and expenditure plan adequately covers the following situations: the source of capital for the national economy's capital construction, increases in the amounts of working capital needed, and the development of all phases of social culture and education. It is also possible with this plan to investigate the various important ratios in the national economy, such as the ratio between investment in fixed assets and investment in working capital and the ratio between consumption and accumulation.

Another difference between the comprehensive financial revenue and expenditure plan and the state budget is that the former is compiled according to the principle of distinguishing on the basis of economic relations. This plan reflects the ascendancy or decline of the various economic sectors and will show within the various economic sectors the uses to which the cash accumulations offered to the state can be put, as well as other changes. Because of this, among the items under revenues, there are separate entries for revenues from the state-operated economy,[7] revenues from the cooperative, public-private jointly operated, and privately operated economies, and from the mobilization of the population's capital, etc. Revenues of the state-operated economy include all of the profits of state-operated enterprises, taxes remitted to the state by state-operated enterprises, other income remitted to the state by state-operated enterprises,[8] state operational income, income from the mobilization of internal resources, etc. Revenues from the cooperative economy are various taxes remitted by cooperative enterprises (including agricultural producer coopera-

tives). Revenues from the public-private jointly operated and
privately operated economies are various taxes and bonds remitted
by public-private jointly operated and privately operated enterprises. The important revenues from the mobilization of the population's capital are agricultural taxes remitted by individual peasants and income from the purchase of bonds by the public.

The state budget is the basic component of the comprehensive
financial revenue and expenditure plan for the entire national economy. In the Soviet Union, revenues and expenditures of the state
budget account for about 80 percent of the national economy's comprehensive financial revenues and expenditures. However, as
China is at present using certain financial plans which are different from those of the Soviet Union, the requirements of state-
operated enterprises for capital construction investment and working capital are provided for out of budget allocations and not directly from the enterprise departments profits and capital depreciation funds. All enterprise profits, after the deduction of bonus
funds and planned losses, are remitted to the state, and capital depreciation funds also appear under budgetary receipts. Therefore,
revenues and expenditures of the state budget in China at present
account for a greater proportion of the national economic comprehensive financial revenue and expenditure plan (approximately 95
percent) than they do in the Soviet Union. Hereafter, however,
changes in the financial system will diminish this ratio.

Because the comprehensive financial revenues and expenditures
plan mirrors certain targets in departmental financial plans, there
is a direct connection between this plan and departmental financial
plans. Moreover, both departmental financial plans and the state
budget are merged in this plan.

There is also a direct connection between the comprehensive
financial revenue and expenditure plan for the national economy and
the credit plan of the State Bank. In regard to expenditures in this
plan, any increase in the allocation of credit capital is reflected in
an amount identical to the surplus in the state budget.

The comprehensive financial revenue and expenditure plan for
the national economy is not a legal instrument but an accounting
instrument whereby the State Planning Commission promotes
financial balance throughout the country and determines the important components of the national economic plan. Although
this plan does not as yet have official government approval, it
is widely used.

Notes

1. Due to space limitations, we will not deal with the credit plan and the cash plan of the State Bank in this lecture. For details, please refer to "Chi-hua ching-chi chi-pen chih-shih" [Basic Knowledge of the Planned Economy], Chi-hua ching-chi, 1956, No. 1, p. 29.

2. This section is based on "1956 nien kuo-ying chi-yeh ts'ai-wu shou-chih chi-hua piao-ke chi pien-chih shuo-ming" [The 1956 Table for the Financial Revenue and Expenditure Plan of State-Owned Enterprises and Notes on Its Compilation].

3. Ko Chih-ta, "Wo-kuo kuo-chia yü-suan ti pen-chih ho t'a tsai kuo-tu shih-ch'i ti tso-yung" [The Nature of the State Budget in Our Country and Its Function in the Transition Period]. Ching-chi yen-chiu [Economic Research], 1956, No. 3, pp. 76-77.

4. State-operated enterprises do not pay an income tax.

5. So-called income from fees refers to the changes made by state organs for performing certain special services for individuals and social organizations. For example, legal fees, social registration fees, marriage certificate fees, and passport fees.

6. Such as regular expenses for people's congresses of all levels, minority nationality affairs, overseas Chinese affairs, political propaganda, etc.

7. State-operated enterprise depreciation funds and foreign trade receipts are listed separately and are not included among receipts from the national economy, a method which facilitates analysis of the ratio between depreciation and capital construction investment and makes comprehensible the foreign trade situation.

8. I.e., remittances from the sale of fixed assets and surplus working capital.

LECTURE 17: THE NATIONAL ECONOMIC BALANCE TABLE

Chu Ch'eng-p'ing*

I. The Basic Tasks of the National Economic Balance Table

The national economic balance table differs from the balance tables used in the sectoral plans of the national economy. It is a comprehensive balance table to balance the whole national economic plan. The formulation of the national economic balance table is based on the sectoral balance tables of the national economy.

The national economy is an integrated whole. Therefore, in formulating the national economic plan, we must not only coordinate the targets with each of the sectoral plans of the national economy so that resources match needs, but must also ensure that the targets for the whole national economy are mutually compatible so that there is an overall balance between resources and needs.

When we formulate the national economic balance table, we can reveal whether or not the production and consumption targets in the national economic plan for the various sectors, the various economic components,[†] and the two major categories[‡] are in conformity with one another; we can show whether or not the targets for the physical quantity and value of the social product are coordinated and whether or not the labor resources of the national economy are consistent with the targets for labor distribution. That is to say, the formulation of the national economic balance table can organically integrate the various aspects of overall social repro-

---

*Chu Ch'eng-p'ing, "Kuo-min ching-chi p'ing-heng piao." <u>CHCC</u>, 1956, No. 9, pp. 27-33.

†Referring to the state operated, cooperative, public-private jointly operated, private capitalist, and individually operated components of the economy. — N. R. L.

‡Referring to the producer and consumer goods sector of the economy. — N. R. L.

duction.* Therefore, the table helps the state planning organs tap the potential of the national economy and use manpower and material and financial resources in the most rational way to promote the growth of the national economy.

From this we can see that the basic task of the national economic balance table is: to reflect and determine correctly the balance of the whole national economy according to the requirements of the economic laws of socialism and moreover to take into account the influence of other economic laws, thus providing a basis for the scientific formulation and examination of a unified national economic plan.

II. The Components and Formulation of the National Economic Balance Table

The whole social reproduction process includes the following three aspects:
  1. the reproduction of the social product;
  2. the reproduction of the relations of production;[†]
  3. the reproduction of the labor force.

Reproduction of the social product and of the relations of production are two integral aspects of the whole social reproduction process. There is no reproduction of the relations of production apart from the reproduction of the social product; and the production of the social product is carried on in the context of certain relations of production. Therefore, in explaining the reproduction of the social product, we are also explaining the reproduction of the relations of production. In describing the reproduction of the social product, due to the existence of laws governing the production and value of marketed commodities, the social product must be expressed both in terms of physical quantity and value. All these determine that the national economic balance table must include the following three components if it is to comprehensively reflect social reproduction:

---

*The term "social reproduction" (she-hui tsai sheng-ch'an) or more fully, the "reproduction of the social product" (she-hui chan-pin ti tsai sheng-ch'an) refers to not only the production of social product but also the processes of exchange and distribution of this product and its ultimate allocation to either consumption or accumulation. — N. R. L.

†This refers to the relation between producer and consumer goods, among the productive sectors of the economy, among various components of the economy distinguished on the basis of the form of ownership, etc. This is discussed more fully below in section III. — N. R. L.

1. The social product balance table: this is a comprehensive material balance table which explains the material content of reproduction. It can reflect the production and uses of the social product.

2. The social product and national income balance table: this is a comprehensive financial balance table which explains the value content of reproduction. It can reflect the processes of production, distribution, and redistribution of the national income and its final uses.

3. The labor balance table: this can reflect the distribution and uses of the society's labor resources.

In addition to the above basic components, the national economic balance table also includes supplementary balance tables and appendices explaining the various aspects of reproduction.

National economic balance tables can be classified as balance table reports or balance table plans according to their intended use. Balance table reports reflect the actual conditions of economic growth in the base period. Balance table plans reflect the growth activities in the plan period.

When formulating the national economic balance table, we must first formulate the national economic balance table report. The national economic balance table report is the basis on which we formulate the national economic balance table plan.

When we have determined the political and economic tasks of the state for the plan period and also have the national economic balance table report in hand, we can begin to formulate the national economic balance table plan. And thus we can approach national economic planning work more scientifically.

The formulation of the national economic balance table cannot be completed successfully in one attempt. It must be revised many times as the formulation of the national economic plan progresses. The preliminary draft of the national economic balance plan can only give a rough indication of the national economic balance in the plan period. Even so, this preliminary draft can still be used to accelerate the process of formulating the control numbers and to relate the preliminary state control numbers to one another so that the control numbers announced by the state will have been examined from the viewpoint of overall balance, thus ensuring compatibility among various targets.

The task in the later stage of formulating the national economic balance plan is to revise the draft balance plan according to the draft plans of the various sectors and regions, to enlarge the scope of the targets in the balance table, and to coordinate further the various targets. At the same time that the balance table is revised, the original control numbers are also revised to facilitate the policies of developing the state control numbers to include even more plan targets and further coordinating among the targets of the state plan.

Therefore, when the national economic balance table is finally completed, the national economic plan is also completed. The national economic plan begins with the formulation of the national economic balance table and ends with the completion of the national economic balance table.

The national economic balance table is not only the most scientific method for formulating the national economic plan, it is also the most scientific method for examining the implementation of the national economic plan. The state planning agencies can use the national economic balance table report to discover disproportions and potentials in the national economy, thus ensuring the fulfillment and overfulfillment of the national economic plan.

III.   The Social Product Balance Table[1]

The basis of social production is the production of material goods. Therefore, the most important part of the whole national economic balance table is the social product balance table. The social product balance table is the core of the whole national economic balance table. Other balance tables must all be formulated around this balance table.

To reflect scientifically the reproduction of the social product, the social product balance table must reflect the following things:

1. The major processes in the reproduction of the social product. In other words, the processes of production, exchange, distribution, consumption, and accumulation of the social product.

2. The proportionate relations and economic relations in the reproduction of the social product. In other words, the proportionate relations and economic relations in social production between producer goods and consumer goods, among the various sectors, and among the various economic components of the national economy.

In addition, the social product balance table must also reflect changes in the material conditions governing the production of the social product and the influence of imports and exports on the reproduction of the social product.

Therefore, the social product balance table can be shown according to the following format:

118

Social Product Balance Table

Targets for the physical composition of social product \ Targets in reproduction of social product	National assets at beginning of plan period	Product at production prices	Value added in exchange process	Product at consumption prices	Imports	Productive consumption	Nonproductive consumption	Of which General population	Of which Nonproduction departments	Accumulation	Exports	National assets at end of plan period
A	1	2	3	4	5	6	7	8	9	10	11	12
I. By economic uses of product												
1. Producer goods												
2. Consumer goods												
II. By sector of origin of product												
1. Industrial products												
2. Agricultural products												
3. Construction products												
4. Restaurant products												

The targets along the rows of the social product balance table classified by economic uses and sectoral origins can reflect the material composition, production, and uses of the social product.

The primary targets along the columns of the social product balance table are the national assets at the beginning and end of the plan period. The total national assets include the two components fixed assets and material reserves. Fixed assets and material reserves can be used for production or consumption. Production-related fixed assets and material reserves are the material basis for expanded reproduction. Nonproduction related fixed assets and material reserves are important conditions for elevating the people's material and cultural standards of living.

Products valued at production prices include only the value of output of industry, agriculture, the construction industry, and the restaurant industry which create use values in the form of material goods. The value of output of the exchange process is the value added in the exchange process. It includes only the output value of freight transport and postal and communication services, domestic trade, foreign trade, and material-supplying and -purchasing which are related to production. When calculating the value of output of production and exchange, the figures should be listed separately by sectors and economic components of the national economy to show the proportions among the various sectors and economic components.

Product valued at consumption value is the sum of the product valued at production prices and the value added in the exchange process.

The material reserves at the beginning of the plan period and the production and imports during the plan period comprise the sources of the total social product. These material resources are mainly used for productive consumption, nonproductive consumption, and accumulation, with some left over for exports.

Productive consumption includes the consumption of fixed assets and working capital in the course of production. Consumption of working capital in the production process is the consumption of raw materials, fuels, and so forth. Consumption of fixed assets in the production process represents the wear and tear on fixed assets in the production process. When calculating productive consumption, the figures should be listed separately by sector, category, and economic component. Only by doing this can we understand the amount and proportions of material consumption in the various sectors, categories, and economic components. In association with the row targets, these figures can show us the relationships between production and consumption among the various sectors and between the two major categories of social production in the national economy.

Nonproductive consumption includes: the personal consumption of all the households and the social consumption of the nonproductive sectors.

Accumulation includes the increases in productive and nonproductive fixed assets and material reserves. When planning accumulation, the figures should also be listed by the various productive sectors, categories, nonproductive sectors, households, and various economic components. Only in this way can we show the amount and proportions of accumulation for the various sectors, categories, households, and various economic components. In association with the row targets, these figures can show the relationships between production and accumulation among the various productive sectors and between the two major categories in the national economy.

From this we can see that with the help of the social product balance table, we can:

1. Determine the scale of reproduction of the social product. This including the gross output of social product; the output of the various productive sectors, the two major categories of social production, and the various economic components; the scale of productive consumption, nonproductive consumption, and accumulation; and the scale of imports and exports.

2. Determine the major proportional relations and economic relations of the reproduction of the social product. The major proportional relations are: the proportional relationship between producer goods and consumer goods, among the various productive sectors of the national economy, among the various economic components, between production and exchange, and between consumption and accumulation. The economic relations are: the relationship between the production and consumption of producer goods and consumer goods and the relationships between production and consumption among the various productive sectors of the national economy.

Therefore, through the social product balance table, the state planning agency can analyze whether the production and distribution of the social product are compatible and thus ensure that the socialist state can expand reproduction at top speed and that the national economy can grow in a proportional and coordinated fashion.

IV. The Social Product and National Income Balance Table

The social product and national income balance table is a money balance table (also known as the financial balance table). Through this balance table, we can explain the production of the social product and the national income in terms of money income, how money is used to distribute and redistribute the national income, and the process through which national income becomes consumption or accumulation.

The simplest format for the social product and national income balance table is shown on the next page.

The first of the row targets in the social product and national income balance table should be the productive realm. And within the productive realm, the following classifications by economic components are appropriate for China's present conditions: state-operated economy, cooperative economy, public-private jointly operated economy, private capitalist economy, and individual economy. In the Soviet Union, state-operated enterprises and collective farming cooperatives are the two major classifications. Then come the nonproductive sectors. The nonproductive sectors can be further classified into: the social, cultural, and welfare sector; the administration and management sector; and the national defense sector. Last are the households. Under China's present conditions, the households can be further classified into: staff and workers, cooperative producers, individual laborers, capitalists, and other households. In the Soviet Union, the major classifications are the staff and workers and the peasants.

Classifications according to the above format in the social product and national income balance table can demonstrate: the roles of various economic components in creating the social product and national income and the direction of changes in these roles; the redistribution of the national income between the productive and nonproductive sectors, among various economic components, and among various classes of people; and the porportionate allocation of the consumption fund among the nonproductive sectors and among the classes of people.

The column targets of the social product and national income balance table should first of all list the social product and then the productive consumption of material resources. According to Marx's scientific definition of national income, national income is social product minus material consumption.

After the national income has been produced, the initial distribu-

Social Product and National Income Balance Table

Targets for the reproduction of the social product and national income / Targets for the composition of the social product and national income

	Production of the social product and national income			Initial distribution of national income				Redistribution of national income			National income by final use		
	Gross social product	Productive-material consumption	Gross national income	Primary income of households	Primary income of enterprises	Transfer primary income of households	Total	Redistribution expenditures	Redistribution revenues	Difference between redistribution revenues and expenditures	Consumption	Accumulation	Total
A	1	2	3	4	5	6	7	8	9	10	11	12	13
I. Productive realm													
1. State-operated economy													
2. Cooperative economy													
3. Public-private jointly-operated economy													
4. Private capitalist economy													
5. Individual economy													
II. Nonproductive sectors													
III. Households													
IV. Total													

tion begins. The initial distribution of the national income can be divided into the primary income of the households and the primary income of the enterprises. In China, the primary income of the households is received in the following four major forms: the wages of the workers and staff of state-operated enterprises, supply and marketing cooperatives, public-private jointly operated productive enterprises, and private capitalist productive enterprises; the wages of members of the handicraft cooperatives; the money income and income paid in kind according to labor days of members of agricultural producers' cooperatives; and the income of laborers in the individual economy. The primary income of the enterprises in the state managed economy includes taxes, profits, and deducations for the enterprise reward fund and social insurance. In the public-private jointly managed enterprises, it includes taxes, the public accumulation fund, the welfare fund for the staff and workers, dividends and interest on government capital in state-private jointly operated enterprises, and dividends and interest on fixed interest on privately owned stocks. In the consumers' cooperatives, the supply and marketing cooperatives, and the handicraft cooperatives the primary income is primarily taxes and profits. In the agricultural producers' cooperatives, it is primarily taxes, the public accumulation fund, and the welfare fund. If primary income obtained by households from the productive realm is listed under the column transfer primary income of households it should be entered under the household category. The primary income obtained by households from the productive realm is the major source of households' total income.

After the initial distribution of the national income, redistribution of the national income starts. The reasons why the national income has to be redistributed in China are:

1. to ensure that the nonproductive sectors and the people who work in them can obtain the necessary income;

2. to achieve the redistribution of income among the various economic components and to ensure that priority is given to the development of the socialist economy;

3. to realize the redistribution of income among the various classes and groups of households so that the material and cultural standards of living between the workers and the peasants can gradually be reduced;

4. to ensure that capital funds are rationally allocated among the various sectors, categories, and regions of the national economy so that new proportional relations among the various sectors,

categories, and regions can be established to meet the requirements of national industrialization.

From these we can see that the redistribution of China's national income is an important means for realizing the general task of China's transition period.

The redistribution of the national income is carried out mainly through budget revenues and expenditures. In addition, prices and the system of banking, credit, and insurance, the social service sectors, the Party, the League, and the labor unions are also used.

After the national income has been distributed and redistributed, it is finally used in two ways: consumption and accumulation. The proportion between the consumption and accumulation of the national income is the most important proportion in the distribution process. To realize national industrialization, it is necessary to increase accumulation rapidly and to increase the proportion of accumulation. However, since increasing the people's standards of living is the purpose of production in China, consumption should also be increased correspondingly. The amount of consumption and accumulation in the national income must be the same as the amount of social product used for consumption and accumulation. This is a major condition for ensuring that the value of the social product is equal to its use value. Specifically, the investment fund must correspond with the availability of construction equipment and materials, and people's purchasing power must correspond with the availability of retail commodities.

The consumption of the national income is divided into the households' personal consumption and the social consumption of the nonproductive sectors.

The personal consumption of the households is calculated by subtracting from their income obtained in distribution and redistribution their expenditures in the course of redistribution. Through distribution and redistribution, the households can obtain income in the following ways: wages of staff and workers; wages of cooperative members; salary income of capitalists; income of cooperative members paid according to labor days; labor income of individual producers; income of households from sideline jobs; income from relief payments, subsidies, scholarships, and one-time bonuses received from state insurance; income from the credit system; food and other physical goods from hospitals, sanitariums, and other welfare departments; interest paid to capitalists; dividend income; land bonuses and remuneration for producer goods paid to members of agricultural producers' cooperatives, and so forth.

The difference between the above income and tax payments, service charges, purchase of public debt, payments to the credit system, payments to the state insurance system, investment and payment for stocks in the cooperatives, membership fees, and other nonconsumption related expenses is the personal consumption and consumption-related accumulation of the households.

The social consumption of the nonproductive sectors is calculated from the difference between the income they receive and the expenditures they make in the course of redistribution. The income of the nonproductive sectors includes: state budgetary allocations for social, cultural, and welfare services, expenditures for national defense and government administration, revenues from services provided to households, direct income from the productive sectors, income from services provided to production enterprises, income from state insurance, income from credit transactions, and membership fees from members of the Party, League, labor unions, and other social organizations. From this income should be deducted taxes and profits paid to the state budget, credit expenses paid to banks, premium payments for state insurance, service expenses, wages paid to staff and workers, the provision of goods and food to households, and so forth. The difference is the consumption and the consumption-related accumulation of the nonproductive sectors.

Here we must point out from the point of view of final consumption [of national income] that, except for national defense and government administration, the consumption by the nonproductive sector such as the transport, post and telecommunications, and municipal public utilities departments of fuel, lighting, office supplies, medical supplies, regular maintenance services and other expenditures, and depreciation of fixed assets should all be regarded as consumption by households received through social consumption. Therefore, they are also part of household consumption.

In order to calculate the amount of household consumption more comprehensively, in addition to the above personal consumption of the households, we should also include the consumption they obtain through social consumption and the benefits accruing to them due to price reductions of consumer goods.

The accumulation of productive enterprises is production-related accumulation. Accumulation by the households and the nonproductive sectors is consumption-related accumulation. The total accumulation of the national income is composed of these two parts.

Accumulation of the productive enterprise is the sum of its primary income and its income from redistribution minus its expenditures in the course of redistribution. The productive enterprise's primary income and its income from redistribution include: the initial income of the productive enterprise, income from the fiscal and credit system, and other income. Income from the fiscal and credit system is the major source of the income which the productive enterprise receives through redistribution. This mainly indicates state budget allocations for fixed assets, working capital, and inventory and loans from banks. The productive enterprise's expenditures in the course of redistribution include: payments and deductions going to the fiscal and credit system and direct payments to the nonproductive sectors. Payments to the fiscal and credit system include the following major items: taxes, profits, and social insurance deductions remitted to the state and principal and interest payments to banks.

V. The Labor Balance Table

To fully tap existing labor resources and ensure the proper distribution of social labor resources between the productive and nonproductive sectors and among the productive sectors is of prime importance in expanding social reproduction. Therefore, the labor balance table is a basic component of the whole national economic balance table.

The labor balance table should reflect the balance between labor resources and their utilization in the national economy. Therefore, a simple format for the labor balance table can be as shown on the following page.

In calculating labor resources, invalids of working age who do not participate in work should be excluded. When calculating the utilization of labor resources, laborers in the productive and nonproductive sectors should be further classified according to their sectors and economic components.

When allocating labor resources, the productive sectors' labor force requirements should be met first. Then the nonproductive sectors' labor force requirements should be ensured. Furthermore, among the production sectors, we should first satisfy the labor force requirements of industrial development. Personnel in administration and management should be reduced as much as possible. The number and allocation of able-bodied people working in the productive sectors depend on the scale of social production,

Labor Balance Table

Targets of labor force reproduction / Targets of labor resource distribution	Number at beginning of year	Increase during year	Decrease during year	Number at year end	Average number in year
A	1	2	3	4	5
I. Labor resources					
1. Adult population with labor capacity					
2. Old and young people actually working					
3. Total					
II. Utilization of labor resources					
1. Those working in productive sectors					
2. Those working in nonproductive sectors					
3. Students of working age					
4. Other population of working age and population engaged in household duties					
5. Total					

the technical level of production, and the level of labor productivity of the various sectors.

*   *   *

In the Soviet Union, the standard of planning work has reached a fairly high level. The national economic balance table used in national economic planning is a fairly complete system. The present national economic balance table of the Soviet Union includes:

1. The social product balance table, namely the balance table showing the production, consumption, and accumulation of the social product. This includes: (1) a comprehensive balance table for the production, consumption, and accumulation of the social product; (2) production and utilization balance tables for the various sectors of the national economy; and (3) a balance table showing the fixed assets of the national economy calculated both according to overall original values and also according to original values after deductions for depreciation.

2. The balance table showing the production, distribution, consumption, and accumulation of the national income. A more complete name for this is the social product and national income balance table. This includes: (1) a comprehensive balance table for the production, distribution, consumption, and accumulation of the national income and (2) an accounting balance table showing the state, the cooperatives, and the households.

3. The labor resources balance table or the labor balance table.

Appendix tables to the national economic balance table are: (1) a table of the major targets in the national economic balance table; (2) a table in which accumulation is classified by types of ownership and economic form; (3) a table in which consumption is classified by types of consumption; (4) a balance table for major material resources; (5) a balance table in which households' money income and outlay are classified by social group and (6) a table of major national economic proportions.

In China, the formulation of the national economic balance table is still in the experimental stage. In 1954, the State Statistical Bureau started to formulate on a trial basis the balance table for the production, distribution, consumption, and accumulation of the national income. At present, it is formulating on a trial basis the social product balance report of the social product balance table. In 1955, the State Planning Commission also started the trial formulation of the balance plan for the production, distribution, consumption, and accumulation of the national income. At present, it is doing preparatory work for the formulation of the whole national economic balance plan.

Note

1. Social product is gross social product, that is, the sum of the output value of various productive sectors.

PART TWO

Lectures on Basic Knowledge of National Economic Plan Tables

LECTURE 1: INDUSTRIAL PRODUCTION PLANNING TABLES

Fang Fa*

I. The Concept of Industrial Production

Industrial production is one kind of material production. It can generally be divided into three parts: (1) The extraction of natural resources or minerals. Examples are the extraction of coal, petroleum, black metallic ores (iron and manganese ores), nonferrous ores (copper, lead, zinc, tungsten, antimony, tin, and molybdenum ores), rare metallic ores (radium, uranium, vanadium, and titanium ores), nonmetallic ores (asbestos, mica, and graphite ores), chemical ores (sulphur, pyrite, fluor-spar ores), and so forth; the cutting of timber; the harvesting of wild fish, shellfish (shrimp, crabs, clams, and mussels), seaweeds (kelp and purple seaweed), and other marine products; the making of sea salt and the extraction of rock salt; the generation of hydroelectric power, and so forth. (2) The processing of agricultural products, such as flour milling, rice milling, oil pressing, sugar making, spinning, livestock slaughtering, milk refining, leather tanning, and so forth. (3) Manufacturing or repairing, such as the smelting of metallic ores into metals, the making of machines from metals, the generation of electricity from various fuels (coal, petroleum, and uranium), machine repairing, and so forth.

II. The Scope of Industrial Production Planning

As mentioned above, the scope and distribution of industrial production within the society is extremely broad. Industrial production is carried on by various sectors, enterprises, and business

*Fang Fa, "Kung-yeh sheng-ch'an chi-hua piao-ke." CCHC, 1957, No. 1, pp. 26-31.

units.* Even the making of clothes and the repairing of bicycles or sewing machines by family members can be regarded as industrial production.

Because of this, to facilitate the formulation and implementation of plans, we cannot include all the industrial activities of the whole society in the scope of industrial production plans. We can only include those industrial enterprises that specialize in industrial production (namely, those industrial production units with administrative and economic independence and independent balance sheets) and the production activities of full-time individual handicraftsmen. Industrial production activities that are either carried out by nonindustrial enterprises (transport enterprises, construction enterprises, agricultural enterprises, commercial enterprises, and so forth) or that are subordinate to or simultaneously managed by business units are generally not included in the state industrial production plan because these activities are subordinate to the important economic activities of these nonindustrial activities (transport, construction...). However, these nonindustrial enterprises or business units can formulate plans for their subsidiary industrial production units. Sometimes, exceptions can be made. For example, both the 1956 and 1957 planning tables of the Soviet Union specified that the industrial plans included only those industrial enterprises having independent balance sheets. However, the output targets included part of the construction materials (such as sawed timber, bricks, prefabricated cement products, and so forth) produced by subsidiary industrial production units. Such exceptions help facilitate the overall balance of these products.

Here we must point out that China's 1956 and 1957 tables both specified that the scope of industrial production planning should include subsidiary industrial enterprises (namely, industrial production units subsidiary to either nonindustrial enterprises or public service units, such as processing plants and other industrial production units subsidiary to farms, construction enterprises, commercial firms, transport enterprises, schools, government organs, and so forth). In some sectors, however, the plans of subsidiary industries were not actually included because the plans of these industrial production units were subject to great changes and the statistical basis of the plans was poor. In some sectors, diffi-

---

*The business units (shih-yeh tan-wei) or business organizations (shih-yeh chi-kou) discussed here are producing units which, unlike enterprises (ch'i-yeh), do not operate in the system of economic accounting. Specific examples are given below in the text. — N.R.L.

culties were encountered even after these plans were included.
Therefore, the question of whether it is necessary or feasible to
include these subsidiary industries in future industrial production
plans of the national economic plan should be studied further. However, in formulating the 1957 plans, we should still include subsidiary industries in the industrial production plan according to the
regulations governing the 1957 national economic planning tables
and, if possible, list them separately.

In China's First Five-Year Plan period, to better reflect and
grasp the socialist transformation of the handicraft industry, beginning in 1954, the value of output and quantity of production of
handicraft industry (including handicraft producers' cooperatives;
handicraft societies for supply, marketing, and production; handicraft production groups; and individual handicraftsmen) was temporarily listed separately from industry and agriculture. But in
the proposal for China's Five-Year Plan, the handicraft industry
(which has already been basically transformed into handicraft producers' cooperatives) is included in industry to facilitate the overall arrangement of the industrial production plan.

The regulations governing the 1957 national economic planning
tables require that the handicraft production plan includes the
handicraft products of the agricultural producers' cooperatives
and the marketed handicraft products of individual peasants. Many
units think that this requirement will lead to difficulties both in
data collection and plan formulation because of the unstable output
of these subsidiary industrial products. Therefore, the question
of whether or not the proposed control numbers in the Second Five-
Year Plan should still include this portion of industrial production
has to be studied further. In formulating the 1957 plans, however,
the relevant regulations governing the 1957 planning tables should
still be followed.

III. The System of Targets in the Industrial Production Plans

Industrial production plans generally consist of the following
targets.
1. Gross Value of Industrial Output. This is the final output of
industrial activities expressed in monetary terms. The output of
industrial production is of many types. Some are concrete goods
(such as cars, machines, flour, and so forth), and some are intan-
gible (such as work of an industrial nature or the value of repairs).
Among physical goods, there are various units of measurement,

such as tons of steel, numbers of cars, meters of cotton cloth, cartons of cigarettes, and so forth. Therefore, it is very hard to represent the gross output of industrial production in physical terms. It is generally expressed in money terms, such as thousands of yuan, or hundred-millions of yuan.

The major purpose of the gross value of industrial output is to reflect the level and rate of growth of industrial output. Suppose the gross value of industrial output in 1956 was 10 billion yuan and the gross value of industrial output in 1957 was 11.5 billion yuan. Comparing the two years using 1956 as the base, we know that the rate of growth of industrial output in 1957 was 15 percent $(\frac{11.5 - 10}{10} \times 100)$. Second, it can also reflect the proportional relationship between industry and agriculture. Suppose the gross value of industrial and agricultural output is 100 billion yuan, of which the gross value of industrial output is 40 billion yuan. Based on these figures, we can calculate the share of gross value of industrial output to be 40 percent $(\frac{40}{100} \times 100)$ of the gross value of industrial and agricultural output. In addition, by means of the following analytical indicators of the gross value of industrial output, other questions of industrial production can also be reflected.

a. The technical level of industry can be reflected by the analytical targets of "modern industry," "factory handicraft industry," and "individual handicraft industry."

The concrete classification guidelines for "modern industry," "factory handicraft industry," and "individual handicraft industry" contained in the current planning and statistical system are: "Modern industry" refers to industrial enterprises using modern technical equipment for their major production activities, such as coal-mining enterprises using hoisting machines to lift raw coal, paper-making enterprises using fourdrinier machines or fourdrinier wire mesh paper-making machines to make paper, flour-milling enterprises using steel grinders to grind flour, machine-building enterprises using various power lathes to cut metals, and so forth. "Factory handicraft industry" refers to industrial enterprises based on manual technology, namely, industrial enterprises without any mechanical power whose production depends only on manual labor and simple tools (such as carpet factories). This also includes industrial enterprises which have some mechanical power machines but whose major activities are still performed manually. "Individual handicraft industry" refers to specialized individual handicraft industries in which the handicraftsman and his family members provide most of the necessary labor and in which no more than three workers and apprentices are hired. Based on the above classification guidelines, it is not difficult to see that the larger the share of "modern industry" in the gross value of industrial output, the higher the technical level of industry as a whole.

b. The proportion between type A and type B industrial production and their relative rates of growth is reflected by the analytical targets of "producer goods production" (that is, type A production) and "consumer goods production" (that is, type B production). We all know that the social product is classified as type A or type B according to its use. The part of the social product used to satisfy production requirements belongs to type A. That used to satisfy livelihood requirements belongs to type B. In general, the rate of growth of type A production should exceed that of type B production. Consequently, the relative share of type A production in the gross value of industrial output steadily increases. This is a basic requirement for expanding social output. In classifying production into type A and type B, we often come across many products (such as coal, electricity, and paper) which can be used as producer goods as well as consumer goods. To achieve uniformity in classification, when we formulate our plans, we should classify each product according to the unified regulations contained in the "Standard Classification List for Industrial Branches" published by the State Statistical Bureau in 1952. For example, the above-mentioned coal, electricity, and paper are to be classified as type A according to the list. Some enterprises (such as rubber plants) produce both type A products (such as automobile tires) and type B products (such as rubber shoes). Under these circumstances, the total product of the enterprises should be divided into type A and type B products, and the value of each type should be calculated separately. If the value of type A products exceeds the value of type B products, the gross value of output of the enterprise should be listed as type A. In the reverse situation, it should be listed as type B.

c. The scale of industrial organization can be reflected by the analytical targets of "large-scale industry" and "small-scale industry." With the exception of individual enterprises which at certain periods of time are suited to small-scale operation, it is generally easier to achieve greater, faster, and better results at lower costs in relatively large-scale enterprises in which costs are low and output large than in relatively small-scale enterprises. The guidelines used by the statistical departments to classify industrial

137

enterprises by scale in the planning work of the past years have
been: "Large-scale industry" refers to enterprises which have
mechanical power and more than sixteen workers or enterprises
which have no mechanical power but have more than thirty-one
workers. "Small-scale industry" refers to enterprises with mechanical power and fewer than fifteen workers or enterprises with
no mechanical power and fewer than thirty workers. Small-scale
industry does not include individual handicraft industry. Independent electricity-generating plants with a capacity of more than fifteen kilowatts are treated as large-scale industry regardless of
the number of people they employ. Those with a capacity of fifteen
or fewer kilowatts are treated as small-scale industry. (Whether
this guideline governing the classification of independent electricity-
generating plants into large- and small-scale industry is appropriate or not can be studied further.)

d. These analytical targets, which are listed separately by industrial branch, can be used to reflect the composition of, and the
proportional relations among, industrial branches. Such questions
as what is the proportional relationship between the extracting
branch and the processing branch, whether the power-generating
branch has been given development priority over other branches,
and so forth can be studied and answered by means of these analytical targets of the gross value of industrial output. According
to the "Standard Classification List of Industrial Branches" published by the State Statistical Bureau, industrial production has
been divided into twenty-eight branches. Within each branch, certain
categories are listed. In our present national economic planning
tables, only the "machine building" category within the metal-
processing branch is listed separately. This is because the
machine building industry is the heart of industry. The "machine
building" category simply refers to enterprises that build various
machines (such as motors, generators, various types of lathes,
and various types of industrial equipment. For details, see "Standard Classification List of Industrial Branches," pp. 6-14). It does
not refer to all industrial enterprises which use machines to manufacture products (such as machine-produced sugar and machine-
produced paper . . .). If the part of an enterprise's output value
represented by "machine building" exceeds half of its gross value
of industrial output, the whole gross value of industrial output of
that enterprise should be classified as "machine building."

e. The analytical targets of economic types can reflect the scale
and rate of socialist transformation in the transition period. For

example, at the Eighth National Party Congress, Comrade Liu Shao-ch'i said: "The output value of state-operated industry in 1949 represented only 26.3 percent of the gross value of industrial output. In 1952, it represented 41.5 percent, and in 1955, it represented 51.3 percent." The three percentages mentioned in the statement were calculated by comparing the gross value of output of all state-owned industrial enterprises with the gross value of output of industrial enterprises of all economic types (state-operated, public-private jointly operated, cooperative, and private).

The methods for calculating the gross value of industrial output can be divided into the factory method, the trust method, the branch method, and the national economy method according to the scope of permitted double counting. The facilitate the formulation, implementation, and inspection of plans, the present planning and statistical systems uniformly use the factory method. As far as the management organ at each level is concerned, the gross value of industrial output calculated by the factory method is the sum of the gross output values of each of the industrial enterprises under that management organ. For a given enterprise, it is the value of the final product of all the industrial activities of the enterprise. However, it is not the sum of the product from the various parts (workshops, work sections) of an enterprise; we cannot allow any double counting of industrial products within an enterprise. For example, when the yarn spun in a textile mill is all woven into fabric, the gross value of industrial output of the plant should only include the value of the fabric, not the value of the yarn, because yarn is not the final industrial product of the mill.

In practice, due to the continuity of industrial production, the final industrial product of an enterprise in a given period (one year, one quarter, and so forth) will not all be embodied in completely finished products. Part of the final product must be in the form of semifinished products or products in-process. (Semifinished products and products in process are distinguished on the basis of which workshop they are from; products which have already completed the final stage of processing within a workshop are semifinished products. In-process products are those that have not passed through the last process. For example, the finished fine yarn in the spinning workshop of a textile plant is semifinished product. The cotton fibres and the coarse yarn in the workshop are in-process products.) There are also some final products which are not embodied in physical goods (for example, the work that goes into repairing an industrial product. After the

139

repair, it is still an industrial product). Therefore, the gross value of industrial output should include the following three basic things:

a. All completed products. This is the total product sold outside the enterprise which is produced either from the raw materials of the enterprise itself or those supplied by units placing orders. In addition to the product sold outside the enterprise, it also includes the product used by other departments of the enterprise which lie outside the cost-accounting scope of the enterprise itself (namely, departments and organizations under the leadership of the enterprise but which do not have the same industrial cost and expenditure department or organization as the enterprise). Examples are the products used by the enterprise's capital construction department, major repairs department, public utilities department, and all kinds of other nonindustrial departments (such as affiliated hospitals, schools, canteens, and dormitories).

b. Work of an industrial character. These include two items: (1) The repair of industrial products, such as the repair of cars and machines... and (2) the individual stages of the processing of industrial products, such as polishing, painting, electroplating, and hole drilling. The common characteristic of these two items is that these industrial activities do not result in new physical goods but merely restore or increase the use value of existing goods. For example, broken machines can be reused after having been repaired. Painted furniture is better looking and more durable than unpainted furniture, and so forth. In calculating the value of work of an industrial character we should include the value of all the labor and materials used by the enterprise itself, namely, the value of labor days and materials or parts supplied by the enterprise itself (either produced or purchased by the enterprise). It should not, however, include the value of materials and parts not supplied by the enterprise itself or the value of objects on which processing or repairing have been done. The scope for calculting work of an industrial character should be the same as that for calculating completed products mentioned above. It also should include only work of an industrial character performed for units outside the enterprise or for departments inside the enterprise which have independent cost accounting. It should not include work of an industrial character performed for the various workshops or production management departments of the enterprise itself.

c. The difference in the value between the beginning and end of a given period of goods in process and semifinished products, tools, and molds produced by the enterprise. In general, the proportionate value of this item does not represent a large share of the gross value of industrial output, but it should be accounted for, particularly for enterprises with comparatively long production cycles. For example, a shipyard starts making 10 ships in the first year and finishes them in the second year. Suppose the total value of the 10 ships is a hundred million yuan. If the value of the shipyard's products which are in process is not included, its gross value of industrial output would be zero in the first year and a hundred million yuan in the second year. This method of accounting naturally cannot realistically reflect the output of the shipyard workers. Again, suppose the motor workshop of an automobile plant has an inventory of 200 units of semifinished products (namely, motors) at the beginning of the year, and at the end of the year there are 500 units. Then, the difference between the beginning of the year and the end of the year amounts to 300 units. If the gross value of industrial output of the automobile plant includes only the value of the finished cars and not the relatively high value of these 300 motors, it naturally cannot fully reflect the total output of the auto workers. Similarly, the difference in the value between the beginning and the end of a given period for the large quantities of tools and sand-casting molds that are made by the auxiliary and carpentry workshops of machine-building plants and that are consumed in the production processes of those plants should also be included in the gross value of industrial output value. On the other hand, however, the difference in the value between the beginning and end of a year of products that are in process or semifinished products is, in the final analysis, not a large share of the gross value of industrial output. Therefore, to simplify the procedures of planning work and to reduce the quantity of work involved in a very large number of calculations, the accounting of semifinished products in the national economic planning tables is limited to those that are listed in the "List of Industrial Products" (published by the State Statistical Bureau in 1952). Products that are not included in the list are omitted from the accounting. The accounting of products in process is also limited to only four types of enterprise (shipbuilding, machine building and repair, automobile manufacturing, and the manufacture and repair of metal structures). Other enterprises can be omitted. When calculating a value differential, we should note that if the figure at the end is larger than the figure at the beginning of the period, the difference in the value between the end and the beginning of the period should be added to the gross value of industrial output. This is because the differential represents the output of the enterprise in that period. If the figure at the end of the period is smaller than the figure at the beginning of the period, this difference in the value should be subtracted from the gross value of industrial output because it represents the amount of output of the previous period which was consumed in the current period.

Since the gross value of industrial output is the final result of the industrial activities of industrial enterprises, the following three items should not be included in it:

a. Output not resulting from industrial production activities should not be included in the gross value of industrial output. For example, the value of work performed by transport departments (car fleet, railway division), postal and telecommunications departments (switchboard, telecommunications office, etc.), supply and marketing departments (purchasing station, marketing station, and shop), design departments (engineering design division, etc.), and scientific research departments (chemical analysis laboratory, material stress laboratory) affiliated with industrial enterprises; the value of output of agricultural production units (livestock ranch and farm, etc.) affiliated with industrial enterprises; the value of services performed by various service units (canteen, laundry, bathhouse, barbershop, etc.) affiliated with industrial enterprises; and the value of work performed by construction and installation departments affiliated with industrial enterprises should not be included in the gross value of industrial output.

b. Products that are not final* should not be included in the gross value of industrial output. For example, products that are produced by the enterprise itself but are used within the enterprise (such as the pulp in paper-making plants and the yarn used for fabric in textile mills) should not be included in the gross value of output. Scrap and waste products are not the goal of production, so although they can be sold, their value still should not be included in the gross value of output. The value of regular repairs necessary for the normal operation of the production facilities should also be excluded from the gross value of output.

c. Industrial products that are not produced by the enterprise itself should not be included in the gross value of industrial output. For example, industrial products purchased from outside the plant and resold without undergoing any processing or tap water,

---

*These are called "intermediate products" in Western national income accounting terminology. — N. R. L.

steam, coal gas, and so forth which are purchased from outside the plant and resold should not be included in the gross value of output.

The above-mentioned uses of the gross value of output and the methods of calculating it only touch on those aspects that are relevant to our present planning tables. Recently, some comrades in the planning and statistics departments raised the question of using net value of output instead of the gross value of output for future industrial production planning (namely, to calculate gross value of industrial output by the national economy method). This question must be carefully studied before any final solution is reached. Those comrades who are engaged in industrial planning work can refer to the articles published in T'ung-chi kung-tso t'ung-hsün [Statistical Work Bulletin] since September 1956 and make suggestions.

Two kinds of prices are used to calculate the gross value of output: constant prices and current prices. Constant prices, also called fixed prices, are those that remain constant over a fairly long period of time. They are used when formulating plans for gross value of industrial and agricultural output to facilitate the observation of trends in society's economic growth at different periods of time, such as changes in the rates of growth of industry and agriculture and changes in various proportions (such as the proportion between producer goods and consumer goods). They also facilitate the inspection of plan implementation by eliminating the factor of price changes. The annual gross value of industrial output in the First Five-Year Plan was entirely calculated according to the average prices in the whole country in the third quarter of 1952 (namely, the average factory prices of the individual industrial enterprises of the whole country in the third quarter of 1952, including production costs, interest, and taxes). Because these same prices are used for the calculations every year, they are referred to as constant prices. Constant prices are determined uniformly by the State Statistical Bureau. Current prices are the actual prices of products at the time when the plans are formulated. These prices are determined uniformly once a year by the state planning organs. The gross value of industrial output calculated at current prices is mainly used to compute the national income. At present, the planning organs do not require the reporting of value of industrial output at current prices.

2. The Value of Commodity Output. The value of commodity output refers to that portion of the products of industrial production activities that can be marketed; that is, the value of that por-

tion of the output that can be exchanged with other enterprises or units. Therefore, the commodity output value is equal to the gross value of industrial output value minus (1) the value of the raw materials used in production that are supplied by units that place orders; and plus or minus (2) the difference in the value between the beginning and the end of the period of products in-process and semifinished products, tools, and molds. (If the value is higher at the end than at the beginning of the period, subtract it; if not, add it.) Because the main function of the value of commodity output is not to reflect the growth of industrial output but rather to calculate costs and estimate taxes and profits, when plans are compiled usually it is only necessary to compile and report the value of commodity production calculated in current prices. It is not necessary to report the value of commodity output in constant prices.

3. The Volume of Output. The volume of output represents output in physical terms. Its main use is to balance the supply, production, and sale of products. Its secondary function is to reflect the actual increase in the scale of production. Therefore, the volume of output not only includes products sold outside the enterprise, but also products that are produced and consumed by the enterprise itself. For example, suppose in a year a certain iron and steel plant produces a million tons of pig iron, of which it refines 800,000 tons into 900,000 tons of steel. In calculating the gross value of output and the value of commodity output, the value of the 900,000 tons of steel and the 200,000 tons of pig iron (the final product of the enterprise) are taken into account. But in calculating the volume of output, the 900,000 tons of steel and the million tons of pig iron are taken into account. The 4.674 million tons of pig iron and 4.12 million tons of steel specified by China's First Five-Year Plan for production in 1957 were calculated in this way by totaling the output volume of the individual iron and steel enterprises.

In formulating the plans for the volume of output, we should adhere strictly to the regulations contained in the list of planned products announced by the higher levels. All products contained in the list of products, regardless of how much the enterprise or the department produces or whether they are for its own consumption or not, should be included in the plan. We should also make sure that the names of the products, their classifications, their order of appearance, and their units of measurement meet the requirements of the higher levels in order to facilitate the work of the summary departments. For example, the list of products requires that "matches" be counted by the "chien" (one chien equals a thousand boxes), but some enterprises count them by the "pao" (one pao equals ten boxes), some count them by the "box," and so on. As a consequence, the comprehensive planning department at the higher level will have to waste a lot of time converting figures, resulting in delay in sending the plans upward.

The list of products is a very important document in formulating plans. In compiling the list of products, the organs at the higher levels should realistically study and determine its content according to both the principle of management by levels and the needs of production, supply, and sale. They should also ensure that the names of the products and their units of measurement are consistent with the requirements in the material distribution list, statistical list, and commodity list to facilitate both comprehensive balance among the individual plans and inspection. The products included in the index of products of the national economic planning tables are all major products (729 in 1957) that greatly affect national construction or the people's livelihood. We cannot include all the products of the society. To guide the economic activities of industrial enterprises more concretely, the plan and management organs of each ministry and province (municipality) can make necessary additions in the variety or specifications of products according to the principle of management by levels and on the basis of the product list used in the national economic planning table.

Producing and trial producing new products is a special target in the system of volume of output targets. Only after 1953 were targets for new products in China included in the national economic plan table, reflecting the objective condition that our country's large-scale economic construction requires a large quantity of new kinds of products which are produced domestically. The 1953 national economic table of the Soviet Union still contained such targets, but after 1955, these targets and tables were canceled. So-called new products refer to those industrial products that have not been produced in the country during the period from the establishment of the People's Republic of China up until the plan period (for an enterprise, a sector, or a region, they refer to products that have not been produced in that enterprise, sector, or region) and which are going to be trial manufactured or manufactured in the plan period. These new industrial products are those that either have not been produced before or that have been produced before but that now differ significantly from similar products in the technology used in production , in their technical characteristics, or in their performance. For example, the trucks produced by the No. 1 Automobile Plant in 1956 and the jet planes successfully trial manufactured by the airplane plant are both new products in the national economy.

4. Technical and Economic Targets. Technical and economic targets are the accounting basis for formulating plans. Because the gross value of industrial output and the value of commodity output are based on figures on the volume of output, the volume of output must be calculated on the basis of technical and economic targets. There are generally five kinds of technical and economic targets for industry: (1) targets for the utilization of equipment capacity, such as the coefficient of utilization of blast furnaces and open-hearth furnaces, and the weft count per minute of weaving machines; (2) targets for the consumption of raw materials, such as the coal consumption rate and the sugar extraction rate; (3) targets for labor force consumption, such as the amount of coal extracted per coal miner per day; (4) targets for product quality, such as the carbon content of coal, the fiber count of yarn, and the weft count of fabric; and (5) targets for the level of mechanization, such as the degree of mechanization in coal extraction (namely, the percentage of coal extracted by machine compared with the total amount of coal extracted using both machines and manual labor) and degree of mechanization in lumber collection and transport.

When plans for technical and economic targets are formulated they should be based on advanced technical and economic targets. Advanced technical and economic targets should lie between the average level reached by most enterprises (workshops or workers) and the level reached by the most advanced enterprises (workshops or workers). The appropriate figures are not obtained simply by averaging the figures that are above average, but are determined after analyzing the favorable and unfavorable factors in the concrete situation, guaranteeing the full utilization of potential, and taking into consideration certain technical and organizational measures. When we calculate the annual levels, we should also follow the above method. They should not be determined on the basis of the average monthly figures or the most advanced monthly figures. The departments in charge should not simply add up the enterprise's targets when integrating and formulating technical and economic targets; they should first study the technical and economic targets compiled by the enterprise according to the above principles and then approve them one at a time under the principle of giving full consideration to extending all advanced experience and exploiting the enterprise's potential. After these targets have been approved, the technical and economic target plan of the departments in charge should be compiled by the method of weighted averaging.

5. Rate of Utilization of Production Capacity. "Production capacity" refers to the maximum possible output in a given period of time (one year, one quarter, and so forth). (For example, a coal shaft with an annual capacity of 3 million tons or a textile mill with an annual capacity of 500,000 p'i of fabric.) Sometimes, due to a lack of skill in technical operation, low labor productivity, slow sales, raw material shortages, or a new plant which has not reached its designed capacity, the actual output is often lower than the production capacity. "The rate of utilization of production capacity" is the proportionate ratio between the actual output (or planned output) and the production capacity. For example, if in a certain year the actual output of the above-mentioned coal shaft with an annual capacity of 3 million tons was 2.7 million tons, then the rate of utilization of this shaft in that year was $\frac{2.7}{3} \times 100 = 90\%$.

On the basis of the rate of utilization of production capacity, the enterprise or the planning organ can study problems like how to further exploit production potential and how to economize on investment and use it in the most critical departments. For example, if society urgently needs certain products in large quantities but the utilization rate of the production capacity for these products is way below 100 percent, then the department in charge can consider ways to strengthen the weak links that prevent the production capacity from being fully utilized and suggest concrete measures to increase output. Again, suppose the rate of utilization of production capacity for product A reaches only 60 percent and the production capacity of product B is no longer adequate to satisfy society's needs but some departments or regions still want to establish plants to produce product A. In these circumstances, the department in charge has a basis for proposing that the investment to establish plants to produce product A be reduced or eliminated and used instead to establish plants to produce product B. Therefore, the rate of utilization of production capacity is an important reference target in formulating industrial plans.

There are three basic factors which determine the productive capacity of an enterprise, namely: (1) the standard utilization of equipment capacity (such as the daily output of a unit of equipment;

(2) the quantity of equipment; and (3) the operation time of equipment (most departments in charge uniformly specify this operation time). In general, the product of these three figures equals the production capacity of the enterprise. For example, if there are 2,000 weaving machines in a certain textile mill, the output per machine per shift is 50 meters, there are 2 shifts daily, and the annual number of work days is 306 (based on 7 legal holidays and 52 Sundays off; 307 days in a leap year), then the production capacity of this mill would be:

50 meters/shift/machine $\times$ 2,000 machines $\times$ 2 shifts/day $\times$ 306 days = 61,200,000 meters.

This is the simplest hypothetical example. In practice, there are constant changes within an enterprise. There are thus many concrete factors that must be considered in calculating the production capacity. For example, the following changes are likely to occur in most branches or enterprises within a year or within every five years: the retirement of old and obsolete equipment, the addition of new equipment, major repairs, renovations, the adoption of new operating methods, changes in labor organization, and so forth. All of these changes will either increase or decrease the production capacity. Therefore, in actually computing capacity, we should follow the above-mentioned basic factors and basic methods of calculation and take into account concrete factors and conditions. While conforming with the uniform requirements, we should make our calculations with reference to concrete situations.

Among the many individual industrial enterprises producing the same product, there are differences in the amount of equipment and in the division of workshops. The specifications of their products and the maximum operation times also vary. To facilitate totaling the production capacity for a given product and to accurately reflect the rate of utilization of production capacity, when each enterprise calculates its productive capacity based on its major equipment, work divisions, and workshops, the conversion rate into standard specification for its products, and the maximum operation time for each enterprise all should accord to the uniformly specified standard of the departments in charge.

LECTURE 2: COMMERCIAL PLANNING TABLES

Sun Chih-fang*

Commerce is the bridge between production and consumption. As material goods move from the production realm to the hands of the consumers, they must pass through certain circulation processes usually known as the product circulation link, colloquially called "doing business." The circulation of commodities not only plays a very important role in the process of expanding social output, it also provides an important link between the urban and rural areas, among regions, and among all sectors of the national economy. It is an important means of consolidating the worker-peasant alliance as well. Therefore, the comrades who are engaged in commercial planning work must establish the point of view of serving production and consumption.

I. The Scope of Commercial Planning

Commerce can be classified into five types according to the nature of its operations: (1) purely commercial enterprises; (2) the commerce which is managed by industrial and handicraft industrial enterprises; (3) restaurants; (4) commerce of service enterprises and the commercial operations they manage; and (5) enterprises which purchase agricultural products. It can be classified into five varieties according to its economic type (basically, there are only four types since peasant trade cannot be regarded as an independent economic type): (1) state-managed economy; (2) cooperative-managed economy; (3) state capitalist economy (including state-private jointly managed commerce, commerce distributed for the state on a commission basis, and commerce distributed by contract for the state; (4) privately managed economy (which can be further classified as resident merchants, itinerant merchants, and stall

---

*Sun Chih-fang, "Shang-yeh chi-hua piao-ke." <u>CHCC</u>, 1957, No. 2, pp. 27-31.

operators and classified as wholesale trade or retail trade); and
(5) peasant trade. Commerce can be classified into two kinds according to the current management system: (1) all the ministries
in the trade system, such as the Ministry of Commerce, the Ministry of Urban Services, the Ministry of Food, the Ministry of Foreign Trade, and the supply and marketing cooperatives and their
affiliated shops and purchasing stations; and (2) all the departments outside the trade system, such as the salt-transporting and
-marketing enterprises of the Ministry of Food Industry, the lumber company of the Forestry Ministry, the state-owned bookshops
of the Ministry of Culture, the newspaper and magazine publishing
department of the Postal and Telecommunications Ministry, the
staff and workers' supply units of the Ministry of Railways and
their affiliated shops. The content of the 1957 plans for state-
managed commercial enterprises includes the commodity circulation plan, the enterprise production plan, the commercial network plan, the capital construction plan, the transportation plan,
the cadre education plan, the labor and wages plan, the circulation
expenses plan, and the financial plan — a total of nine plans.

From these, we can see that the commercial plan not only covers a great deal but is also relatively complex. Here, we cannot
discuss all its aspects in detail but must limit ourselves to the
most important part of the commercial plan — the commodity circulation plan, which is the core of society's present commercial
plan. All the other plans, such as the capital construction plan,
the labor and wages plan, and so forth will be discussed separately
in later lectures and will not be discussed here.

We know that the circulation of commodities is a process of buying and selling of socially produced commodities so that they are
transferred from the production realm to the consumption realm.
Its characteristics are: (1) the objects of circulation are commodities and (2) buying and selling must take place. Based on the
above characteristics, the scope of the commodity circulation plan
generally includes the following four kinds of activity: (1) direct
sale of products by production units to the consuming units; (2) sale
of products by production units to commercial organizations;
(3) trade among wholesale units and sales by wholesale units to
retail units; and (4) sale of products by commercial organizations
to consuming units. Things that do not belong within the scope of
commodity circulation include: (1) the provision of services alone,
in which money payments are involved but no goods are delivered
(for instance haircuts, baths, theater entertainment, rides on motor

vehicles, health care, and so forth); (2) the transfer of goods which does not involve buying and selling (such as payment of agricultural taxes, gifts, and the transfer of commodities within an enterprise); (3) the mutual buying and selling of goods among peasants (such as the exchange of seeds, fodder, and other agricultural and side-line products); and (4) the unified distribution of goods by the state to state-managed and state-private jointly managed enterprises.

II. The Formulation of the Tables for the 1957 Commercial Plan

The 1957 commercial plan tables began with the principles of simplification and usefulness, and moreover they are cognizant of the new situation arising from the basic completion of the socialist transformation and are compatible with the First Five-Year Plan as well as being determined by the principle of control by levels. The State Planning Commission, where necessary, combined the purchase and sale circulation plan for commodities (basically this is the wholesale circulation plan), the retail circulation plan and the plan for the procurement of agricultural products and consolidated or eliminated other tables where possible.

The tables used by the provinces, the municipalities directly under central authority, and the autonomous regions were not changed significantly. Since the question of "who wins over whom" has been basically answered with the completion of socialist transformation and since the socialist component in the commodity circulation realm now occupies a dominant position, the "wholesale plan for privately managed commerce" and the "table for calculating the proportion of socialist retail commerce" were eliminated. At the same time, some revisions have been made in the method of formulating the retail commodity circulation plan in order to reflect the transformation and arrangement of privately owned commerce adopted in the branches and regions and to strengthen the planned management of privately owned commerce and small merchants and peddlers who are undergoing socialist transformation. The formulation of the plans of privately operated industry and small peddlers undergoing socialist transformation is no longer the responsibility of the system of state-managed commerce and supply and marketing cooperatives but has been shifted to the transformation departments. This serves actually to strengthen retail planning, to strengthen the unified organization of the socialist commerce of business departments, to improve the service to consumers and to satisfy the ever increasing needs of urban and rural residents. With the continuous growth of industrial and agricultural production, the people's purchasing power increases correspondingly. We must raise the quality of commercial planning work even further and must constantly study the changes in the needs of urban and rural residents. To do this, we have added the "plan table for the commodity composition of retail sales" (namely, the table of the composition of social purchasing power expenditure.) To embody the local sources of commodity supply that are controlled by state-owned commerce and supply and marketing cooperatives and moreover to coordinate industrial plans with commercial plans, we have added the "plan table for the domestic purchase of major commodities by state-owned commercial enterprises and supply and marketing cooperatives (namely, the plan table for the purchase of industrial products).

Based on the present level of work and actual needs, the "urban" and "rural" targets have been eliminated from the planned targets. This is because under the present method of calculating the people's money income, the income from the sale of the peasants' agricultural and sideline products is generally regarded as their major income. On the other hand, the income of the staff and workers and other nonagricultural people is computed according to their industrial system. Under these circumstances, separate calculations for urban and rural presents many problems. However, in order to study the commodity supply problems of the large and medium-sized cities and industrial, mining, and forestry regions, we have stipulated that the purchasing power of municipalities which are under the direct jurisdiction of the province and have more than 100,000 people, key-point cities which are undergoing major construction but have fewer than 100,000 people, and industrial, mining, and forestry regions should also be reported individually when formulating the social purchasing-power plan. Thus, we can both reduce the work load and also satisfy the actual work requirements.

III. The Major Components of the Commodity Circulation Plan

The commodity circulation plan is divided into three individual components of purchase, sale, and storage of commodities. It can also be classified into the wholesale commodity circulation plan and the retail commodity circulation plan according to the nature of circulation. Its major targets are as follows:

1. <u>Total volume of purchases and sales</u>. This is the monetary expression of the total commodity circulation picture. It reflects, on the one hand, the total amount of goods controlled by the commercial sector in the plan period. On the other hand, it reflects the capacity for supplying goods to the people. It is determined with reference to the rates of growth of industrial and agricultural production while also taking into account the commodity needs of the urban and rural population. Thus, we must formulate it according to the principle of "demand and feasibility." On the one hand, we should make demands on the production branches in accordance with changes in people's purchasing power and needs in order to stimulate the growth of production. On the other hand, we must also direct consumption according to production feasibility. While gradually increasing their production, we should distribute scarce commodities fairly, taking into account past consumption levels. We must do our best to discover new products and substitutes to satisfy the requirements of the consumers. In other words, we must make suitable arrangements and adjustments in the composition of our commodity needs. For example, with the rapid increase in the cultural and living standards of the people, the demand for paper has far exceeded the growth of its production. Taking the sale of machine-made paper in 1952 as the base of 100, its sale was 120.5 percent in 1953, 132.2 percent in 1954, and 145.2 percent in 1955. The projected sale in 1956 is 200.0 percent. Even with such a broad increase, we still cannot satisfy the demand. On the other hand, the amount of paper produced by indigenous methods has declined, from 290,000 tons in 1954 to 260,000 tons in 1955. It was still declining as of 1956, which increases the need for machine-made paper. Under these circumstances, when we formulate plans, based on the state control numbers, we should rationally supply machine-made paper to the branches which have the greatest need, and at the same time we should strive to organize the production of paper by indigenous methods to satisfy the more general needs.

2. <u>Domestic purchases</u>. This is the gross monetary value of products purchased by commercial enterprises from domestic sources. It reflects the proportional relationships between the commercial sector and the industrial and agricultural production sectors and among the commercial branches. These relationships must be mutually compatible and balanced without any dislocations or incompatibility. The targets of domestic purchases included the following:

a. Products purchased directly by the unit itself (namely, state-managed commercial enterprises or supply and marketing cooperatives; the same applies below) from the industrial production departments of state-owned industry and local-state owned industry, public-private jointly operated industry, privately owned industry, handicraft producers' cooperatives, and individual handicraft industry.

b. Products purchased directly by the unit itself from the agricultural production branches of state-owned farms and local-state owned farms (including tractor stations), agricultural producers' cooperatives, agricultural mutual-aid teams, and individual peasants.

c. Products purchased directly from industrial and agricultural enterprises affiliated with various business units (such as commercial enterprises and transport enterprises).

d. Products purchased directly from industrial and agricultural enterprises affiliated with the units themselves but which have independent accounting.

e. Commodities purchased through other units (namely, those products that are accounted for in the unit itself).

f. Commodities paid for with budgetary allocations. These are commodities purchased by government financial agencies at all the levels to be resold.

The purchase targets should be based on the quantity of output; moreover, for different products the quantity produced and the quantity purchased are not the same. For industrial products, the output figure is generally the purchase figure. For agricultural and sideline products, the commodity output is the difference between the output and the part retained by the peasants (including that kept for seed, fodder, and the peasants' own consumption). (The commodity output includes the agricultural tax paid in kind. When calculations are made, we must avoid both double counting and omissions.) For commodities like cotton and cured tobacco which are handled by one branch, the commodity output is the amount of purchases by that branch. Commodities like live pigs which are handled by more than two branches should be distributed according to certain operational proportions. The parties involved should be closely coordinated on this matter. Here we refer mainly to commodities that are subject to unified purchase and planned purchase. For commodities that are not subject to planned purchase (such as minor native products and products of the handicraft industry and a portion of the local industry), some rough figures should be arrived at based on production conditions and taking into account the estimated degree of plan fulfillment in the last period and the responsibilities assigned by higher levels (usually a target expressed in money terms). We know that many agricultural products cannot be sold in the year they are produced; examples are food grain, cotton, and oil-bearing crops. Only part of the output can be sold in the output year. The rest is sold the next year. Therefore, two calendar years elapse between the marketing season of one year and another. For example, for food grain, the season extends from July of one year to June of the next year; for oil-bearing crops, from October of one year to September of the next year. (The establishment of a uniform schedule for the whole country has facilitated plan integration. The exceptions are those regions which market all of their output in the same year.) But the commodity circulation plans are calculated by the calendar year (or plan year), namely, from January 1 to December 31. As a result, the amount of purchases in one plan year has to be computed from the commodity output in two agricultural years. Suppose the output of cotton in 1955 in one province was 3 million tan and the amount marketed was 2.7 million tan. Of these: the amount marketed between September and December 1955 was 2 million tan, and the amount marketed between January and August 1956 was 0.7 million tan. The output in 1956 was 3.5 million tan, and the amount marketed was 3.2 tan. Of these: the amount marketed between September and December 1956 was 2.6 million tan and the amount marketed between January and August 1957 was 0.6 million tan. Then, the amount purchased in 1956 was 3.3 million tan = 0.7 million tan + 2.6 million tan. It is not the amount marketed out of the 1956 output, that is, 3.2 million tan. In general, the formula for converting the amount of agricultural products marketed during two years into the amount purchased in one plan year is as follows:

Amount of purchase = (Last year's output × Marketed rate − Amount marketed last year) + (Current year output × Marketed rate − Amount to be marketed next year).

3. Domestic sales (namely, the sum of wholesale and retail sales). This is a measure of the capacity of commercial enterprises to supply material goods (including industrial raw materials, producer goods, and consumer goods) to the domestic market. It is expressed in both physical and money terms. When the plan is formulated, we should do our best to embody in it the policies and responsibilities of serving industrial and agricultural

production and urban and rural consumers. We should distribute commodity supplies according to Party and state policies, targets set at higher levels, and the proportion of public and private operations. This proportion guarantees the steady growth of socialist commerce and can also facilitate the maintenance of private commerce during the socialist transformation. Furthermore, we can use it to gradually transform private commerce and strengthen plan management. The scope of targets for domestic sales includes:

a. Commodities sold by the unit itself directly to the commercial enterprises of the various economic sectors (state-owned commerce, supply and marketing cooperatives, public-private jointly operated commerce, private commerce, and so forth) for resale.

b. Commodities sold by the unit itself directly to industrial production branches and agricultural production branches of various economic components for use in their production.

c. Packaging materials, storage and transport equipment, processing tools, and fodder for marketed livestock sold directly by the unit itself to commercial enterprises.

d. Commodities sold directly by the unit itself to agencies, organizations, and people for their consumption.

e. Commodities sold through other units.

f. Commodities paid for through budgetary allocations. These are materials supplied by enterprises to government finance departments of the regions according to allocation coupons.

g. Commodities sold to industrial enterprises, agricultural enterprises, and restaurants affiliated with the unit itself but having independent economic accounting.

The sales targets should be set such that the total sum of goods is built on an active, steady, and reliable basis. They are generally determined with reference to the commodity income and expenditure balance table of the branches concerned. Therefore, it is necessary to consider domestic purchases, imports and exports, inward transfers and outward transfers,* increases in or reductions in inventory, and other factors. At the same time, we must see to it that they are in line with related targets in other branches (for example, the purchase and sales targets of state-owned com-

---

*The inward and outward transfers (t'iao-ju t'iao-ch'u) refer to the transfers of commodities into or out of given regions within China which are carried out by the central government. — N. R. L.

merce and the supply and marketing cooperatives must be properly coordinated) in order to guarantee harmonious conduct among all the branches of the national economy. After gross sales are determined, we must first separate the gross amount of wholesale from the retail within the branch itself. Then within the wholesale targets, the distribution proportions must be determined by branches and economic sectors. The differentiation between wholesale and retail can be handled according to the regulations published by the State Statistical Bureau. But the State Statistical Bureau classifies commodities by their uses. This is not quite the same as calculating the total volume of circulation of commodities according to social purchasing power. For example, the producer goods purchased by the fishery producers' cooperatives are classified for statistical purposes as wholesale, but the money income of the fishermen is based on the sale of marine products. Therefore, monetary expenditures include not only noncommodity expenditures and savings, but also include the purchase of producer goods to expand output and consumer goods for personal livelihood needs. (The State Statistical Bureau has already stipulated that agricultural producer goods be treated as retail). All such matters must be considered uniformly in the future.

4. Export supplies and import purchases. Export supplies refer to commodities sold by domestic commercial enterprises or by enterprises that purchase agricultural products to the various specialized companies of the Ministry of Foreign Trade for export (including the portion that is exported on behalf of the Ministry of Foreign Trade). Import purchases refers to imported commodities purchased by domestic commercial enterprises or by enterprises that purchase agricultural products from the specialized companies under the Ministry of Foreign Trade or purchased directly from public-private jointly operated importers. From this, we can see that export supplies and import purchases are targets that are coordinated between the domestic commercial plan and the foreign trade plan. They are also the major basis for guaranteeing a balance between foreign exchange income and expenditure. With the continual increases in the country's socialist industrialization and in the people's living standards, we have to import many machines and much equipment, industrial raw materials and ores, and certain consumer goods. At the Eighth Party Congress, Comrade Chou En-lai pointed out in his "Report on the Draft Second Five-Year Plan to Develop the National Economy": "During the First Five-Year Plan, 40 percent of the machines and equipment

required for national construction had to be imported." Therefore, actively organizing sources of supply and fulfilling export demands are instrumental in accelerating our socialist construction.

5. Commodity reserves. These include actual inventory, inventory in transit,[1] and inventory in process,[2] namely, all owned material reserves. This is also expressed in both money and physical terms. In determining the amount of reserves, we should generally consider factors such as the market circulation pattern of the commodities, transport conditions, seasonality, and commodity perishability. Since commerce is responsible for serving the production branches and the consumers, the quotas for inventories should not be fixed mechanically. They must be adjusted according to objective conditions. For some commodities, the inventory may be increased for some time or in some places in order to maintain and arrange for production. Suitable reductions in the inventory of some commodities may also be necessary because of distribution difficulties or temporary shortages.

6. The total volume of circulation of retail commodities. This is the monetary value of the amount of commodities needed by the urban and rural populations of the regions and the supply of commodities by the retail commercial organizations. At present, China's total retail commodity circulation includes commodities sold directly to either the urban and rural populations or to agencies and organizations for consumption and products sold directly to peasants for use in production.

Total social retail commodity circulation is the monetary expression of the sum of the retail commodities supplied by the commerce, restaurants, industrial enterprises, and handicraft production branches of all the economic components. It does not, however, include peasant trade. The 1957 planning tables stipulate peasant trade as a reference target; it is not to be included in the state plan targets. It is to be listed separately in the money income and expenditure balance table of the people. The determination of the total volume of circulation of retail commodities, on the one hand, depends on the purchasing power of the urban and rural population and social organizations. On the other hand, it depends on the capacity for supplying commodities. Therefore, it is necessary to compute the above two aspects accurately.

When each branch formulates its plan for the volume of circulation of retail commodities, they should propose their total volume of retail sales for the plan period on the basis of directives from higher levels and moreover on the basis of the relative importance of that branch in the field of retail commodity circulation during the plan period. Moreover, with regard to the responsibility for transforming privately owned commerce, small merchants, and peddlers, their business volume should be determined by a combination of the goods that will be applied to these units by the wholesale commodity circulation plan and an estimate of that portion which they will buy and sell themselves with reference to data obtained from surveys and research (such as the number of workers, the average living standard, and so forth).

The formulation of the plan for the volume of retail sales is still in an experimental stage. This is because China's commercial organizations are established mainly according to wholesale links. This is necessary to guarantee both the supply of raw materials to production branches and the transformation of capitalist industry and commerce. The expected results have already materialized. At the same time, privately owned commerce is gradually being transformed into state capitalist commerce. The transition from indirect planning to direct planning can only be carried out gradually. Therefore, there are still certain objective difficulties at present in establishing a full-fledged plan for the volume of retail sales. Of the fifty items in the 1957 retail commodity list published by the state planning agencies, the State Statistical Bureau requires reporting on only nineteen. All the branches should conscientiously prepare the retail statistics for the above-mentioned commodities in order to create favorable conditions for expanding the retail commodity planning list in the future. In formulating the plan, the retail sales plan of the state-owned specialized company or the supply and marketing cooperative in charge of the commodity can generally be the major component (for example, in the case of cotton, the fabric sales figures of the textile company should be used for computation), while taking into account the wholesale plans of private merchants (both those who have and have not yet been transformed) and the estimated change in inventories. For example, the formula for computing the retail quantity of cotton is as follows:

Retail quantity of cotton = Retail sales of textile product company + Retail sales by other companies under Ministry of Commerce + Retail sales of other state-owned enterprises (namely, state-owned enterprises outside Ministry of Commerce system) + Retail sales by supply and marketing cooperatives + Retail sales by jointly owned commerce and retail sales by small merchants and peddlers in the course of socialist transformation.

7. <u>Plan table of the commodity composition of retail sales.</u>
Simply put, this table classifies the expenditure of purchasing
power into the major categories of food, clothing, services, housing, and fuel. In the past, we were only concerned with drawing
up the composition of the sources of purchasing power; we did not
draw up the composition of social purchasing power expenditure.
This one-sided knowledge about purchasing power was thus not
very useful in formulating the branches' commodity circulation
plans. For example, some reacted, "The frame is too broad, it
does not suffice in the specific use." Consequently, we have added
this table this year. After it is calculated, it will reflect the proportion of each type of commodity in social purchasing power and
will be very useful in formulating the branch commodity circulation plans. This requires that all the business units do their best
to coordinate with and help the planning committees at every level.
Because the method for classifying commodities and the current
statistical classification method are not yet consistent with each
other, many difficulties will be encountered everywhere in formulating the table. Comrades of all regions are requested to suggest
concrete computation methods and improvements based on their
practical experience.

The formulation of all of the targets in the commercial plan
must be based on the branch plans. That is, they must be filled
out by examining and comprehensively balancing all the branch
plans. Therefore, the planning agencies at each level need not
distribute the relevant tables to all the branches to be filled out.
Naturally, some planned targets must still be filled out by the
relevant branches, such as the volume of retail sales, the table
of the commodity composition of retail sales, and so forth.

IV. The Basic Method of Formulating Commodity Circulation Plans

The basic method of formulating commodity circulation plans
is the balance method. This balancing method is constructed on
the basis of carrying out "demand and feasibility." As far as
commodity circulation plans are concerned, "demand" refers to
the purchasing power of the urban and rural population; "feasibility" refers to the capacity for supplying commodities. These two
aspects do not immediately balance. Only after repeated computation and many revisions can this balance be achieved.

The first tool used in the balance method is the balance table for the distribution of material resources. It is the basis for determining the capacity for supplying retail commodities and for formulating commodity circulation plans. "Resources" consist of such targets as inventory at the beginning of the period, domestic production, imports, transfers from outside the province or municipality, and so forth. "Distribution" consists of such targets as the quantity of goods supplied for retail sale, for industrial uses, military uses, exports, consumption by the peasants themselves, transfers outside the province or municipality, inventory at the end of the period, and so forth. The content of the balance table can be appropriately increased or reduced according to how the commodities are handled. This balancing work does not belong only to the comrades who manage comprehensive commercial plans. Comrades who manage specialized plans and even comrades who only manage specific commodity plans must also get involved. Will this cause duplication of effort? I think not. On the contrary, because people have different jobs, their different viewpoints may be of some use in mutual accounting. In computing this table, comrades in each specialized branch can still list their own branch operation figures under each target. This way, on the one hand the proportion of their own branch operations can be observed, and on the other, the figures on commodity purchases and sales can be initially determined. We must accumulate relevant data on a regular basis, including such things as production figures, the direction of commodity circulation, local and national consumption levels, and the consumption levels of regions with similar economic characteristics. These are indispensable economic data for plan formulation.

Another tool used in the balance method is the table for computing social purchasing power (computed by means of the social organizations' purchasing-power table and the people's money income and expenditure balance table). This is the basic factor in determining the total volume of circulation of retail commodities. It is composed of the urban and rural people's purchasing power and the social organizations' purchasing power.

The urban and rural people's purchasing power is determined by the money income of the urban and rural population (including the wages of the staff and workers and the money income of other nonagricultural people, the money income of the agricultural population from the sale of agricultural and sideline products, the other money income of the people, and money remitted to them); the noncommodity expenditures of the urban and rural population such as rent, utilities, culture and entertainment, and children's education; and the amount of money used for public debt purchase and savings deposits. Its computation formula is as follows:

Purchasing power of urban and rural population = Money income of urban and rural population − Noncommodity expenditures − Public debt purchase and additions to savings deposits − Money remitted out = Increase or decrease in money holdings of the population (namely, increase or decrease of cash held by the population).

When we make the calculations for each region according to the above formula, we must bear in mind the money that is in the process of circulating (that is, the circulating purchasing power). So far, we still lack a well-developed method for computing the circulating purchasing power and the ready cash of the population. Please study this problem and make suggestions or share your practical experience with us.

The social purchasing power should be computed according to the planning tables established by the state planning agencies (namely, purchasing power tables 1 through 7). Concrete targets will not be discussed in detail here.

Since computing social purchasing power involves every sector of the national economy and the targets are complex, the amount of work is comparatively large. For some regions, a rough idea of the market capacity can be obtained by simply looking at the quantity of currency added to circulation in the cash flow plan of the bank. This inevitably involves many repetitions and omissions (for example, noncommodity expenditures which have not been deducted and commodity purchases by agencies, organizations, and enterprises which are mostly made through account clearances rather than cash payments). However, a rough idea can still be obtained.

The balance between social purchasing power and total volume of circulation of retail commodities must be established on a fully reliable basis. If the capacity for supplying commodities is less than social purchasing power, market chaos in the form of rapidly rising prices and inflation in the plan period will result, leading to destruction and losses in the national economy. Therefore, in formulating plans, we must overcome and solve this weak link. Under the socialist system, the law of planned (and proportional) development of the national economy plays a decisive role. The proportional relationship between production and consumption must be closely coordinated.

Notes

1. Inventory in transit includes commodities which have been subtracted from the inventory of the seller but not yet included in the inventory of the buyer and commodities for which ownership has been obtained (by virtue of purchase certificates) and which have been duly entered as purchases and reserves but which have not been received.

2. Finished products still to be returned by industrial production branches which have been entrusted raw materials by commercial branches for processing.

LECTURE 3: TRANSPORT PLANNING TABLES

Ch'en T'ieh-cheng*

I. The Scope of Transport Planning

The transport industry can generally be divided into two different types.

One is transport within the productive branches. It serves only the production of a given enterprise and is one component of the production process. An example in the coal-mining industry is the transport of extracted coal from the mine shaft to the surface. In the forestry industry, it is the transport of timber from the felling area to the sawmill. And in a factory, it is the transport of parts or semifinished products from one workshop to the next workshop. This kind of transport takes place within the unified organization of production work and belongs directly to the productive sphere. Transport within the production branches includes many different types of transport, such as railways, automobiles, tractors, sky lifts [t'ien-ch'e], cable cars, conveyor belts, pipelines, and animal power.

The other kind of transport provides external links among enterprises or among various sectors of the national economy. Marx characterized this kind of transport as "it appears as a continuation of a process of production within the process of circulation and in the process of circulation."[†] Examples are the transport of coal from Fu-shun to the Anshan Steel Mill and the transport of tangerines grown in the south to the north for consumption. This kind of transport is carried out by the independent public transport industry. The public transport industry also includes many

---

*Ch'en T'ieh-cheng, "Yün-shu chi-hua piao-ke." <u>CHCC</u>, 1957, No. 3, pp. 29-33.
†Karl Marx, <u>Capital</u>, Vol. II (New York: International Publishers, 1967), p. 152.
— N. R. L.

types of transport. For example, at the present time, China has railway transport, inland waterway transport, maritime transport, highway transport, air transport, and so forth. And inland waterway transport, maritime transport, and highway transport include both modern means of transport (steamships, automobiles) and traditional means of transport (wooden sailboats, animal-drawn carts, pack animals, and so forth).

The scope of the national economy's transport plan basically includes the latter kind of transport (carried out by the public transport industry) using all types of transport.

The national economy and the people place two types of demand on the transport industry, namely, freight transport and passenger transport. Therefore, in the transport plans for each type of transport, there is a separate plan for freight transport and for passenger transport. But in the civil aviation transport plan, in addition to freight transport and passenger transport, there is also a separate plan for mail transport.

II. The Basic Task of Transport Planning

The basic task of the transport plan is to ensure the full satisfaction of the needs of the national economy and the people for freight and passenger transport through the most rational use of each means of transport. That is to say, an overall arrangement of each means of transport must be properly worked out so that the national economy's and the people's demands for transport will be fully satisfied with the smallest amount of labor (including live labor and embodied labor).

At the same time, the transport plan is also the basis of demands for producer goods made by the transport industry on other sectors of the national economy. This is because the transport industry (especially the railway transport industry) is one of the country's biggest consumers of material goods. Its need for some products (such as locomotives, railway cars, and boats) almost determines the amount of work of the industrial branches producing them. Therefore, accurately determining the transport industry's need for producer goods on the basis of the transport plan can, on the one hand, ensure the realization of the transport plan and, on the other, reflects the scale of demand placed on industrial production. This facilitates arranging the national economy's industrial production plan.

III. The Composition of Transport Planning Tables and Their System of Targets

The composition of transport is as follows: (1) those belonging to the system of targets for the volume of transport: the freight and passenger transport plan table, the plan table for the composition of freight, the plan table for through freight transport via rail and water, and the plan table for freight transport requested by consigning departments; (2) those belonging to the system of technical-economic targets are the plan table for technical-economic targets for means of transport and the separate operating plan for locomotives and cars within the railway transport plan; (3) the balance table for the means of transport (or the plan table for the increase or decrease in the means of transport); (4) the plan table for the repair of the railway's fixed assets; and (5) the plan table for work. The following is a brief description of the functions and content of these tables and the methods of estimating certain major targets.

1. Tables Belonging to the System of Targets for the Volume of Transport

a. The Freight and passenger transport plan table. The targets for the volume of freight and passenger transport that are determined in this table form the basis of the transport plan. It represents the transport needs of the national economy and the people. At the same time, it also represents the transport assignments the transport industry should complete for the national economy and the people. The major targets that express the volume of transport are:

1) The volume of freight transport. The volume of freight transport is the number of tons of freight delivered. It is a major target reflecting the link between the transport industry and other sectors of the national economy. The most important task in the formulation of the freight transport plan is to achieve within the freight transport plan an accurate reflection of the proportionate development between the volume of freight transport and the quantity of output.

The major method for determining the target for the volume of freight transport is the balance method, that is, formulating an economic balance table for transport for each good. However, the balance method can only be applied to bulk freight transport.

For freight which is small in quantity and has great variety, the coefficient method and the method of estimating according to the proportionate volume of freight transport are used. Furthermore, in determining the targets for the volume of freight transport for certain bulk freight, we are often limited by inadequate economic data and cannot necessarily use the balance method. The following is a brief description of some present methods of calculation.

a) The balance method. In formulating the transport plan, up-to-date knowledge of the production, supply, and sales of each major good is essential for determining targets for the volume of freight transport with the balance method. In recent years, when formulating the rail transport plan, we have begun to use this method to determine the volume of freight transport for certain important, bulky goods whose production is regionally concentrated such as coal, crude oil and oil products, iron ore, and iron and steel.

The economic balance table for transport represents the relationship between the sources of various goods and the demand for them in the area where they are produced in the plan period. From this we can determine the quantities that must be transported. Therefore, there are three basic components to the economic balance table for transport: (1) sources, which include the quantity of output and other sources of goods (such as imports) in the plan period and the inventory at the beginning of the plan period; (2) products not transported, which includes consumption by the producing units themselves, sales in the producing areas, and inventory at the end of the plan period; and (3) the volume of transport. The items listed in the economic balance tables for the transport of various goods can be appropriately changed according to concrete situations. For example, in formulating the railway transport plan, we now use the following format for our economic balance table for coal transport (see page 70).

b) Method coefficients. This method of determining volume of transport on the basis of the quantity of goods provided during the plan period (for food grain it is based on the volume of government purchases) and the specified transport coefficient. The transport coefficient is a ratio of the volume of transport to the quantity of output, but it is not fixed. Therefore, in applying the method of coefficients we must first analyze the data from past years as well as factors in the whole economic process from production to consumption which may affect the transport coefficient in the plan year. Examples are the enlargement of the transport network,

Economic Balance Table for Coal Transport

	Base period	Plan period
I. Sources		
1. Quantity of output		
2. Industrial process coal and increased weight of coal		
3. Transport turnover of graded coal		
4. Quantity of inventory at the beginning of the plan period		
II. Product not transported by rail		
1. Quantity consumed by producing units		
2. Quantity of local sales (not transported via rail)		
3. Quantity wasted in washing and grading coal		
4. Quantity transported directly by water routes		
5. Quantity of coal produced not along the rail line		
6. Quantity of current year reserves (the part not transported outside)		
7. Quantity of inventory at the end of the plan period		
III. Duplicated traffic		
IV. Volume of railway transport (I - II + III)		

changes in the proportion of freight carried by each type of transport, the development of new economic regions, changes among production, supply, and sales, increases or decreases in imported goods, the thorough realization of major government policies, and the implementation of new economic measures. We now use this method of estimation to determine the traffic of certain goods carried by rail and other types of transport.

c) Quota method. For example, the traffic of mineral-type construction materials (bricks, tiles, sand, gravel, and so forth) is determined on the basis of each 100 million yuan of construction and installation work, that is, the average number of tons of mineral-type construction materials that must be transported per 100 million yuan of construction and installation work. However, these quotas are not fixed either. They are subject to large variations according to changes in the composition of construction and installation work, changes in design standards, the development of campaigns for economizing on materials, and the degree of reliance on locally available materials. Therefore, in formulating

168

plans, we must fully analyze factors affecting changes in quotas in the past and the concrete situations in the plan period before new quotas are estimated.

d) Proportional method. For example, the volume of freight transport of goods that are small in quantity and for which economic conditions are difficult to assess can be estimated according to their proportionate share of the volume of freight transport of these goods in total freight transport in previous years.

In practical application, the above methods can be used to supplement one another. For example, after the volume of coal transport has been calculated by the balance method, it can be verified by the transport coefficient method. The volume of transport determined by the quota method and the method of coefficients can also be verified by the proportional method. Only through multifaceted and repeated study and verification and continuous revision can the targets of volume of freight transport be realistic.

In addition to the above methods for determining targets of the volume of freight transport according to the national economy's need for transport, at present for those shipping routes where the transport capacity of trucks and of lighters on inland waterways is inadequate, we can use the method of determining the volume of freight transport on the basis of transport capacity. That is, we first determine the total volume of freight transport according to the maximum transport capacity during the plan period. Then we analyze and study the goods that objectively need to be transported during the plan period and determine the volume of transport for each important good, taking into account the Party's and government's policies. The needs of the national economy which are still unsatisfied are included in the freight transport plan of traditional means of transport. In sum, no matter which method of estimating is used, a thorough economic investigation of the sources of supply and the supply routes is essential for determining freight traffic targets.

In addition, in formulating transport plans, every transport branch must also pay full attention to the comprehensive utilization of each type of transport. Otherwise, the full utilitization of existing transport capacity and the (relatively) balanced growth of each type of transport may be adversely affected. Furthermore, the freight transport time may be lengthened, thus adversely affecting the growth of the national economy.

2) Turnover of goods. The turnover of goods is one of the major targets representing the work load of the transport industry.

The size of the work load in freight transport depends not only on the volume of freight transport (tons delivered), but also on transport distance. The turnover of goods is a composite target of the volume of freight transport and transport distance. Its unit of measurement is ton-kilometers (or ton-nautical li for water transport). The turnover of goods is also the basic data for estimating the demand for vehicles, boats, and fuels, the amount of repair of fixed assets, and the plans for labor, costs, and financial receipts and payments.

The method for estimating the turnover of goods is to multiply the volume of freight transport by the average freight transport distance (kilometer or nautical li). Thus, the basic work of determining the target for the volume of freight transport and determining the average freight transport distance is the primary task in estimating the turnover of goods.

The average freight transport distance reflects the geographical distribution of the productive forces, the degree of rationality in the relations between the producing and the marketing areas, and the level of comprehensive utilization of each type of transport. The average freight transport distance is calculated separately for each different category of good that is included within the scope of targets for the volume of freight divided by commodity category. The best way to determine the average freight transport distance targets is to make the calculations on the basis of the regional production and sales balance tables for major goods. However, at the present time, we are not equipped to do this. We can only look at the average transport distance expected to be covered in the base period for each type of good and take into account changes in the distribution of production and consumption (namely, changes in the flow of goods) in the plan period to arrive finally at a composite average transport distance for the total volume of transport.

3) The volume of passenger transport. This is the number of passengers on cars (boats or airplanes) measured at the departure of their trips. It does not include free passengers (for example, staff and workers of the railway and their dependents who travel for free). The volume of passenger transport depends on the mobility of the people, and the mobility of the people depends in turn on: the level of development of the national economy and culture, the people's standard of living, the geographical distribution of cities and rural areas and industrial and mining enterprises, the population density, the distribution of the transport

network, the major policies of the state, and so forth. In determining passenger traffic targets, we must carefully study the above factors for the plan period.

4) Passenger turnover. The meaning and function of this is basically similar to the turnover of goods. The unit of measurement is passenger-kilometer (or passenger nautical li for water transport). In determining this target, we must take into account changes in passenger traffic and fully study factors contributing to increases or decreases in passenger travel in the plan period.

In addition, in the railway freight transport plan, there is also the target for the "average number of cars loaded each workday." The "average number of cars loaded each workday" referred to in this target is the number of cars loaded computed on the basis of a four-axle car. That is, the loading of each four-axle car is counted as one car, and the loading of each two-axle car is counted as half a car. The "average number of cars loaded each workday" is the basis for estimating the number of railway cars needed and for formulating the technical work plan in railway transport. At the same time, this target facilitates the Ministry of Railway's daily supervision of transport businesses.

b. The plan table for the composition of freight transport. This is a table for calculating what in the railway transport plan are targets for the volume of freight transport and the average transport distance for eleven types of goods. (There are twelve types in the inland waterway and maritime transport plan represented in the tables for freight traffic and goods turnover.) The targets for the composition of the volume of railway freight transport are: coal, coke, crude oil and oil products, mineral ores, iron and steel, mineral-type construction materials, timber, cotton, food grain, salt, and other. The classification of goods is not fixed. It varies and is set according to the conditions and concrete situations at various times. More detailed classifications can be made on the foundation of the above classification of goods in the transport planning tables at the grass-roots level of various transport industries. The major principles in classifying goods are as follows: (1) Select goods which represent a sizable proportion of the volume of freight transport, such as coal, iron, steel, timber, food grain, and mineral-type construction materials. The total volume of freight transport can be closely estimated from the volume of freight transport of these bulk goods. (2) Select goods that are significant to the national economic life or transport work even though their proportion of the total freight traffic may be small. Coke and cotton are examples of the former. Crude oil and oil products that have to be carried by special vehicles and boats (tank cars and oil tankers) are examples of the latter. (3) Be sure that the years will be able to be compared with one another. And (4) pay attention to integrating all the types of transport.

c. The plan table for the volume of through freight transport via rail and water. The purpose of this table is to integrate planning for through transport between the railways and either the inland waterways directly under the central government or the coastal waters in order to gradually expand the scope of through transport, strengthen planning for cooperation among all types of transport, be good at comprehensively utilizing rail and water routes, and shorten the transit time of goods, thus accelerating the turnover of goods.

The targets for the volume of through freight transport are in the form of tons of freight transported jointly along railways and either inland waterways or coastal routes classified according to the port or station of transport and the type of goods. The volume of through freight transport includes separate targets for the volume of railway, inland waterway, and coastal freight transport. That is to say, the goods that are sent through transport that are included in targets in the volume of railway, inland waterway, and coastal freight transport are expressed once again in this table.

d. The plan table for the freight transport requested by consigning departments and the work of compiling freight transport plans of the consigning departments must be formulated with close coordination between the transport branches and the goods-consigning branches. This way, on the one hand, the transport branches must continuously analyze present and future sources and flows of goods with a view to satisfying the transport demands of the national economy. On the other hand, the consigning branches must furnish the plan for requested freight transport as a reference and basis for the formulation of freight transport plans by the transport branches. This enables the transport branches to better predict the trend of growth of traffic, make timely preparations, and arrange for capital construction of transport equipment in good time in order to ensure the satisfaction of all the consigning branches' transport requirements. This, in turn, is one of the major conditions for ensuring that the production, capital construction, and product circulation tasks of all the branches consigning goods will be completed. As of 1957, some major goods-consigning branches have started formulating the plan for requested freight transport for railways, inland waterways directly under the central government, and coastal water routes. These plans consist of requests for freight transport classified by the type of freight, the point of dispatch, and the point of arrival (by railway substations and ports).

2. Tables Belonging to the System of Technical and Economic Targets

a. Technical and economic target tables for means of transport. The technical and economic targets in the transport plan are mainly targets for the utilization of equipment capacity, namely, targets for the rate of utilization of the means of transport. Targets for the rate of utilization of the means of transport are quality targets which ensure the fulfillment of targets for the volume of transport, and at the same time, provide the basis for formulating means of transport balance tables. Such targets to a large extent determine increases in the labor productivity in the transport industry and decreases in transport costs.

Since the method of transport for each means of transport differs, the targets for the rate of utilization that are specified for them also vary. At present, major targets already approved by the state are as follows:

1) The major targets in the railway transport plan are:

a) Freight car turn-around time. Freight car turn-around time is the time period (one workday is the unit of measurement) between the beginning of the first loading of a freight car, through the unloading and up to the second loading. Shortening the freight car turn-around time would not only reduce the number of cars needed, but also increase the amount of transport work that could be obtained from a given number of cars. At the same time, shortening the freight car turn-around time would also imply shortening freight transport time, consequently accelerating the turnover of goods.

Freight car turn-around time includes the time spent at the loading and unloading stations, the time spent at the transfer stations, and the time in transit. Therefore, in determining the target for car turn-around time, we should pay attention to: (1) eliminating or reducing circuitous transport and reducing empty-car mileage to reduce the total turn-around distance; (2) around-the-clock loading and unloading — whenever possible, heavy goods should be loaded and unloaded with machines to shorten the cars' waiting time; (3) reducing the number of transfers at technical stations (by using express trains) and shortening the transfer time at technical stations in order to shorten the total time spent at the technical stations; and (4) increasing the speed of the trains and thus shortening their total transit time.

b) Average load per freight car. This is the average weight (in tons) of freight carried by a car. Increasing the average net carload can result in fewer cars carrying even more freight. At the same time, increasing the average net carload is also one measure for fully utilizing the hauling capacity of locomotives. Even when the total weight hauled by the freight train is constant, the relative weight of goods in the total weight hauled would be increased and the relative weight of the cars would be reduced, thus the output of ton-kilometers of freight transport would be increased. The major factors affecting the average load per freight car are: changes in the proportions of heavy and light freight, changes in the type of cars used, and the extent of utilization of the cars' technical loaded quantity (fixed load quota). In determining the target for the average load of a freight car, we must pay attention not only to absolute increases (because the average load naturally increases if the proportion of large cars is increased), but more importantly to increases in the load coefficient. And the main way to increase the load coefficient is to use cars rationally and to improve the packaging specifications for goods and the loading methods.

c) Freight locomotives' kilometers per day. This is the average number of kilometers traveled by each locomotive per day. It is a basic target for the utilization of locomotives. It is also an absolute figure for estimating the need for locomotives. Increasing the kilometers per day of operating locomotives is one of the major methods of economizing on locomotives or increasing the amount of transport work without additional locomotives. In determining the target for locomotives' kilometers per day, we must fully consider the distance between the points traveled by freight trains in their fixed operating zones, changes in the running speed of the trains, and changes in the locomotives' ratio of idle time (including time spent in its own zone and other zones) to running time.

d) Average gross weight hauled per freight locomotive. This is the average gross weight of the cars hauled by a freight train. By increasing it, we can proportionately reduce the need for operating locomotives and increase the carrying capacity of the railroad tracks. In determing the target for average total weight hauled per freight locomotive, we must take into account: changes in the composition of the type of locomotives and cars, restrictions imposed by the length of the track between stations and changes in the profile of the track, changes in the running speed of the trains, changes in the gross load of freight cars, changes in the proportions of trains operating on tracks with varying hauling quotas, and so forth. At the same time, we must also increase the coefficient of utilization of the hauling capacity of locomotives, that is, make the target of gross weight hauled by locomotives closer to the standard for weight hauled by locomotives (the hauling quota).

2) The major target in the inland waterways and coastal transport plan is the quantity of output per boat-ton in the plan period (for tugs, it is the quantity of output per horsepower in the plan period). The output per boat-ton in the plan period is a composite target for the utilization of boats. It expresses the number of ton-kilometers of transport work produced by each ton of boat (or each horsepower) in the plan period. In determining this target, we should pay attention to: increasing the boat's technical running speed, increasing the travel time coefficient, increasing the boat's load (or the tonnage hauled by the tug), and increasing the boat's operating time. That is to say, we must consider how to improve the technical operation of the boat and the arrangement and loading of freight, reduce the mooring time at ports (especially nonproductive mooring time), shorten the maintenance time, and improve the quality of maintenance work.

3) The main target in the truck transport plan is the annual output of truck-tons. This is a composite target for the truck utilization rate. It expresses the quantity of output per ton of truck in the plan period and is estimated in ton-kilometers. In determining this target, we must consider improving organizational measures in transport work; increasing the trucks' operating rate, namely, increasing the number of days the trucks work and reducing the number they are idle; increasing technical speed and increasing the running time in order to add to the distance traveled per truck per day; and reducing the proportion of trucks traveling empty and fully utilizing trucks' load capacity.

4) The main target of the civil aviation transport plan is the "quantity of output per hour of transport aviation," which is the number of ton-kilometers produced per plane per hour. It too is a composite target. We determine this target mainly by estimating the plane's commercial loading capacity (namely, the plane's total

carrying capacity minus the weight of the flying personnel and fuel equals the capacity available for commercial transport), its flying speed, and the aviation transport rate. Since this target is calculated on a per plane basis, changes in the proportions of the types of planes often lead to large changes in the average target for all the planes. Therefore, in addition to determining the average target for all planes, we must also set targets for each type of plane.

The technical and economic targets should be actively and realistically based on the advanced quotas so that they are above the average level reached by the various units (or workers).

b. Table for the operating plan of railway locomotives and cars. The targets in this table are all estimated targets. Its goal is to compute the number of kilometers traveled by locomotives and cars and the gross ton-kilometers hauled by locomotives within the plan period on the basis of the turnover of goods and passengers. These are then used to determine the demand for locomotives and cars. Afterward, the balance between transport capacity and the volume of transport is obtained by means of the balance table for locomotives and cars.

3. Balance Tables for Means of Transport (or Tables of Estimated Increases or Decreases in Means of Transport)

Another important task in formulating transport plans is to determine the total demand and replacement need for means of transport in order to ensure a balance between transport capacity and the volume of transport and also the fulfillment of traffic targets.

We must estimate transport capacity from two aspects. On the one hand, we must determine technical and economic targets for the rate of utilization of the means of transport. On the other hand, we must estimate the amount of means of transport in the plan period (including the amount at the beginning of the year, the increase or decrease during the plan period, the amount at the end of the year, and the average amount in use during the whole year — the amount used on the amount managed). For example, the annual transport capacity of an inland waterway transport enterprise is equal to the product of that enterprise's average annual boat tonnage and the average annual quantity of output per boat-ton. Balance tables for means of transport are formulated to achieve a balance between transport capacity and the quantity of transport and to ensure the fulfillment of transport targets by determining the demand and replacement need for means of transport and

176

estimating transport capacity on the basis of technical and economic targets.

When the capacity of transport equipment is below the national economy's demand for it (as in the case of China's truck transport), the quantity of transport is basically determined by transport capacity. Therefore, when formulating transport plans, it is particularly significant to calculate accurately transport capacity by using the table of estimated increases or decreases in the means of transport.

4. The Plan Table for the Repair of the Railway's Fixed Assets

The targets for the repair of fixed assets contained in the transport plan are unique among the national economic plans. Why are there no repair targets for fixed assets in the industrial production plan? This is mainly because the transport industry's fixed assets have the following two characteristics.

a. There are comparatively more fixed assets in the transport industry. In transport, labor is applied directly to means of labor (cars, boats, and so forth), and not to objects of labor (goods, passengers). The operation of the means of labor simply results in the movement of goods and passengers. For example, the job of an engineer is mainly to drive the locomotive in order to take the cars to their destination. Only then can its load of goods (or the passengers it carries) be delivered. Industrial production is different because in industrial production, labor is applied directly to objects of labor (raw materials or semifinished products). For example, the job of a carpenter is mainly to saw and plane the timber to make it into tables and chairs. Therefore, this determines the need to have comparatively more fixed assets in the transport industry. At present, the fixed assets of China's transport industry comprise about 30 percent of the fixed assets of the whole economy. The fixed assets of the Ministry of Railways are the largest of all the economic sectors.

b. The fixed assets of the transport industry are largely mobile. This is particularly true of railroad cars which are used in common within the whole country. Cars that are under the jurisdiction of one management bureau today may be under the jurisdiction of another tomorrow. The day after, they may be under the jurisdiction of yet another management bureau. They do not belong to any one enterprise or unit. The result can be that everyone is merely concerned about using them, and their repair may be neglected.

177

Precisely because of the above, targets for the repair of fixed assets in the transport plan have special significance for ensuring that the large fixed assets of the transport industry are properly maintained and for strengthening the planning and supervision of the maintenance work.

The repair plan for fixed assets includes money targets and physical targets. The money targets consist of the major expenses of repairing fixed assets. The physical targets consist of the amount of repair work to be done on the tracks, locomotives, and cars.

5. The Work Plan for Ports

The work plan for ports is an independent part of the transport plan. This is because ports are operated as an independent business system. Ports are important links in the economic work of maritime transport. The loading and unloading of boats and the technical supplying of boats are all done at ports. Therefore, the quality of maritime transport depends largely on the quality of work at the ports. More importantly, the amount of work at the ports also includes the loading and unloading capacity and the amount of loading and unloading connected with overseas transport on foreign vessels. This is why the work plan for ports is an independent part of the transport plan.

The work plane for ports is formulated on the basis of individual ports. It consists of two systems of targets: One is quantitative targets — the operational targets of each port, including the loading and unloading capacity, the quantity loaded and unloaded, and the amount of operations. The other is qualitative targets, including such things as the port's coefficient of mechanized operation and the average loading and unloading quotas per work shift.

LECTURE 4: AGRICULTURAL PRODUCTION PLANNING TABLES

Liu Hsien-kao*

I. The Concept of Agricultural Production

Like industrial production, agricultural production is also one of the social material production activities. Its content includes plant growing (the growing of all kinds of farm crops, such as food grain and cotton, and afforestation) and animal husbandry (the raising of domesticated livestock, poultry, silkworms, and marine life). However, unlike industrial and other production sectors, agricultural production is characterized by the fact that expanding agricultural output is closely related to natural reproduction. For example, the production processes of planting crops and raising livestock are simply the natural reproduction processes of crops and livestock. At the same time, agricultural products are the means for their own reproduction. For example, wheat can be used as seeds to produce identical wheat, and livestock can produce identical livestock. This characteristic of agricultural production determines that agricultural production activities are greatly restricted and affected by natural conditions.

II. The Scope of Agricultural Production Planning

The 1957 national economic planning tables stipulate that the scope of agricultural production planning includes the agricultural production activities of state-owned and locally administered state agricultural enterprises, agricultural producers' cooperatives, mutual-aid teams, and individual peasants. Agricultural production activities carried on by nonproduction agricultural organiza-

*Liu Hsien-kao, "Nung-yeh sheng-ch'an chi-hua piao-ke." CHCC, 1957, No. 4, pp. 30-33.

tions such as farms or experimental stations which conduct scientific research are not included.

State-owned and locally administered state agricultural enterprises, such as farms, ranches, and agricultural-machine and tractor stations, are owned by the people as a whole. They are advanced forms of socialist agricultural production organizations. Although they are now still relatively unimportant in China's agricultural production, their planning is direct planning and is an important part of the national agricultural planning.

Agricultural producers' cooperatives have become the major form of organization for China's agricultural production. Therefore, the production activities of agricultural producers' cooperatives have become the major content of the state agricultural plan. However, agricultural producers' cooperatives are not state-owned enterprises. Their means of production do not belong to the whole people; they are partly or wholly owned by the collective. Therefore, the state plan does not control the agricultural producers' cooperatives; it can only be a reference guide for them.

The agricultural production activities engaged in by the mutual-aid teams, individual peasants, and individual members of agricultural producers' cooperatives are included in the state plan through indirect planning in order to reflect the scale of production of agricultural products and to facilitate balancing agricultural products.

However, agricultural production is very complex. It is affected by natural conditions, and the land area is very broad. Therefore, the state agricultural production plan does not include all the agricultural production activities of every social economic component mentioned above. It only includes the major parts of agricultural production. Secondary agricultural production which does not greatly affect the national balance is not controlled.

As in 1956, in order to bring into play local agricultural production activism, the method of keeping "two separate accounts" for the state and the provinces or municipalities is still used in 1957 for agricultural production planning. In other words, the state's agricultural production plan is sent down only to the provinces and municipalities. Having guaranteed the fulfillment of the state plan targets, the provinces and municipalities can adjust the plan targets. The basic unit in agricultural planning is the hsien. After the plan targets set by the provinces and municipalities are sent down to the hsien, they can be sent to the agricultural producers' cooperatives and the peasants in various forms according to the concrete conditions of each region.

III. Major Targets in Agricultural Production Planning

The 1957 agricultural production plan targets were determined according to the principle of "simplifying targets." The major targets are as follows:

1. Sown Area, Yield per Unit of Area, and Gross Output of Major Crops

The 1957 planning tables include the sown area, the yield per unit of area, and the gross output of food grain (listed by rice, wheat, root tubers, and miscellaneous grain), soybeans, cotton, jute, ramie, flax, sugarcane, sugar beets, peanuts, and rapeseed. They also include the total area sown, the area sown to industrial crops, and the area sown to other crops. The area sown to oil-bearing crops and the green-manure crop area are listed separately. In order to avoid rigidly controlling agricultural planning, the state sends down only the plans for the area sown, the yield per unit of area, and the gross output of food grain (not separately listed by type of grain), soybeans, cotton, jute, peanuts, and rapeseed. The other targets are all set by the provinces, municipalities, and autonomous regions.

Sown area. Arable land that is sown to crops is known as the sown area. Sown area differs from arable land area. It is calculated by the number of times a piece of arable land is planted within one year. For example, if two crops are sown in a year on one shih mou of arable land, the sown area is two shih mou.

Generally speaking, there are only two ways to increase crop yields. One is to raise the crops' yields per unit of area. The other is to expand the sown area. The total sown area listed in the agricultural plan is the sum of the area sown to food grain, industrial crops, and other crops. One important element in agricultural planning work is to study the composition of the sown area (the proportion of the area sown to various crops in the total sown area) and its changes. This is because the proportional relationships within agriculture are determined mainly through the composition of sown area.

By comparing the total sown area and the area of arable land, we can estimate the multiple-cropping area and the multiple-cropping index. The amount by which the total sown area exceeds the area of arable land is the multiple-cropping area. The ratio of the total sown area to the area of arable land is the multiple-

181

cropping index. For example, suppose the sown area is 120 mou and the area of arable land is 100 mou, then the multiple-cropping area is 20 mou, and the multiple cropping index is 120 percent. The multiple-cropping area and the multiple-cropping index are indices reflecting the degree of utilization of arable land.

Yield per unit of area. The amount of crops harvested from a unit of area is the yield per unit of area. It is usually expressed as the yield per shih mou or per hectare. There are three ways to estimate the yield per unit of area: (1) By the sown area, which is the usual method for formulating and assessing plans. The formula is: yield per unit of area = gross output ÷ total sown area. The yield by unit of area estimated according to the sown area can reflect the average level of agricultural production. (2) By the harvested area, which is the method used to assess the impact of natural calamities on agricultural production. The formula is: yield per unit of area = gross output ÷ total harvested area. (3) By the area of arable land. The formula is: yield per unit of area = gross output ÷ area of arable land. The yield per unit of area estimated by the area of arable land can embody a concentrated reflection of the effects of, and the need for, all the measures for increasing agricultural output (including increasing the multiple-cropping index). It is a quality target in the agricultural production plan. The results obtained from these three methods of estimating the yield per unit of area are different. For example, suppose the area sown to food grain crops in a certain agricultural producers' cooperative is 1,800 mou, the harvested area is 1,600 mou, the arable land devoted to food grain crops is 1,000 mou, and the gross output of food grain is 400,000 chin. Then, the yield per mou of food grain crops would be: 222 chin by the first method of estimation, 250 chin by the second method, and 400 chin by the third method.

Because the target for the yield per unit of area can comprehensively reflect the effects of, and the need for, each technical measure, such as building water conservancy projects, leveling land, improving soil, improving farm tools, extending good seed strains, increasing fertilizer applications, preventing diseases and pests, and improving farming techniques and farming systems, it is very important in agricultural planning.

Gross output. This is the gross crop output of a given sown area. Its formula is: Gross output = sown area × yield per unit of area. The gross output reflects the final result and scale of crop production, so many million chin of food grain, so many thousand tan of cotton, and so forth. The 1957 planning tables specify that food grain should be counted in its unprocessed state. Four chin of root tubers are to be counted as one chin of food grain. Soybeans (including yellow beans, green beans, and black beans) are to be counted in the form of dry seeds, cotton is to be counted before ginning, cured tobacco is to be counted as dry tobacco leaves, sugarcane is to be counted by the stalks, and sugar beets by the root tuber only. Peanuts are to be counted in the form of dry, unshelled peanuts. On the one hand, such specifications make it possible to reflect correctly the results of crop production, and on the other, they facilitate the balancing and estimation of industry's demand for agricultural products.

2. Livestock

In the 1957 planning tables, the numerical target for livestock includes the large animals — cattle, water buffaloes, horses, mules, donkeys, and camels — and small livestock — sheep, goats, pigs, and so forth. The state only specifies the planned numerical target for pigs; the targets for all the other livestock are determined by the provinces, municipalities, and autonomous regions.

The number for a particular type of livestock includes livestock of varying ages, sexes, and uses (muscle power, meat, hide). It mainly reflects the scale of development of livestock herds. The formula for estimating the number of livestock is: Total number of livestock throughout the country in the plan year = number of livestock at the beginning of the year + estimated number of young livestock to be bred during the plan year − number slaughtered − number of deaths. If the estimate is for only one region, the sale and purchase of livestock must also be taken into account.

The number of livestock is a stock figure.[1] The 1957 plan specifies that the number of livestock refers to those existing on December 31 of a given year. This way, uniformity with other national economic plan years can be achieved. At the same time, livestock breeding is largely completed by the end of the year, and there is relatively little change in the number of livestock.

3. Afforested Area

This refers to the area of barren mountains and wasteland suitable for tree planting which people have afforested. The 1957 planning tables specify that the afforested area does not include scattered tree planting, such as trees planted near homes, villages, roads and the water, or already afforested areas in which additional trees are planted.

Forests can be classified as protective forests, lumber forests, special-use forests, and "other forests" according to their uses. Protective forests are planted to reduce or prevent natural calamities caused by wind, sand, flood, and drought and thus increase agricultural output. Examples are wind-breaking forests, sand-breaking forests and watershed forests. Lumber forests are planted primarily to produce lumber (such as construction timber). Special-use forests are planted mainly for their fruits, bark, leaves, and rubber. "Other forests" refers to forests falling outside the above categories, such as firewood and charcoal forests, scenic forests, and so forth.

Protective and lumber forests occupy a very important position in the total afforested area. Planned development requires that the area planned for protective and lumber forests be listed separately when formulating the plan for the afforested area. The area for special-use forests and "other forests" should be determined by the local administrations.

4. Gross Output of Cultivated Aquatic Products

This refers to the gross output of fish, shrimp, crab, shellfish, and seaweed raised by man. However, it does not include the harvesting or gathering of these same wild marine animal and plant products*; nor does it include the output of lotus seed, lotus root, trapa bicornis, or similar marine plant products. Fish is an important nonstaple food. Part of it can also be used as industrial raw materials. At the same time, the output of fish is a very large part of China's output of aquatic products (in 1955, fish represented 75 percent of the gross output of aquatic products). Therefore, the output target for fish is listed separately among the planned targets for cultivated aquatic products so that it can receive full attention in the course of the plan.

5. Gross Value of Agricultural Output

This is a monetary expression of the total results of agricultural

---

*The value of these natural products is included in the gross value of industrial output. — N. R. L.

production activities in one year. It reflects the scale of agricultural production. The rate of growth of agricultural output can be obtained by comparing the gross value of agricultural output for various years. The position of agriculture in the whole social product can be gauged by comparing the gross value of agricultural output with the whole social product. The gross value of agricultural output is also important for estimating the net value of agricultural output, agricultural labor productivity, and the income of peasants. The composition of gross value of agricultural output embodies the proportional relations within the whole agricultural sector. Studying the composition of the gross value of agricultural output and correctly arranging for the development of each agricultural branch are the basic tasks in formulating the agricultural plan.

The State Planning Commission and the State Economic Commission must estimate and study the gross value of the country's agricultural output when formulating long-term and annual plans. Because the ownership system in agricultural production is mainly collective and since agricultural planning is not highly centralized, the plan for the gross value of agricultural output plan sent down by the state is not region-specific. It does not even require the provincial, municipal, or hsien planning commissions to estimate the gross value agricultural output. If necessary, however, the provincial, municipal, or hsien planning commissions can estimate it themselves.

To facilitate comparison among the gross values of agricultural output of past years, the gross value of agricultural output must be computed at constant prices. However, when estimating the national income, the gross value of agricultural output is computed at current prices.

According to the regulations of the State Statistical Bureau, the scope of the gross value of agricultural output includes the three components of plant growing, animal husbandry, and subsidiary farm business. Plant growing and animal husbandry represent about 80 percent of the gross value of the country's agricultural output. The value of subsidiary farm output represents about 20 percent. The value of subsidiary farm output refers to the value of the production of the following four items: (1) the spare-time harvesting and gathering of wild animals, plants, and mineral matter; (2) the preliminary processing of agricultural products (rice and flour milling done by the peasants themselves); (3) the self-supply handicraft industry (such as making clothes, shoes, and socks for personal use); (4) the fees earned by peasants during their spare time for processing raw materials furnished by other consumers. Actually, these activities do not constitute agricultural production, and their computation is also far from accurate. Therefore, some people suggest that the value of the output from subsidiary farm output should not be included within the gross value of agricultural output. Whether the value of the output of tractor stations should be estimated separately and whether the gross value of agricultural output should include internal double-counting are also questions currently under study. There is still no consensus about them. (For questions relating to the methods of estimating the gross value of agricultural output, one can refer to T'ung-chi kung-tso t'ung-hsün [Statistical Work Bulletin], 1956, No. 22, and T'ung-chi kung-tso [Statistical Work], 1957, Nos. 1 and 4.)

6. Targets for Technical Measures of Agricultural Production

These include arable land area, irrigated area, the number of agricultural-machine and tractor stations, and so forth. They are included in the plan as target measures for ensuring an increase in agricultural output.

Arable land area. This refers to the land area which is devoted to growing various crops and requires periodic ploughing and hoeing. Newly reclaimed land, land abandoned for less than three years, and land lying fallow for the year are also included because they are quite similar to arable land. Arable land is divided into paddy fields and dry fields. Paddy fields refer to fields with ridges that can hold water permanently during the crop-growing period. Land which cannot hold water permanently is dry land. To determine the effective arable land area and to facilitate the arrangement of the area sown to various crops, the target of "arable land area usable in the current year" must be listed separately in the plan. The planned target for arable land area should be computed on the basis of the arable land area at the end of the year. The main way to increase the arable land area is to reclaim barren land. The increase in arable land area resulting from reclamation in the plan year should be listed separately to reflect the scale and rate of reclamation.

Irrigated area. This refers to the arable land area which can be regularly irrigated during the crop-growing period from fixed or permanent water-conservancy or irrigation facilities. The irrigated area is estimated according to the arable land. It includes paddy fields and irrigated land. An increase in the irrigated area depends mainly on building and repairing irrigation and water-conservancy projects or facilities. But it is also possible to increase the irrigated area by strengthening irrigation management and extending experience in scientific water use on the basis of the existing irrigation and water-conservancy projects and facilities. Due to natural calamities, some of the irrigation and water-conservancy projects or facilities are destroyed or damaged every year. The irrigated area has to be reduced accordingly. In order to raise the quality of the projects and to reduce unnecessary decreases in the irrigated area, the 1957 planning tables have a separate listing for the target of "irrigated area attained at the end of the year." We can see the development of irrigation by comparing the irrigated area and the arable land area existing at the end of the year.

Agricultural-machine and tractor stations. The 1957 planning tables specify the numerical target for agricultural-machine and tractor stations, the numerical target for tractors, the target for the area serviced, and the target for the total amount of tractor work. Of these, estimates of the total amount of tractor work are still too inaccurate, so the state cannot assign such targets for the present.

The number of tractors is computed on the basis of a "standard unit." The number of standard units is computed by converting tractors of varying hauling capacities into standard units. The plan specifies that a standard unit is equal to fifteen horsepower. For example, a "Stalin 80" tractor has sixty horsepower. After conversion, it is equal to four standard tractor units.

The area serviced refers to the arable land plowed by the tractor stations for the agricultural producers' cooperatives or individual peasants. This target reflects the scale of agricultural mechanization. To simplify calculations, one mou of arable land is counted as a single mou no matter how many different operations and how many similar operations (such as raking it twice) are performed on it.

The total amount of tractor work is a composite target reflecting the work situation of tractor stations. It is equal to the sum of all the operations performed by the tractor stations. However, there are many different kinds of tractor operations. A uniform standard should be used for computation. According to the regulation, different kinds of operations should be converted to work output based on plowing old land.* The conversion standard used is known as the "conversion coefficient to plowing old land." It is based on the fuel consumed in completing all different kinds of operations. For example, suppose it takes 2.4 chin of gas for a tractor to plow one mou of old land and 0.8 chin of gas to sow one mou. Taking the plowing of one mou of old land as 1.0, then the coefficient to convert sowing to plowing old land is: $0.8 \div 2.4 = 0.33$. The same procedure is used for other operations. Suppose a certain tractor station plows 500 mou of old land and sows 500 mou. Its total work is then: $(500 \times 1) + (500 \times 0.33) = 665$ (mou).

IV. The Purchase Plan for Agricultural Products

At present, there are shortcomings in the method of handing down the state's agricultural production plan targets; the plan targets controlled by the state often conflict with the concrete local conditions. The production activism of the peasants is thus adversely affected. In September 1956, the "Directive of the Party Central Committee and the State Council concerning Strengthening Production Leadership and Organization in Agricultural Producers' Cooperatives"† pointed out that "the central government must gradually move from specifying production plans to specifying the purchase and distribution plans for agricultural products." Therefore, the state planning tables specify that from 1957 onward, the purchase plans for agricultural products will be formulated on a trial basis. The initial targets in the purchase plan for agricultural products include the total purchased amounts of food grain (rice, wheat, and miscellaneous grains), soybeans, cotton, jute, ramie, cured tobacco, peanuts, rapeseed, tea leaves, domesticated silkworm cocoons, tussor cocoons, rubber, live pigs, wool, and other major agricultural products, seventeen in all. The major task of the state purchase plan for agricultural products is to gradually replace the agricultural production plan as a guide to agricultural production. Therefore, the scope of the plan, the plan years, and the content and computation methods of the targets in the purchase plan for agricultural products are all iden-

---

*Literally "ripe land" — land that has previously been cultivated as opposed to land being brought under cultivation for the first time. — N. R. L.

†Jen-min jih-pao (People's Daily), September 13, 1956. The English-language text released by the New China News Agency is reproduced in Documents of the Chinese Communist Party Central Committee, Vol. 1 (Hong Kong: Union Research Institute, 1971), pp. 407-430. — N. R. L.

tical to those in the agricultural production plan. The advantage of replacing the current agricultural production plan with the purchase plan for agricultural products is that the agricultural producers' cooperatives can arrange their production according to their own needs after having fulfilled the state purchase quotas for agricultural products. Hence, the production activism of the masses can be fully brought into play.

The purchase plan for agricultural products in agriculture differs from the purchase plan for agricultural products in commerce. The purchase plan for agricultural products in commerce does not guide agricultural production directly. For example, the 1957 cotton-purchase plan was formulated on the basis of the estimated production of cotton in 1956. It did not have any direct role in guiding cotton production in 1957. The bases on which some targets are computed are also different. For example, in the purchase plan for agricultural products in commerce, food grain was computed on the basis of marketable grain, peanuts were computed on the basis of shelled peanuts, and so on.

During the trial formulation stage of the purchase plan for agricultural products, many problems will certainly arise. We hope that we can all study more and pay more attention to accumulating experience.

Note

1. All plan and statistical figures which reflect the conditions or levels at a particular point of time are known as stock figures. The number of livestock is a stock figure representing the number of livestock on a certain day of the year.

LECTURE 5: CAPITAL CONSTRUCTION PLANNING TABLES

P'eng Jung-ch'üan*

I. The Concept and Content of Capital Construction

Capital construction is the increase in or replacement of fixed assets,[1] or simply the expanded reproduction of fixed assets.

Fixed assets are the material and technical basis for production. Since social production is based on expanded reproduction, there must be expanded reproduction of fixed assets, that is, there must be capital construction. It is thus easy to see the very important role of capital construction in national economic growth.

Capital construction includes all work related to the increase in and replacement of fixed assets. Of this, some is related to increasing the value of fixed assets, and some, while not increasing the value of fixed assets, is directly related to capital construction or is work which must be completed before the projects under construction can be activated.

The following is a concrete description of the characteristics of capital construction from three aspects:

1. Capital construction can be classified by the nature of the projects into:

a. Construction work. This refers to permanent or temporary structures, such as the construction of plants, generating stations, all kinds of industrial buildings, all kinds of transportation lines, and all kinds of civilian housing; the laying of power and communication cables; the value of all the structures forming parts of buildings, the heating and sanitation equipment plus their installation and painting; the construction of foundations and supports for machinery, and the construction of boilers and all kinds of special furnaces and pipelines; irrigation and water conservancy projects;

---

*P'eng Jung-ch'üan, "Chi-pen chien-she chi-hua piao-ke." <u>CHCC</u>, 1957, No. 5, pp. 29-33.

the cultivation of perennial crops; the excavation of new mine shafts and the exploratory deep drilling for natural gas and petroleum; the landscaping of work sites; recommended geological surveys connected with construction; and the special construction measures to provide protection from air attacks, fires, water damage and poison.

b. The installation of machinery and equipment. This refers to the assembly and installation of permanent and temporary production, power, weight-lifting, transport, gear-driven, medical, and experimental equipment; the construction of working platforms and ladders attached to equipment; the laying of pipes and cables attached to installed equipment; and the electrical and thermal insulation and painting of installed equipment.

c. The purchase of machinery and equipment, tools, and instruments. Machinery and equipment is classified into that which needs installation and that which does not need installation. Equipment that needs to be installed refers to equipment which can be used only after it is assembled and installed on foundations or supporting frames, such as boilers for industrial production, steam turbines, and fixed electricity generators. Equipment that does not need to be installed refers to that which can be operated without being fastened to a fixed space or onto supporting frames, such as automobiles, tractors, and earth movers.

Tools and instruments can be divided according to whether they are used for production or for operation and management or for daily living.

d. Other capital construction. This refers to the training of cadres, the expropriation of land, and the purchase of buildings for newly constructed workshops in new or renovated projects.

2. Capital construction can be classified by sector into industrial construction; construction in agriculture, forestry, water conservancy, meteorological services; survey and design agencies; transport, postal and telecommunications services; cultural and educational services; sanitation and health services; scientific experiment and research services; urban public utilities and service industries; and administrative agencies.

3. Capital construction can be classified according to the form of expanded reproduction of fixed assets as new, renovation or restoration.

a. New projects refer to those built from the ground up. However, if the value of the fixed assets added to an existing plant exceeds more than three times the replacement costs of its original fixed assets, the project is regarded as new.

b. Renovation projects refer to those that expand the scale, increase the area or volume, and add machinery and equipment to existing plants and buildings such as to increase their designed capacity so they can produce even more products. Or they involve the reinstallation of parts of the equipment or the renovation of parts of the building to correspond to the production requirements of new products.

c. Restoration projects refer to those that restore damaged buildings to their original forms.

Major repairs simply restore the original value of the fixed assets and extend their years of service but do not add new value to them. They are therefore not included in the content of capital construction.

II. The Scope of Capital Construction Planning

The scope of the capital construction plan in 1957 includes the fourteen activities of industry, agriculture, forestry, water conservancy, meteorology, transport, education, sanitation, culture, broadcasting, athletics, urban public utilities, construction, and labor reform that are under the jurisdiction of either the ministries or directly subordinate agencies of the State Council or of the people's councils of each province, autonomous region, and municipality and their subordinate special districts, hsien and lower levels (The construction of elementary schools is included only if it is carried out at the special district or hsien level or above.) The scope of the plan includes: all new, renovation, or restoration construction projects and their preparatory work, at which work will either begin in 1957 or at which work will continue from last year, that are managed by enterprises, business units or administrative agencies which are under state management, local-state management, public-private joint management, and Chinese-foreign joint management, that are within any of the [14] above departments; and the purchase of fixed assets by existing enterprises. But the following are excluded:

1. Capital construction carried out by labor unions and co-operatives. Since they are mass organizations or collectively owned economic entities, their construction projects should be approved by their respective leadership organs.

2. Capital construction financed independently by the enterprise reward fund and workers' welfare fund of state-owned and locally administered enterprises are also approved by the plant managers or labor union organs and need not be approved by the state.

However, if the construction is jointly financed by the state and the above-mentioned funds, it should be included in the state plan. This is because construction projects are an integrated whole and cannot be mechanically separated on the basis of the amount of capital funds into those parts which are and are not included in the national plan. Moreover, this kind of mechanical distinction would create difficulties in statistical and accounting work.

3. Geological prospecting work and survey and design work. These activities directly serve capital construction. However, the State Planning Commission specified in 1955 that these expenses should not be included within the capital construction plan, but should be financed directly from the state budget and regarded as service expenses.

The reasons why the costs of geological prospecting for resources are not included in the capital construction plan are: First, this activity is generally carried out before work is begun on the construction projects. If these expenses are included within capital construction investment, then long before work is started on the project investment and construction progress targets must be approved. Obviously, these advance approvals without any guaranteed returns are premature and unpractical. Moreover, if these expenses are included, they create statistical and accounting difficulties which cannot be resolved for a long time. Second, geological prospecting work is divided into the two stages of surveying and prospecting. The first stage has no concrete object, and although the latter has a concrete object, in the course of the actual work, it is difficult to separate it from the survey work. Therefore, it is not appropriate to include the costs of the prospecting stage within the capital construction plan. However, the costs of exploratory drilling for petroleum and natural gas and the costs of geological prospecting stipulated by the project designs are included within the capital construction investment plan. This is because exploratory drilling is a stage of the construction work. Furthermore, we already produce petroleum and natural gas, and undertaking and carrying out geological prospecting is one stage of this process.

The costs of survey and design work are not included within the capital construction plan because, if they are included, design fees must then be based on the gross construction costs. Under these circumstances, the designing units, in order to get a larger design fee, often act in an unprincipled fashion and inflate the construction costs of the projects, raise the design standard, recommend luxury facilities, increase the safety coefficients, reject standard designs and design patterns that can be repeated at very low costs, and prefer only large projects, thus adversely affecting the arrangement of state design assignments. Second, when the designing capacity is increased, the design of some projects can be completed well ahead of the time of construction. If design fees are included in the capital construction plan, they create statistical and accounting difficulties that cannot be resolved for a long time. However, the fees paid for designs made by domestic survey and design units that are not financed by the state budget and for designs made in the enterprises themselves should be included in the capital construction plan. This is because the state does not pay the current expenses of these units. They have to charge their clients fees, and their clients can only pay them out of the capital construction investment fund. However, with design capacity becoming more centralized, design units and enterprise design personnel not financed by the state budget are few in number. Their design assignments are also few. Therefore, even if these design fees were included in the capital construction plan, the overall effect, though unfavorable, would still be negligible.

4. The increase of fixed assets and miscellaneous small capital construction projects to carry out technical and organizational measures and for the trial manufacture of new products. These projects and purchases cannot easily be managed according to the procedures for capital construction planning. For example, technical and organizational measures are mainly rationalization proposals suggested by existing production enterprises. They cannot be controlled by capital construction departments. Furthermore, if these expenses are included in the capital construction plan, the enthusiasm of the enterprise may be adversely affected. They are therefore not included in the capital construction plan and instead the finance departments distribute special funds to enterprises under each branch for their use. But this arrangement also has drawbacks: First, special fund appropriations dissipate state funds and adversely affect the commitment to heavy industry. Second, these projects are not easily delineated from projects included in the capital construction plan. Funds for the two purposes are often

mixed up, creating confusion in financial management. Third, though these projects are not included within the plan, difficulties in balancing construction materials, machinery and equipment, and work capacity are still created. Therefore, the preliminary opinion of the relevant branches favors including these projects in the capital construction plan in the Second Five-Year Plan after the management system has been suitably simplified.

5. Capital construction performed abroad by state organs, such as the Ministry of Foreign Trade and the Ministry of Foreign Affairs. Since these projects are carried out overseas and have no effect on the domestic balance of construction materials and work capacity or on organizational work, they are not included in the state capital construction plan.

The scope of the First Five-Year Plan and the scope of the annual plans were basically identical, but there were some differences. The 1957 annual plan, compared with the First Five-Year Plan, added construction projects carried out at the level of special district or hsien or below within each province, autonomous region, and municipality, construction projects carried out by administrative agencies at the central level, housing construction in the military branches, construction projects jointly financed by either enterprise reward funds, or worker welfare funds, with state budgetary appropriations, geological prospecting stipulated by the project designs, design work not financed by the state budget which is done by domestic survey and design units, and design work carried on by the enterprise itself. The reasons why these have not been included in the long-term plans have either been due to inadequate consideration or lack of favorable conditions.

III. Capital Construction Planning Tables and Their Major Targets

In 1957, the ministries under the State Council and the people's councils of each province, autonomous region, and municipality all used seven tables and one appendix table for capital construction planning. These are based on the 1956 capital construction planning tables. They were drawn up and revised and supplemented according to the spirit of management by levels and the principle of simplifying tables and taking into account the comparability of the annual plans of the First Five-Year Plan and the requirements and level of present planning work. These tables are composed of two categories, the distribution of investment and the results of investment. The former reflect how investment is distributed according to administrative units, the composition of investment, regions, and key-point construction projects. The latter reflect the results of investment as measured by the increases in production capacity, fixed assets, and residential area. The following explain the purposes and the concept of each major target of these two categories of tables:

1. The investment distribution tables include the capital construction investment plan, the plan for the composition of capital construction investment, the plan for investment divided by province, autonomous region, and municipality, and the table of detailed explanation of above-norm construction projects — four tables in all.

a. The purpose of the various investment distribution tables. The purpose of the capital construction investment plan is to reflect the scale and rate of growth of the expanded reproduction of fixed assets and the proportion of investment in each sector and to study further the proportional relationship between central and local, heavy industry and light industry, raw materials industries and processing industries, industry and agriculture, and industry-agriculture and communications-transport so that they will correspond to the requirements of planned (proportional) growth, and we can thus determine the investment quota for each sector and each province (municipality). The plan for the composition of capital construction investment reflects the proportionate amount of construction work; the amount of installation work; the value of machinery and equipment, tools, and instruments; and other capital construction in order to facilitate the rational distribution of investment funds among all the components. At the same time, the amount of construction and installation work and the value of machinery and equipment are bases for comprehensively balancing work capacity and the supply of construction materials and machinery and equipment and for determining the reserve needs for construction materials and appropriations for machinery and equipment for the following year. The investment plan by province (municipality) reflects the scale and rate of growth of construction in each region and key-point cities and thus facilitates the analysis of the proportional relationship in investment between the interior and the coastal regions and the proportion of investment in new industrial cities. It helps solve the internal coordination problems within each region. The above-norm construction unit table is a basic table for capital construction planning. It reflects the targets for construction scale, construction rate, production capacity, and utilization of fixed assets of major construction units and their major projects. Through it, we can study the coordination among big, medium, and small enterprises and between key points and secondary points, and we can further determine the amount of investment of major construction units and the timing and quantity of increased production capacity in order to satisfy the needs of national economic development.

b. Major targets in the tables for the distribution of investment.

1) The amount of investment. This is a monetary expression of the amount of capital construction. Like the target for the value of output in industrial production that expresses the physical quantity of products, this is the most important target reflecting the scale of construction. Because there are many different kinds of construction projects with different units of measurement, they cannot be added together as physical units. They can only be expressed in monetary terms. At the same time, the amount of investment expressed in monetary terms also reflects the overall construction expenses of a construction project.

The annual amount of capital construction investment is not equivalent to the state budget appropriations for capital construction. This is because the amount of investment represents the physical amount of construction, namely, the value of labor, materials, machinery and equipment, and certain other related work invested in a construction project. Included in this is the value of machinery and equipment and construction materials purchased in the previous period for this period's use and the value of machinery and equipment and construction materials purchased this year for this year's use. However, it does not include the value of machinery and equipment and construction materials purchased this year and reserved for use in the next period. The major source of funds is state budgetary appropriations, but it [the amount of investment] includes other sources of funds. Financial appropriations are merely the quantity of funds for construction projects provided by the state budget. They include the value of materials and machinery and equipment reserved for the next period's projects and deductions for the enterprise reward fund from construction projects managed by construction units. However, they do not include the value of the surplus machinery and equipment and construction materials from the previous period which does not require state appropriations in the present period or other assets and money that can be used for construction projects this year; nor do they include the value of machinery and equipment which does not cost anything or which is distributed through account transfers, the value of unpaid labor services performed by military and civilian manpower, enterprise reward funds that are used in conjunction with state appropriations, and other funds outside the state budget. However, these are included in the amount of investment. In addition, the account clearances between the state and the construction units (such as the current profits of self-operated projects that are paid to the state and capital depreciation funds, income from the sale of mineral and lumber products obtained during project construction, and net income from the sale of obsolete fixed assets) are reflected in the investment value, but are not reflected in state budgetary appropriations for capital construction. Therefore, the

Amount of capital construction investment = Capital construction appropriations − Value of materials and machinery and equipment reserved for next year + Surplus from previous year that can be used this year in the form of materials, machinery and equipment, other assets, and cash − Deductions for enterprise reward fund from construction projects managed by the construction units + Profits and depreciation fund from construction projects managed by the construction units + Value of machinery and equipment that is transferred but does not require a state appropriation + Value of unpaid military and civilian labor services + Other funds from sources outside the state budget + Income earned during execution of construction projects.

The growth percentage of the amount of investment is obtained by comparing the amount of investment in the plan period with the expected (or actual) amount of investment in the base period. This percentage is the target which reflects the rate of growth of capital construction investment. Its computation formula is:

Growth rate = (Amount of investment in the plan period − Amount of investment expected in the base period) ÷ Amount of investment expected in the base period × 100.

2) The amount of construction and installation work. This is the monetary value of the amount of work completed by construction workers in building construction and the installation of machinery and equipment. It usually represents about 60 percent of the gross national amount of capital construction investment. It is a target of decisive importance in the capital construction plan. How well the amount of construction and installation work is com-

198

pleted directly affects the completion and activation of projects and thus the fulfillment of production and operating plans. At the same time, this target reflects the production activities of the workers. It is one of the bases on which the contract plan is formulated and the work capacity and major construction materials are comprehensively balanced. At present, the method for comprehensively calculating labor requirements is to divide the amount of construction and installation work in the plan period by the average labor productivity of each construction and installation worker. The method for comprehensively calculating the demand for structural steel, lumber, cement, and other major construction materials is to multiply the experiential quota of the quantities of structural steel, lumber, and cement that have been required for each ten thousand yuan of construction and installation work times the amount of construction and installation work in the plan period.

3) Value of machinery and equipment. This target is realized through procurement and supply activities. It is therefore directly determined by the production plans of the domestic material production branches and the supply plan for foreign imports. The way in which the value of machinery and equipment is entered in the plan varies according to conditions. The value of machinery and equipment that has to be installed and whose installation will begin in the plan period can be included in the plan. The value of machinery and equipment that does not require installation and of machinery and equipment reserved for later use that does require installation must be included in the plan only after it is transported to the work site or warehouses, received by the construction unit, and entered in the fixed assets account. When arranging the composition of investment, we must maintain a reasonable proportion between the value of machinery and equipment that has to be installed and the amount of installation work according to the characteristics of the plan period.

4) Construction units. Any construction project that has an overall design and an overall construction budget can be regarded as a construction unit. In one construction unit, there can be many project items with independent production capacities and project benefits. For example, a construction unit for an industrial enterprise involves building major production workshops, subsidiary production workshops, transport, power, cultural and welfare facilities, and other project items. These project items can be carried out at one or several work sites. At present, the factory areas and housing areas of many industrial enterprise construction

units are divided between two construction sites. There are also construction units which involve only one project item and no supplementary projects, such as the construction of an independent administrative office building.

The construction unit is the object of capital construction. It reflects the type of construction project. Therefore, the type of construction must be specified in detail. For example, a construction unit for a coal mine requires the following details: xx open mines, xx vertical shafts, xx slanting shafts, xx horizontal tunnels. There is a difference between the construction unit and the basic planning unit: A construction unit that does not have a planning organ or does not have the conditions to formulate plans is not a basic planning unit. At present, all the construction units for large plants and mines are usually also basic planning units. However, construction units that are not for plants or mines, such as food grain warehouses, shops, and middle and elementary schools, often have their plans formulated and implemented by the managing units of the hsien (municipality) where the construction units are located. The basic planning units in such cases are the food-grain bureau or the cultural and educational bureau of the hsien (municipality).

To facilitate management by level, construction units are classified as those that are above—norm or those that are below—norm according to the size of their overall amount of investment. All construction units which are larger than or equal to the stipulated norm are above—norm units. Those which are smaller than the stipulated norm are below—norm units. Above—norm construction units are the major objects of capital construction investment. They are centrally managed and controlled by the state. These units should be listed individually in the above—norm construction unit table. The above—norm project items should also be listed separately. Through the above—norm construction unit table, the state can control the concentrated use of investment and its construction content in order to guarantee the construction of key-point units. For below—norm construction units, the state merely approves the total amount of investment. They are left to the control of the various ministries, provinces, autonomous regions, and municipalities. When the ministries, provinces, autonomous regions, and municipalities submit the drafts of their plans, they only need to list the gross amount of investment, the amount of construction and installation work, and the fixed assets to be activated. The construction units need not be listed individually.

The size of the norm is determined according to the type of business to which the construction unit belongs.* At the same time, the norm must also be revised and supplemented according to changes in the jurisdiction of management by level during different plan periods, expansion of the construction scale, and increases in various types of construction. For example, before 1957, the state stipulated that all new electricity stations, coal shafts, petroleum extraction and refining, railways, highways, river ports, sea harbors, and tractor stations would be treated as above-norm units regardless of the size of the investment involved. In 1957, however, the norms were based on the size of the investment.

After all the investment targets of the projects related to each construction unit have been formulated, the plan for the amount of capital construction investment can be formulated according to the management system or type of business to which that construction unit belongs. The plan for the composition of capital construction investment can be formulated according to the composition categories, and the investment plan by province, autonomous region, and municipality can be formulated according to the location of the construction unit. For a construction unit that spans more than two provinces, autonomous regions, or municipalities, the amount of investment is estimated by the proportion of its projects allocated to each province, autonomous region, or municipality. For the detailed table of above-norm construction units, the targets for the total amount of investment and the amount of construction and installation work for a given project is formulated based on the gross estimated (budgetary) value or the comprehensive estimated (budgetary) value of the above-norm construction unit and the above-norm project item and the value of its construction and installation projects. The amount of investment and the amount of construction and installation work in the plan period are calculated separately on the basis of the estimated (budgetary) value of the project items and the value of construction and installation projects carried out by the construction units in that year. For below-norm construction units, only the sum of the amount of investment and the amount of construction and installation work in the plan period are listed.

  2. The tables of investment results include the plan for new

---

*Norms were established for each category of capital construction. They ranged from 5 to 10 million yuan in heavy industry and 3 to 5 million yuan in light industry. State Statistical Bureau, Ten Great Years (Peking: Foreign Languages Press, 1960), p. 47. — N. R. L.

production capacity that results from investment, the plan for new fixed assets that results from investment, and the housing construction plan, three tables in all.

a. The purpose of various tables of investment results.

The ultimate goal of capital construction is to increase fixed assets and production capacity in the national economy and thus satisfy the needs for the growth of production and services and gradually raise the people's material and cultural standard of living. Therefore, the scale and rate at which fixed assets and production capacity are increased to a large extent determine the pace of our socialist construction. They are very important targets in the capital construction plan.

The plan for new fixed assets* is a monetary indicator of the quantity of all kinds of new fixed assets and their planned rates of growth. On the basis of the proportional relationship between the quantity of new fixed assets and the amount of investment (coefficient of activation), we can study the activation rate of all kinds of fixed assets in order to accelerate the work, save investment expenses that do not increase fixed assets, and rationally raise the coefficient of activation.

The plan for the increase in production capacity is a physical indicator of the result of increased designed capacity of all kinds of production facilities, and increased structures, and their planned rate of growth. This plan is closely related to the development plan of production and operations. The increase in production capacity is directly determined by the required development of production and operations. Therefore, the correct formulation and fulfillment of this plan is very significant for ensuring the development of production and operations.

The housing construction plan reflects the scale of housing construction and the increased quantity of housing in each region. Through it, we can study the rate of growth of housing in order to adequately meet the people's needs.

b. The concept of "activation" and its scope.

In the capital construction plan "activation" refers to the idea

---

*Literally "the plan for fixed assets that start to be used" or "the plan for the activation of fixed assets" (tung-yung ti ku-ting tzu-ch'an chi-hua). This concept is apparently identical to the more commonly used "new fixed assets" or "the increase in fixed assets" (hsin-tseng ku-ting tzu-ch'an) which I use in the translation here. Shigeru Ishikawa, National Income and Capital Formation in Mainland China: An Examination of Official Statistics (Tokyo: Institute of Asian Economic Affairs, 1965), p. 135. — N. R. L.

that construction items that are part of a construction unit and can independently generate results are handed over after they have been completed, inspected by the contracting parties, and approved by the agencies at the higher levels. The quantity of new fixed assets listed in each investment result table includes that part of the investment that will start to be used in the plan period and that part of the investment in the base period that will start to be used in the plan period. However, it does not include the quantity that will start to be used as a result of technical organization measures and other investment outside the plan; nor does not it include the original production capacity and project benefits of units being renovated. Moreover, reductions in the existing quantity [of fixed assets] due to retirement, dismantling, or moving and change of affiliation are not deducted.

c. Major targets in the various tables of investment results.

1) Targets for the capacity of major production equipment and project benefits. There are many ways to indicate the production capacity of the construction unit. Some are indicated by the production capacity of the whole project. Some are indicated by the production capacity of project items that are major links in production. For example, the production capacity of the cement plant construction unit is represented by the capacity of the cement grinder. The production capacities of other equipment such as the kiln and gravel-maker are not represented. Based on the principle of the necessity for comprehensive balance work for the national economy and the principle of management by level, the state instituted a unified index and units of measurement only for the capacity of major production equipment and project benefits and required that each branch fill them in accordingly. Each branch can also make suitable adjustments according to needs.

Production capacity is calculated according to the designed production capacity of the completed project or the designed project benefits, not according to estimated level of output. For example, the annual designed capacity of a newly constructed cement plant was 100,000 tons. It was activated in the third quarter. Suppose the operation reached the designed level, and the half yearly output was 50,000 tons. The activated production capacity of that plant should be 100,000 tons, not 50,000 tons.

2) New fixed assets. These can be classified as productive, working, and nonproductive according to their nature and uses. New fixed assets which result from investment include all kinds of construction projects, equipment installation projects, ma-

chinery and equipment qualified as fixed assets, the purchase value of tools and instruments, land expropriation expenses, the purchase value of houses and structures, the purchase value of productive livestock and draft animals, relocation compensation for households, graves, and crops situated at the work sites, and management expenses of the construction unit (including technical supervision fees). However, they do not include cadre-training expenses, the purchase value of inexpensive and easily worn tools and equipment that is included within the construction budget, relocation expenses of enterprises, and transfer expenses of construction agencies. The part of the amount of investment reserved for future allocation is not included either. The value of fixed assets that are included in the comprehensive budget of the project items must only be included in the value of new fixed assets when the project items have been completed, inspected, and approved by the higher levels. Some common independent expenses not included in the comprehensive budget of project items are site leveling and other preparatory work, land expropriation expenses, relocation compensation expenses, site cleanup expenses after the project is completed, management expenses of the construction unit (including technical supervision expenses). If it can be determined that they belong to certain project items, they should be entered in the plan following the activation of these projects. If it cannot be determined that they belong to definite project items, then following their activation their value should be entered in the plan on the basis of their share of the construction budget. The cultivation of perennial crops should be included in the annual plans according to the yearly work load. For exploratory deep drilling for natural gas and petroleum, new fixed assets are calculated in the Soviet Union according to the success rate in prospecting work. In other words, a proportionate success rate is computed on the basis of past data and experience. And the new fixed assets are the product of the number and depth of wells drilled in the plan period and this experiential quota. However, there is no such quota in China at present. Therefore, for the time being, exploratory drilling work for specific construction objects is included in the plan for new fixed assets. Otherwise, it is treated as expenses. If there is output from the actual prospecting, it is then included in the plan of new fixed assets. The quantity of new fixed assets can be calculated by the following formula: New fixed assets in the plan period = the amount of investment in projects that are uncompleted at the beginning of the period + the amount of

investment in the current period — the amount of investment in
the current period that does not increase the value of fixed assets
— amount to be distributed — the amount of investment in uncompleted projects at the end of the period.

3) Housing. This refers to family dwellings and group dormitories. Also included are housing for school faculties and staffs,
student dormitories, purchased dwellings and dormitories, permanent dormitories and dwellings for staff and employees built with
the third category construction budget of the contract-letting unit
under the central direction of specialized construction enterprises,
and dormitories and dwellings renovated from nondwelling-type
buildings with state investment. However, buildings for special
uses, such as military barracks, prisons, and temporary and permanent work sheds housing construction workers are not included.

Within the amount of housing construction investment, in addition to the construction costs of housing itself, the outdoor projects
in the residential area, such as drainage channels, gas pipelines,
electrical lighting cables, heating ducts and boiler rooms, neighborhood roads, and kitchens, toilets, and bathrooms attached to
dwellings or serving several households, are also included. However, it does not include investment on independent project items
such as the common mess halls, toilets, or bathrooms serving the
whole residential neighborhood.

The housing construction area starts from the outside walls of
the building. It includes the bedrooms, living rooms, kitchens,
toilets, bathrooms, storage rooms, and hallways, but it does not
include the courtyards, balconies, and stairways beyond the outside walls of the building. The area of a multistory building is the
sum of its floors.

Note

1. Please refer to Chi-hua ching-chi, 1955, No. 5, p. 26.

LECTURE 10: LABOR AND
WAGE PLANNING TABLES

Cheng K'ang-ning and Hsia Wu*

I. The Significance of Labor and Wage Planning

China is a populous and labor abundant country that is still very
backward economically. The purpose of accurate labor planning is
to rationally utilize China's labor resources and arrange for labor
employment; to determine the rate of increase of labor productivity
in each sector of the national economy in the plan year; and to rationally distribute the labor required by each sector of the national
economy and build up labor reserves in order to guarantee the basic needs of the national economy for skilled workers and cadres.

Wages are the monetary expression of the share of the social
product obtained by the staff and workers according to the quantity
and quality of their labor. Wages affect the vital interests of the
staff and workers. Accurate compilation of the wage plan not only
organically links the personal interests of the staff and workers
with the collective interests and their present interests with their
long-term interests so that they care about their own labor results
and bring their enthusiasm to build socialism into play, but at the
same time, it is also important in harmonizing the worker-peasant
relationship and consolidating the worker-peasant alliance.

The labor and wage plan is an organic component of the whole
national economic plan. It is closely related to other parts of the
national economy. The plan for staff and workers is formulated
according to the plan for production and business. It rationally
distributes the labor force according to the development needs of

---

*Cheng K'ang-ning, Hsia Wu, "Lao-tung kung-tzu chi-hua piao-ke." CHCC,
1957, No. 10, pp. 29-33.

production and business in each sector of the national economy in order to guarantee the fulfillment and overfulfillment of the plan for production and business. The plan for staff and workers is also an indispensable basis for formulating the cadre-training plan. The wage plan also constitutes indispensable data for formulating the cost and financial plan. At the same time, the wage plan greatly affects the commodity circulation plan. There are definite proportional relations between the total amount of wages and the total amount of commodities circulated. In addition, the various figures in the labor plan are closely related to the calculations for the residential area plan, the cultural, educational, and health plan, the financial plan, and the financial budget. Therefore, accurate labor and wage planning plays an important role in guaranteeing the planned (proportional) growth of the national economy.

II. The Scope of Labor and Wage Planning

In principle, the labor plan should include the whole of social labor. However, in practice, we must still adopt different methods and requirements according to the characteristics and conditions of each economic sector and each economic type. At present, China's labor plan can be classified into the direct planning component and the estimated planning component according to their nature, functions, and methods. The former portion of the plan consists basically of commands. The latter portion of the plan merely provides references for policy consideration and decision making.

The direct planning component of the 1957 labor and wage plan includes independent industrial and commercial enterprises that are state-owned, locally state-owned, owned by supply and marketing cooperatives, and jointly managed by public and private organizations; agriculture, forestry, water conservancy, and meteorological services sponsored or owned by the state; capital construction units and communications and transport enterprises; urban public utilities; cultural, educational, and health operations; state financial organs and state organs; and people's organizations. However, for the labor plans of the state organs and people's organizations, the State Economic Commission merely itemizes the number of personnel permitted and their wages for these units according to the financial budget and the data provided by the

Personnel Commission of the State Council* when it reports the plan to the State Council. It did not require each ministry and province to furnish this part of the labor and wage plans. Furthermore, the number and wages of staff and workers cf state organs and people's organizations outside the permitted personnel quota and the number and wages of staff and workers in units affiliated with state organs and people's organizations were not listed. The estimated planning component of the 1957 labor and wage plans required that each province and municipality report estimated labor and wage figures for private enterprises. However, in reality most of the provinces and municipalities did not report. Moreover, the provinces and municipalities were not required to report estimated employment in the individual economy and cooperative economy.

Therefore, the scope of the 1957 labor and wage plan was not very complete. This meant that the labor and wage plan could not fully reflect the situation and problems in the employment of social labor and could not embody an overall national picture of labor allocation.

According to the policy of "overall planning with individual consideration and comprehensive arrangement," we must appropriately expand the scope of labor and wage planning. Therefore, the 1958 planning tables stipulate that the scope of the labor and wage plan is as follows: The direct planning component includes all the staff and workers and their wages of the enterprises and business units which are under the jurisdiction of each ministry, province, and municipality and which are owned by the people as a whole, by supply and marketing cooperatives, and by joint public-private groups with fixed stock and fixed dividends, and also of government agencies, Party organizations and their affiliated units. The estimated planning component requires that each province and municipality estimate the number of people employed as individual laborers (excluding household labor and staff and workers employed by families), those employed by the privately owned economy (including the joint public-private economy in which stocks and dividends have not yet been fixed), and those employed by the cooperative economy (excluding agriculture and agricultural sidelines).

---

*The State Council's Personnel Commission (pien-chih wei-yüan-hui), and its predecessor the Personnel Bureau (jen-shih chü), is responsible for the promotion and transfer of personnel working in government and mass organs. Franz Schurman, Ideology and Organization in Communist China (Berkeley: University of California Press, 1966), pp. 184, 186. — N. R. L.

The 1958 requirement that the labor and wage plan of state agencies and people's organizations and their affiliated units be directly planned presents some difficulties. This is because in the past, the ministries, provinces, and municipalities did not directly formulate this part of the plan, and the planning departments seldom collected or accumulated relevant data for it. However, the accounting and personnel departments do have these data. Moreover, in 1956 the statistical departments conducted a survey of labor and wages in state agencies and people's organizations and their affiliated units. If the planning departments conscientiously collect these data through the relevant units, the data problem can be solved. Of course, this part of the plan can only be properly formulated with close collaboration between the planning departments and the Personnel Commission.

In his report on government work to the Fourth Session of the First National People's Congress,* Premier Chou pointed out in connection with labor employment that "for a long time to come, the major direction of labor employment will still be participation in agricultural labor. The handicraft industry and service industries will also be supplementary sources of labor employment."[†] Following the spirit of this directive, the 1958 planning tables require each province and municipality to provide "estimates of labor employment in the individual, privately owned, and cooperative economies." The planning commission of each province and municipality must collect data from the statistical departments, labor administration departments, handicraft-industry management departments, industrial and commercial administration departments, and other business departments and must invite their suggestions concerning this aspect of the work in order to do a good job in arriving at these estimates. In addition, we hope that each province and municipality will also describe under "comments" the number of unemployed, the number of senior high-school graduates who have failed the college entrance examination, the number of junior high-school graduates in urban areas who have failed the senior high-school entrance examination, and other information on labor resources in their areas and also make suggestions for future actions. This way, the conditions and planning of labor employment from the provinces and municipalities to the whole nation can be quite fully reflected.

*June 26-July 15, 1957, in Peking. — N. R. L.
[†]Chou En-lai "Report on Work of the Government." Jen-min shou-ts'e (People's Handbook — Peking: Ta-kung pao, 1958), pp. 201-214. — N. R. L.

III. The System of Targets in the Labor and Wage Plan

There are three types of targets in the labor and wage plan:
(1) labor productivity targets; (2) target numbers of staff and
workers; and (3) wage targets.

1. Labor Productivity Targets

Labor productivity is the output of a worker in a given period
of time, or the amount of labor time spent in producing a given
unit of output. The larger the output in a given period of time or
the shorter the time spent in producing a given output, the higher
is the labor productivity. In other words, labor productivity is
equal to output or amount of work divided by labor time. Labor
productivity is an important target reflecting the efficiency of
economic activities in an enterprise, sector, or the whole society.
It is generally possible and necessary for all material production
branches to calculate labor productivity. It is not necessary for
nonmaterial-production branches to do so.

The expressions and computation methods for labor productivity
vary according to the different purposes they are required to serve.
In general, there are the following kinds:

a. Labor productivity can be expressed in three forms: in value terms (by the gross value of output, the net value of output, the
value of marketed commodities calculated at constant prices and
budget prices); in physical terms; and by time norms. For example, a construction worker completed 4,000 yuan worth of work
in one year. This is labor productivity expressed in value terms.
A coal miner dug up 1.5 tons of coal in one day. This is labor productivity expressed in physical terms. The number of hours required to make one machine is labor productivity expressed in a
time norm. There are various bases and reasons for adopting
each of the expressions of labor productivity mentioned above.
For example, labor productivity expressed in physical terms can
be used to reflect directly the level of labor productivity. This is
suitable for enterprises with simple products or for industrial
branches. However, the products of every sector in the national
economy are many and varied. It is difficult to get a comprehensive figure by using this method alone. Therefore, labor productivity targets in value terms are mainly used in labor planning.

b. The method of calculating labor productivity varies according to the time unit adopted. Thus, labor productivity can be cal-

culated by the hour, day, month, quarter, and year. Hourly labor productivity does not take rests and breaks into account. It reflects the actual output of a worker in an hour. Daily labor productivity takes into account the breaks, absences, late arrivals, and early departures within a day. For example, in an 8-hour workday with a half hour break, a worker actually works for 7.5 hours. If he makes fifteen units of product altogether, his hourly labor productivity is two units, and his daily labor productivity is not sixteen units, but fifteen units. Monthly, quarterly, and annual labor productivity must consider not only the breaks and absences within one day, but also the work stoppages, absences, and leaves for days at a time. In the state plan, we have now adopted the target of annual labor productivity. That is, the annual gross value of output or the amount of work is compared with the number of workers in the whole year. Some people have suggested that the number of productive personnel* or the population of the whole enterprise be used to calculate labor productivity. There are advantages to these methods of computation. Namely, if the number of staff and service personnel and other indirect productive personnel or the number of nonproductive personnel were reduced, labor productivity would be increased. Otherwise, labor productivity would be reduced. This encourages the enterprises to reduce the number of indirect and nonproductive personnel. At present, we are still studying whether or not we will adopt this method of computation.

c. There are two ways to measure labor productivity in a comprehensive way, namely, the output value method and the index method. Because the comprehensive methods are not the same, they lead to rates of growth of labor productivity which are not the same. At present, the output value method is used in planning. That is, the output and number of workers in each enterprise in both the base year and the plan year are totaled separately. Then the gross output of each year is divided by the total number of workers in each year to obtain the labor productivity for the two years. Through comparison, the rate of growth of labor produc-

---

*During the First Five-Year Plan the workers and employees in industry, capital construction, and transport and communications were divided into "productive" and "nonproductive." The former included all those engaged in the production of principal products, and the latter included all other persons employed. John Philip Emerson, Nonagricultural Employment in Mainland China: 1949-1958, International Population Statistics Reports, Series P-90, No. 21 (Washington, D.C.: U.S. Government Printing Office, 1965), p. 46. — N. R. L.

tivity in the plan year can be computed. The following table shows labor productivity using the output value method:

	Output value (thousand yuan)			Number of workers (persons)			Output per worker (yuan)		
	1957	1958	1958 as % of 1957	1957	1958	1958 as % of 1957	1957	1958	1958 as % of 1957
Total	10,000	12,600	126.0	3,000	3,727	124.2	3,330	3,380	101.5
Enterprise A	6,000	6,600	110.0	1,000	1,000	100.0	6,000	6,600	110.0
Enterprise B	4,000	6,000	150.0	2,000	2,727	136.4	2,000	2,200	110.0

The above table shows that the labor productivity has been increased by 10 percent, in both enterprise A and enterprise B. But the comprehensive labor productivity shows an increase of only 1.5 percent. The reason is not that the production or labor organizations of the two enterprises are poor, but that there has been a change in the composition of production between the enterprises. The number of workers and output value of enterprise B, where labor productivity (output value per worker) is lower, have grown faster than those of enterprise A. Therefore, when we use comprehensive measures of labor productivity calculated by the value of output method it can only reflect and correspond to changes in the composition of output. At present, China is undergoing socialist construction. Large-scale plants and enterprises using new technology are continuously being put into production. Therefore, changes in the composition of output will generally raise labor productivity. Only in individual cases will labor productivity be reduced. To eliminate the effect of changes in the composition of social output on labor productivity and to observe the increase of labor productivity in enterprises when targets for comprehensive labor productivity are calculated, we should analyze and compare labor productivity using the index method. If the index method is used to calculate a comprehensive measure, then the combined labor productivity of enterprises A and B increased by 10 percent, correctly reflecting the respective rates of growth of labor productivity in enterprises A and B. The method of using the comprehensive index method is as follows:

[(Percent increase of labor productivity in enterprise A × Number of workers in enterprise A in plan year) + (Percent increase of labor productivity in enterprise B × Number of workers in enterprise B in plan year)] ÷ (Number of workers in enterprise A in plan year + Number of workers in enterprise B in plan year) = [(10% × 1,000) + (10% × 2,727)] ÷ (1,000 + 2,727) = 10%.

The method of estimating labor productivity is still an important problem being studied by the economic branches and economic scientific research branches. In general, however, the methods of calculating should vary according to the conditions and requirements. In order to be able to summarize and to facilitate comparison of data from past years, and to be able to reflect the influence of all kinds of factors on labor productivity, and to be able to carry out mutual arrangements between other related aspects of the national economic plan, and moreover to give rise to an expression that is timely and not too complex, the method of calculating labor productivity in the state plan is stipulated to be the value method of calculating comprehensive labor productivity. The index method is merely a supplementary method for analyzing problems. At the same time, labor productivity in industrial enterprises is to be expressed in terms of the gross value of output completed by a production worker in one year. In construction and installation enterprises, it is to be expressed in terms of the amount of work (budget value) completed by a construction and installation worker in one year. In transport enterprises, it is to be expressed as the amount of transport work (in ton-kilometers or nautical miles) completed by a transport worker (in railway transport enterprises, an engineer) in one year. We should point out that labor productivity calculated by the production worker in industrial enterprises and the construction and installation worker in construction and installation enterprises still cannot fully reflect increases in labor productivity. This is because there are also a large number of staff and workers in these industries that are not directly related to production. This method of estimating must be studied further. In order to improve the work of calculating labor productivity in a planned way, the 1958 tables require that the labor productivity of construction and installation enterprises should be calculated not only on the basis of [the number of] construction and installation workers, but that each ministry, province, and municipality should calculate labor productivity on the basis of [the number of] production workers (including construction and installation workers, affiliated and auxiliary production workers, transport workers, and so forth).

The 1957 labor and wage planning table required that, in addition to calculating labor productivity in industry, construction and installation, and state-owned transport enterprises, that labor productivity also be calculated for the survey and design, geological prospecting, and commercial branches. However, since the number of staff and workers in these branches is determined mainly according to the employment quota and because the method of computing labor productivity in the above branches is still not perfect, it was often impossible to reflect accurately changes in the actual work efficiency. Therefore, the 1958 tables do not require the formulation of labor productivity plans in the survey and design, geological prospecting, and commercial branches. Each relevant ministry and each province and municipality can choose its own method of computation according to its needs.

There are many factors that affect the increase of labor productivity. For example, increases in labor productivity in industrial enterprises depend mainly on improvements in technical equipment, reforms in the organization of production and labor, and increases in the technical, cultural, and political level of the workers. In the long run and according to general law, increases in labor productivity depend mainly on improvements in technical equipment. However, China's economic construction must proceed on the present economic and technological basis. On the one hand, we must construct some big modern enterprises up to international standards to be the backbone of industry in order to strengthen China's economic and defense capacity and to create favorable conditions for mastering the world's advanced technology. On the other hand, we cannot ignore the use and construction of medium and small enterprises. Therefore, increases in China's labor productivity will still depend for a relatively long time to come on improvements in production and labor organization and the rational utilization and distribution of the labor force.

2. Target Number of Staff and Workers

The term staff and workers refers to laborers who do not own producer goods and whose major source of income is wages. The staff and workers plan reflects the level of employment, the size of the rank and file working class, and their distribution among all the sectors of the national economy. On a national basis, the number of staff and workers should include all the working personnel of enterprises, businesses, state agencies, and people's organizations belonging to each sector, region, and economic type. In terms of an enterprise, it should include production personnel, the working personnel of auxiliary and affiliated production units, and all the working personnel of affiliated units serving the livelihood needs of the staff and workers. However, since China's

individual economy, privately owned economy, operating units run
by the people, and various cooperative economic organizations still
do not possess the means to directly formulate plans, the 1958
planning tables require that the number of staff and workers (including apprentices) employed by the above units not be included
in the number of staff and workers of branches subject to direct
planning. Instead, it should only be included in the employment
figures of the individual, privately owned and cooperative economies. They also require that the number of staff and workers
employed in them be enumerated. Due to the present lack of survey and statistical data, the 1958 tables do not require an estimate
of the number of staff and workers employed by agricultural cooperatives.

The 1958 tables further require that staff and workers be classified into official staff and workers and temporary staff and workers. Official staff and workers refer to those who are employed
to do regular work and whose length of employment is not specified. Official staff and workers also include probational staff and
workers and trainees. Temporary staff and workers refer to those
who are hired to do temporary work and whose length of employment is specified (usually not exceeding a month; if they are employed for more than one month, a new employment contract must
be signed). They are dismissed after the job is completed or at
the end of the employment period. Temporary staff and workers
also include seasonal workers and domestic workers employed
by enterprises. Temporary staff and workers can usually be recruited on the spot. They are mostly manual laborers and require
no training. Their wages are comparatively low, and their welfare
benefits also differ from those of the official staff and workers.
Therefore, temporary and official staff and workers differ in terms
of their source, distribution, training, wages, and welfare benefits.
Separate plans have to be formulated for them. However, because
the number of temporary staff and workers in cultural, educational
and health business units, agencies, and organizations is small and
there is a lack of such data, for the time being in 1958 the above
branches are not required to formulate plans for temporary staff
and workers.

The 1957 and 1958 planning tables require that the number of
staff and workers be calculated according to the annual average
number and the year-end number respectively. The annual average number refers to the average number of workers during the
year. It reflects the quantity of labor in one year. We have adopted

the annual average number of persons to be consistent with the estimates of the targets for annual labor productivity, annual gross wages, and annual average wages. At the same time, having the annual average number of persons facilitates our formulation of the construction plan for staff and workers' dwellings and the plan for providing the staff and workers with welfare facilities. The year-end number of persons refers to the number of persons employed on December 31 of the year. Changes in the number of staff and workers, the distribution of the labor force, and the training and distribution of cadres in the plan year must all be computed on the basis of the year-end number of persons. Therefore, we must adopt the year-end number of persons target in formulating annual plans.

To see whether the staff and workers are rationally distributed among each sector of the national economy, to grasp the changes in the number of staff and workers among each sector of the national economy, and to calculate the distribution and redistribution of national income, we must classify all the staff and workers by the sector of the national economy in which they are employed.

The 1958 planning tables specify that the number of staff and workers be classified into nine categories according to the nature of the activities of the sector of the national economy in which they are employed: industry; capital construction (construction and installation, survey and design, geological prospecting); agriculture, forestry, water conservancy, and meteorology; transport (railroad, ocean, inland waterway, and air transport) and post and telecommunications; commerce, restaurant and service enterprises; urban public utilities; cultural, educational, and health units; state agencies; and people's organizations. The nature of the work and business activities of the staff and workers employed by a branch or a unit are many and varied, and it is very difficult to strictly classify the staff and workers according to the real nature of their work. Under the present conditions, we can only roughly classify the number of staff and workers by sector. Therefore, the 1958 tables specify the following concrete ways of classifying the staff and workers by sector of the national economy:

a. All the staff and workers of independent industrial enterprises and capital construction units (including the staff and workers of sideline production organs, transport organs, and cultural, educational, health, and welfare units led by the above units) are regarded as engaging in industrial or capital construction labor. They are listed as the staff and workers of the industry and capital

216

construction sectors respectively. Those among them who are engaged in activities other than industrial production do not have to be further classified by sector.

b. In addition to independent industrial and capital construction units, the staff and workers employed by the business units led by each ministry and the departments and bureaus of each province and municipality are primarily classified according to the nature of the main business activities that are managed by each ministry and each department and bureau (there are some exceptions as explained in [c] below). For example, all the staff and workers of the education operating units led by the Ministry of Education and the Departments (Bureaus) of Education of the provinces and municipalities (including the staff and workers in these units who are engaged in noneducational activities) are all classified as working personnel of educational units. However, the staff and workers employed in education units which are not led by the Department (Bureau) of Education are not classified as working personnel of educational units even though they are engaged in education work. For example, the staff and workers employed in the children's elementary schools and the evening schools for staff and workers which are run by industrial enterprises and construction and installation enterprises are included in the number of staff and workers listed under the "other activities" category in the industrial enterprises and capital construction units respectively.

c. In the case of some independent business units whose business activities differ greatly from the major activities of the leadership departments above them and which have a large number of working personnel, their staff and workers are classified by the nature of their own business activities. For example, the Salt Company under the Ministry of Food Industry system, the Lumber Company under the Ministry of Forestry Industry system, the Transport Company under the Ministry of Acquatic Products system, the Pharmaceutical Company under the Ministry of Health system, and the New China Bookstore and the International Bookstore under the Ministry of Culture system all belong to commerce according to the nature of their business activities. The number of staff and workers involved is also relatively large. And while their organizational structure has been established along vertical lines, these activities are also under the leadership of the Commercial Departments (Bureaus) of the provinces and municipalities. Therefore, the 1958 tables list the staff and workers of the above units in the commercial sector. Similarly, the number of staff and workers in the livelihood supply shops of the Ministry of Railroads system should also be listed in the commercial sector. Therefore, it is also specified that the Ministry of Railroads should separately list the target for the number of such staff and workers in order to facilitate their inclusion among the staff and workers of the commercial sector in the final synthesis made by the State Economic Commission.

d. The number of staff and workers employed in organs affiliated with state agencies and people's organizations is listed as a separate target. This is because the number involved is relatively large, and the nature of their work also differs from that of the state agencies. They are therefore not included in the number of staff and workers of the state agencies and people's organizations, but constitute an individual target. Moreover this target is further divided into separate targets for material-technical supply organs and scientific, cultural, educational, and health units so that the State Economic Commission can easily include them among the number of staff and workers of the commercial and the cultural, educational and health sectors.

The above methods of classifying staff and workers according to sectors of the national economy basically reflect the nature of activities engaged in by the staff and workers of each sector. They are also consistent with the regulation governing the methods for labor and wage statistics. Because the planning departments are capable of satisfying this requirement, it is still a reasonable regulation and can be implemented. Some comrades think that the classification of the number of staff and workers by sectors of the national economy should be based on the nature of each group's activity. They believe that this method is scientific, and it is also followed by the Soviet Union. The so-called classification by the "nature of each group's activity" can be explained with the example of an industrial enterprise. Only the industrial production personnel are classified as industrial labor. The working personnel of farms affiliated with the enterprise are classified as agricultural labor, the transport workers who work outside the plant are classified as transport labor, the major repairs personnel are classified as capital construction labor, the working personnel of the health clinic and hospital are classified as health services labor, those who work in the mess halls are classified as restaurant industry labor, those who work in schools are classified as education labor, those who work in the library and clubs are classified as cultural services labor, those who work in bathhouses and barbershops are classified as service labor, and so forth. This is a comparatively scientific method of classification, but the targets have to be very detailed, and there is a large amount of summary work. Furthermore, this is not the present practice of the statistical departments, and the number of cadres in the labor planning departments is limited. If this method were adopted, it would be very difficult to synthesize, check, and send down the plans. Therefore, in the 1958 revision of the tables, we did not adopt this idea.

3. Wage Targets

There are two wage targets: (1) the total amount of wages and (2) the average wage. The total amount of wages is an important national economic target. It reflects the income level of the working class. At the same time, it is also an important component of social purchasing power. It is closely related to the amount of commodities in circulation. Total wages includes all compensation paid to workers and staff whether in money or in kind and also wagelike subsidies which must be paid to staff and workers on the basis of legal provisions. Regardless of the source of the funds, they should all be included within the total wages. Furthermore, total wages include all the wages of persons, whether they are registered or not registered. However, total wages does not include the following payments: one-time awards to the staff and workers for inventions, technical improvements, rationalization suggestions, being labor competition winners, and being model persons; supplementary wages and payments of institutional welfare expenses; and various payments related to labor protection, outside duties expenses, travel expenses, family living expenses, and subsidies for trainees and students.

Wages paid during work stoppages and overtime wages in enterprises should be included in the total wages actually paid and should be accounted for accordingly. However, the work assignments for the plan year are usually calculated on the basis of normal working conditions. No work stoppages or overtime work are planned. Therefore the planning tables of past years specified that the planned total wages could include wages paid to working personnel on legal holidays and vacations in enterprises with continuous operations (such as iron and steel refining, electricity generation, railway transport, and so forth). However, wages paid for overtime and work stoppages due to poor management of the enterprises themselves are not included in the planned total wages. If the wages actually paid exceed the planned amount because of work stoppages and overtime which result from poor management, it is a kind of man-made waste. In addition to being accounted for as such, effective measures must be taken to cover this deficit.

The planning data of past years shows that the wages paid to nonregistered persons were very small. Many units did not plan for them at all. At the same time, the total wages for nonregistered persons consisted mainly of wages paid to temporary staff and workers who worked less than one day at major business activities and less than five days at secondary business activities. However, the 1958 tables have changed the method of estimating the number and wages of temporary staff and workers. The total wages for temporary staff and workers already include the wages of all temporary staff and workers. Thus, the total wages of nonregistered persons consist mainly of payments for literary work. But such payments are already required to be noted at the end of the tables. Therefore, the 1958 planning tables do not require the formulation of a total wage target for nonregistered persons.

The average annual wage refers to the average wage income of a staff member or worker in one year. The average wage target is mainly used to observe and compare the wage levels of each type of personnel in each sector. However, because there are already many plan targets and because labor planning work is still not well grounded, it is not feasible to have more detailed classifications of personnel, thereby increasing the number of average wage targets for even more categories of personnel. Therefore, we usually pay more attention to studying the average wage target for personnel as a whole. However, the average wage target for personnel as a whole is even more comprehensive and is affected by many factors. We should do more study on how to correctly use the average wage target.

LECTURE 11: CADRE PLANNING TABLES

Ch'en Chi-ch'eng and Ch'en Chih-chang*

The cadre plan is a component of the national economic plan. It contains two major parts: the plan for training new skilled workers and the plan of the need for specialists. The major purpose of formulating this plan is to determine the quantity, quality, and speciality of cadres that can be trained through various means according to the long-term and annual development needs of capital construction, production, and other businesses and to rationally distribute them according to those needs. At the same time, in the process of formulating the cadre plans, each planning unit may discover problems relating to the need for, and the training of, cadres and may suggest various measures to solve these problems in order to satisfy the national economy's need for cadres.

Some people ask why the plan to train new skilled workers is included in the cadre plan. What then does the word "cadre" mean? The word cadre was translated from a foreign language. It refers to persons with a certain level of technique and professional knowledge who assume leadership and backbone roles in various work units. There are also two interpretations of this explanation: one is that cadres refer to mental laborers who work in Party, government, and military agencies, people's organizations, and every economic sector. This is now an accepted interpretation in society. Another is that in addition to the above persons, it also includes manual laborers who assume backbone roles in grassroots units of industry, construction, geology, and other undertakings. Technicians are an example. The latter interpretation applies to the cadres referred to in China's present national economic plan.

---

*Ch'en Chi-ch'eng, Ch'en Chih-chang, "Kan-pu chi-hua piao-ke." <u>CHCC</u>, 1957, No. 11, pp. 35-37.

I. The Plan for Training New Skilled Workers

1. The Concept of New Skilled Workers

New skilled workers refer to: (1) workers who were originally ordinary laborers who have mastered certain skills and professional competence for the first time after undergoing training; and (2) workers who originally possessed certain techniques and professional competence and who have mastered other techniques and professional competences after training to meet the requirements of new posts. New skilled workers do not include: (1) workers who can do their jobs after being introduced to them only briefly and without undergoing specialized technical and professional training; (2) skilled workers whose level of technical theory and operating skills improves on a continuous basis.

2. Ways to Train New Skilled Workers

At present, there are three major ways to train new skilled workers:

a. Workers' technical schools. These provide a way to train middle-level skilled workers with more comprehensive skills. Workers who have been trained this way should possess relatively systematic and complete knowledge of technical theory and operating skills and should be able to quite readily understand new operating methods and skills. However, because of various limitations of practical training organizations and conditions, at the present time new skilled workers trained this way have not achieved the same degree of operating skill as that reached by new skilled workers trained through apprenticeship.

b. Training classes. These are generally a way of training workers in specialized techniques and professional theoretical knowledge. Examples are the training classes for the professional personnel in the postal and telecommunications departments.

c. Apprenticeship. This method involves having the highly skilled workers and apprentices sign contracts under which the masters guide the apprentices individually or in groups to learn techniques directly in the course of the production process.

Each of the above three methods has different characteristics. Which of them should be adopted depends on the time required, the complexity of the job, the source of funds, and the state policy of building the country with diligence and thrift.

3. Methods of Formulating the Plan to Train New Skilled Workers

The plan to train new skilled workers is composed of three targets: the "total number of trainees," the "number of trainees who will graduate," and the "number of recruits." The "total number of trainees" refers to the number of persons who have still not completed their training in the base period plus the number of newly recruited trainees in the plan year. Part of them are being trained to meet needs during the plan year and part of them are being trained to meet needs in later years. The "number of trainees who will graduate" refers to the number of persons who will be promoted to worker status through satisfying training requirements and passing examinations. The "number of recruits" includes the total number of persons recruited internally and from outside.

The plan for the number of new skilled workers who will graduate is based on an accurate estimate of the need for new skilled workers. This is because the need for new skilled workers is based on the production (business) and capital construction tasks. It reflects the overall need for new skilled workers in the plan year. Whether or not the need is accurately determined directly affects the degree to which the enterprises' need for new skilled workers will be satisfied. If the need is overestimated or underestimated, there will be a glut or shortage of trained workers. Therefore, it is very important to formulate the need for new skilled workers more accurately and realistically.

The need for new skilled workers is composed of the following three parts: (1) the number of new skilled workers which must be added within the plan year because of work increases in production (business), construction and installation, geological prospecting, and survey and design; (2) the number of new skilled workers needed to prepare newly constructed or renovated enterprises for operation; (3) the number of workers needed to replace those who have resigned due to old age, military enlistment, and long-term transfers for training purposes. The concrete computation methods are as follows:

a. The number of new skilled workers required by an increase of work is estimated from the increase of work in the plan year in production (business), construction and installation, geological prospecting, and survey and design and from the planned employment quotas. We also take account of possible factors that may increase labor productivity. This number is basically the same as the number of additional workers in the labor plan. The only differences are: (1) the number listed in the labor plan is basically an average number, while the number used to indicate the need for new skilled workers due to work increases is an actual number; (2) the labor plan includes workers that do not require training and temporary workers; and (3) the labor plan does not reflect the number of additional new skilled workers required by an enterprise for nonindustrial production, or other activities. Therefore, while we compile the plan for training new skilled workers on the basis of the labor plan, this must be supplemented with the above three factors. Only then can we avoid overestimating the need for new skilled workers.

b. The number of new skilled workers needed to prepare newly constructed and renovated enterprises for operation. At present, some units interpret "production-preparation workers" as being everyone, whether worker, apprentice, or trainee, who prepares newly constructed or renovated enterprises for operation. This is not consistent with the regulations on labor planning. The labor plan stipulates that production-preparation working personnel (workers) refers to "all relevant working personnel (workers) who participate in production preparation starting from the date when preparations are made to construct or to renovate plants and mines to the date when they are in operation, but it does not include people undergoing training or those still in school."[1] The need for production-preparation workers which is listed in the plan for training workers should be calculated according to the interpretation stipulated in the labor plan.

To satisfy the needs of newly constructed and expanded enterprises when they officially start production, it is extremely necessary to send a certain number of workers in advance to the newly constructed units to become acquainted with the blueprints and the new technical processes. At present, the needs of newly constructed enterprises for production-preparation workers are estimated according to the requirements of the above tasks and are based on the fixed number of staff and the personnel schedule for new plants. The concrete computation method is as follows: Suppose the construction of an enterprise requires two years and will be completed in 1958. After the whole plant is put into operation, it will need 1,000 skilled workers. Due to the needs for construction, installation, trial production, and familiarization with new technical processes, the number of workers who should arrive in 1957 represents 10 percent of the total number of workers required. In this case, 100 production-preparation workers are required in 1957. The percentage of staffing actually required must be based on the concrete situation of the enterprise and the minimum proportion of advance staffing required by the progress of construction.

   c. The number of workers needed to replace those who retire due to old age, military enlistments, and long-term transfers for training purposes. This part of the need is generally based on the number of resignations in past years and is estimated on a percentage basis. That is, we see what percentage of workers retired for the above reasons during the several years before the plan year and use it to figure out how many replacements will probably be needed in the plan year. For example, suppose 1956 is chosen as the standard. If the number of registered persons* was 1,000 at the beginning of 1956 and the number of persons who left their jobs for the above reasons during the whole year was 10, then the percentage of resignations was 1 percent. To estimate the number of replacements in the plan period, we simply multiply the number of registered persons at the beginning of the plan period by the percentage obtained as above. If the number of registered persons in the plan period is 2,000, the number of replacements needed in the plan year will be 20. Admittedly, this calculation is not completely accurate. There is a certain degree of uncertainty. However, according to past experience, this computation method can usually still roughly reflect the replacement needs. We understand that in the Soviet Union, this proportion is set at 3 to 5 percent of the registered persons. In China, the present proportion is around 2 percent or even less. This is the general situation. In some enterprises at the grass-roots level, we can also directly estimate the replacement needs in the plan period according to the age structure, health conditions, and cultural level of the workers.

   The sum of the above three numbers of people constitutes the total need for new skilled workers in the plan year. However, in determining the plan for training new skilled workers, we must also consider other possible sources (such as demobilized military technicians) before we can formulate an accurate plan.

   How can the "number of recruits" be calculated? Since the national directive about lengthening the training period of apprentices

---

*State regulations of the time required each enterprise to maintain a register of all workers and staff, both permanent and temporary. — N. R. L.

was proclaimed, the apprentices and trainees recruited in the plan period have generally been trained for the needs of later years. Therefore, it is a very important and also very difficult problem to make the number of recruits correspond to the requirements of later years. Generally speaking, the target number of recruits should, on the one hand, be based on the long-term plans for capital construction, production tasks, and employment quotas. On the other hand, it must also take into account adjustments made to capital construction and production tasks during the plan year. To avoid discrepancies between the long-term requirements and the training plan, when we calculate the number of recruits we must first consider the needs of newly constructed enterprises that can surely be completed and pay little or no attention to items that are less likely to be completed. The requirements should be classified into those for: (1) newly constructed or renovated enterprises; (2) production (business) enterprises; and (3) other purposes.

Since there is generally some surplus personnel in many units, when determining the sources of new skilled workers it is necessary to tap internal potential and send some youths in the plants, mines, enterprises, and organizations with training potential to schools and plants to learn techniques. Only when necessary do we select from society a portion of the youths who are to undergo training. Therefore, under the target number of recruits, the target for recruits from society should be listed separately in order to control the number of persons recruited from society.

II. The Plan for Specialists Who Are Needed

1. The Scope of Specialists

This refers to graduates of institutes of higher education and middle-level vocational schools.

2. The Method of Formulating the Plan for Specialists Who Are Needed

Specialists are engaged in all kinds of jobs in each sector of the national economy. Some participate directly in productive labor, such as teachers and physicians. Some do not participate directly in production; they organize and manage production, such as technicians and engineers in construction and installation and industrial production units. The requirements for specialists who participate directly in production can be computed according to the tasks decided on by the state and the amount of work that a person can handle. For example, the annual need for medical personnel can be estimated according to the annual state development plan for health services (expressed by the number of hospital beds and the number of out-patient clinics) and the quotas for medical personnel required to staff hospitals of a certain size and to take care of a certain number of beds.

It is more complicated to determine the needs for additional specialists not directly engaged in production. First, we must determine the number of workers. Then the requirements for each type of technical personnel are computed with reference to the number of technical personnel that a certain number of workers should have. For example, to compute the number of additional specialists required to complete construction and installation projects, we must first estimate the number of workers needed to complete the amount of construction and installation work for that year. The formula is:

Number of construction and installation workers = [(Amount of construction and installation work (square meters or tons) × Number of workdays required to complete each square meter (or ton)] ÷ Number of effective workdays per worker per year.

Then, on the basis of the number of construction and installation workers needed in that year, we can estimate the number of additional specialists needed by using the following formula:

Number of construction and installation workers needed in the year × Number of technicians required per thousand construction and installation workers − Existing number of construction and installation technicians × Proportions of senior and middle-level technicians among them × Proportions of each type of specialized technicians = Number of each type of additional senior and middle-level specialized technicians needed for the year.

The tasks of each sector of the national economy are many and varied. However, to facilitate computation, we have classified them according to the nature of the work into survey and design, construction and installation, geological prospecting, and scientific research.

When estimating the need for additional specialists, we should fully take into account factors affecting the quotas for technicians. We should focus on the various types of plants, such as newly constructed and renovated plants, and accurately determine the quotas for technicians (expressed as so many technicians per thousand workers) in order to facilitate an accurate estimate of the need for additional specialists in the various fields. In general, the following factors affect the norms for technicians:

a. Plants and mines producing different types of products require different numbers of technicians.

b. Plants and mines with different technical equipment also require different numbers of technicians.

c. The production organization of plants and mines.

d. The present number of technicians in plants and mines.

e. The quality of specialists trained by schools.

We should seriously study the above factors for each enterprise and should gradually accumulate experience in order to compute accurately the need for each type of specialist. The Soviet Union has done a great deal of work on this aspect and has accumulated a considerable amount of experience in the training and distribution of specialists. We should learn from this experience.

After the norms for technicians are determined, another important job is to study and determine the specialties needed of the additional technicians and who should do what. For example, in a metallurgical enterprise with an annual output of a million tons of steel, the number of metallurgical engineers, metallurgical technicians, mechanical engineers, and the number of other specialized engineers, technicians, and assistant technicians required should be studied in collaboration with the experts.

Determining the needs for additional specialists is a new job in China. We lack experience in this respect. The relevant units should jointly study and sum up their experience.

Note

1. See 1958 National Economic Planning Tables, p. 190.

LECTURE 12: COST AND CIRCULATION EXPENSE PLANNING TABLES

Cheng Chih*

I. The Scope of Cost and Circulation Expense Planning

The scope of cost and circulation expense planning is classified according to each different sphere of the national economic plan. It can be roughly divided into the following types:

1. Cost plans for industrial products. All industrial enterprises and units which specialize in industrial production and have independent economic accounting should formulate cost plans. The scope of the formulation not only includes industrial enterprises of the industrial branches, but at the same time, industrial enterprises of nonindustrial branches (such as the Ministry of Railroads, the Ministry of Food, and the Ministry of Commerce). However, it does not include the industrial enterprises and handicraft enterprises affiliated with industrial branches, nonindustrial branches, and business units because these units do not have the necessary bases for planning and statistical work; nor do they possess the means for independent economic accounting. If they are required to formulate cost plans, difficulties will arise in the course of the work. In 1957 the cost plans for industrial products that are produced under state management refers to the industrial enterprises and units directly under the jurisdiction of each ministry of the State Council; those for local industrial enterprises and units are to be controlled by the provincial (municipal) people's councils.

2. Transport cost plans. All public transport enterprises that have the means for independent economic accounting should formulate transport cost plans. The extent of the formulation includes:

*Cheng Chih, "Ch'eng-pen ho liu-t'ung fei chi-hua piao-ke." CHCC, 1957, No. 12, pp. 30-33.

railroad transport, water transport, air transport, road transport, and so forth. However, it does not include the various transport that takes place within production branches because that only serves the production needs of a particular enterprise and is a component of the production process. Take the transport of lumber in forestry as an example. The cost of transporting the timber from the cutting site to the sawmill or to the lumber storage yard by enterprise-owned railroad cars, trucks, or tractors should not be included in the transport cost and should be treated as part of the cost of forest products. In 1957 the scope of the state managed transport cost plans is: enterprises directly under the railroads, and maritime, and river transport, and enterprises and units of the aviation branch. The cost plans for public roads and other inland water transport are controlled by the relevant ministries of the State Council and the various provincial (municipal) people's councils.

3. The scope of formulating the cost plans for construction and installation projects and for state-owned farms and tractor stations should only include those construction enterprises, state-owned farms, and tractor stations capable of independent economic accounting. However, due to the large changes in the plans of these units at present, the reporting time of their plans cannot be uniform. Also, the conditions of the units are different. It is difficult for the state to control the cost plans of these units. Therefore, from 1957 onward, they are to be controlled by the various ministries of the State Council and the various provincial (municipal) people's councils.

4. The product circulation expense plan differs from the various cost plans mentioned above. Product circulation expenses are expenses incurred by commercial enterprises at the various links (transport, storage, marketing) of product circulation. The scope of formulating the product circulation expense plan is: commercial enterprises and units with independent economic accounting, including the enterprises and units of commercial branches (such branches as commerce, food, foreign trade, and cooperatives). At the same time, it also includes noncommercial branches (such as the Salt Bureau of the Ministry of Food Industry, the Lumber Company of the Ministry of Forestry, and so forth). In 1957, the state exercises control over the circulation expenses of the above-mentioned units. At the same time, it also required the people's councils of each province (municipality) to supervise the cost plans of the commercial enterprises of their own province (municipality).

II. Cost and Circulation Expense Planning Tables and Their Systems of Targets

1. Cost Plan for Industrial Products

The main targets of the cost plan for industrial products are: (1) production expenses of industrial enterprises; (2) overall costs of marketed commodities; (3) total cost of comparable products; (4) the rate of and the amount of cost reduction for comparable products. These targets are included separately in the budget of production expenses for industrial enterprises (Cost Table No. 1) and the cost plans for industrial products both by type of product and by cost item (Cost Tables Nos. 2 and 3). The following is an explanation of the functions, content, and computation methods for the major targets of these tables.

a. Industrial enterprises production expenses budget table.

It can be divided into the following three major parts:

1) Industrial enterprises production expenses. Production expenses of industrial enterprises is the major target of the cost plan. It is a total of all the expenses incurred by the enterprise in the course of their production activities. It not only includes the various expenses related to production, but also expenses unrelated to production, such as the expenses involved in major repairs of buildings and of other structures using the productive capacity of the enterprises themselves, the expenses incurred in the performing of other services by the enterprises' transport divisions which do not have independent economic accounting, and the expenses incurred in nonindustrial activities by the workers of the enterprises.

The essential elements of the industrial enterprises production expenses are: (1) raw materials and major processed materials; (2) auxiliary materials; (3) purchased fuels; (4) purchased power; (5) wages; (6) supplementary wage expenses; (7) depreciation charges; (8) other cash outlays. These expense items are classified by economic origin and the nature of the expenses. That is to say, we are only interested in what the expenses are, regardless of the roles these expenses perform in production activities. For example, purchased fuels can be used both in the production process and for heating the workshops, but in estimating production expenses, they are all included in the item of "purchased fuels." Another example is wages that include both the wages of the workers of the core workshops and those of the administrative and technical personnel. They also include the wages of those in the auxiliary workshops and of the whole staff of the enterprise management structure. Therefore, the industrial production expenses budget can guarantee that the cost plans are consistent with other national economic plans (such as labor, production, finance, and material supply plans — the same is true for the following). For example, the item of "the wages of production workers" in the production expenses budget corresponds to the total quantity of wages in the labor and wage plan. The quantity of raw materials and major processed materials corresponds to the need for raw and processed materials in the material supply plan. At the same time, the structure of the various elements of production expenses are in keeping with those in the financial plan. Therefore, we can use them in calculating the working capital needed by the enterprises, as well as in calculating the national income.

Because the industrial enterprise production expenses can directly relate the cost plans of industrial products to other plans, they can be used to exercise cash supervision over the norms for the consumption of raw and processed materials and fuels and the use of industrial fixed assets, working capital, labor resources, and miscellaneous expenses. They motivate enterprises to continuously extend advanced experience, adopt new techniques, and reduce production expenses in order to reduce the cost of products.

2) Production expenses of the gross value of industrial output.

These are industrial enterprise production expenses net of expenses involved in the major repair of buildings and structures done by the enterprises themselves, transport activities outside the plants not subject to independent accounting, nonindustrial activities which do not constitute part of the gross value of industrial output, plus or minus apportioned expenses and advance deductions.

Apportioned expenses are one-time outlays which are apportioned annually to the cost outlay. Before the expenses have been fully apportioned to the cost, they must be paid from working capital. The major items covered by these apportioned expenses are the enterprise's purchase of special tools and the cost of cheap and easily worn out articles.

Advance deductions are the opposite of apportioned expenses. These expenses are deducted in advance and in later production periods are charged as expenses. For example, the packaging-materials expenses reserved for next year's production are advance deductions.

3) Production expenses for the value of marketed output. These

are the production expenses of the gross value of industrial output plus the balance of products-in-process, semifinished products, and self-produced cheap and easily worn-out products at the beginning of the plan period, minus the balance of products-in-process, semifinished products, and self-produced cheap and easily worn-out products at the end of the period. The method for estimating the balance of products-in-process, semifinished products, and self-produced cheap and easily worn-out products is: the calculation of the balance at the beginning of the period must be based on the account entries or actual inventory taking. However, calculations of the balance at the end of the period must be based on the quantity of labor used on the products-in-process and semifinished products and on the norms for the consumption of all kinds of materials.

The sum of the production expenses for marketed output value and nonproduction expenses equals the total cost of marketed commodities.

In formulating the production expenses of industrial enterprise, we should pay attention to the following several aspects:

First, we should not include the raw and the major processed materials provided by the ordering parties themselves when calculating the value of the expenses for raw materials and major materials.

Second, the same raw or processed materials can be listed as raw and processed materials for one product and listed as auxiliary materials for another product. Therefore, when formulating industrial enterprise production expenses, we must classify these materials with reference to the concrete conditions of the enterprise and categorize them as primary or secondary, listing them as "raw materials and major materials" or as "auxiliary materials." However, they cannot be listed both as "raw materials and major materials" and as "auxiliary materials" in the production expenses. Fuels are an exception. To reflect accurately the proportion of raw and processed materials and of fuels, if the same materials are used as raw and processed materials as well as fuels, they can be listed separately.

Third, the method of apportioning "nonproductive expenses." Nonproductive expenses include two different things. One is the expenses incurred by the enterprises to train cadres and conduct scientific research. The other is expenses involved in the marketing of products. The methods of apportioning them to cost are different for each of them. The former expenses are apportioned to cost in the same way as are workshop operating expenses and enterprise management expenses. Marketing expenses are apportioned only for the products which are sold. Thus, the cost of products which are not sold should not include marketing expenses.

b. Industrial products cost planning tables (Cost Tables Nos. 2 and 3).

China's national economic planning tables specify that industrial product cost plans should be formulated and classified according to major marketed commodities and cost items. Industrial cost plans (Cost Table No. 2) formulated on the basis of major marketed commodities specify the unit cost level of each major marketed commodity. Industrial cost plans formulated on the basis of items of cost (Cost Table No. 3) reflect the cost composition and the proportions of all the marketed commodities and comparable products. They also specify the amount of reduction for each item of cost for comparable products. The following major targets are included in these two tables:

1) Total cost of marketed commodities. The accounting objects of this target are the total amount of marketed commodities that enterprises expect to sell. The cost of semifinished products and products-in-process must be deducted from it since they are not part of the marketed commodities.

The total cost of marketed commodities is based on the unit cost of each type of product. The unit cost estimate of the product is generally divided into direct expenses and indirect expenses. Direct expenses are those that can be directly apportioned to the product cost, such as raw materials and major processed materials, auxiliary materials, fuels and power consumed in the technical processes, wages for production workers, and supplementary expenses. These items should be formulated with reference to the production plan, the labor plan, norms for the consumption of raw and processed materials, fuels, and power, and norms for work time of each product. The determination of the above norms must be based on the average advanced norm of the enterprises. There should also be some definite plans for technical and organizational measures to ensure economy on raw and processed materials and increases in labor productivity. Indirect expenses are those that cannot be apportioned to the cost of certain products. These expenses are generally classified under the three comprehensive items of "workshop operating expenses," "enterprise management expenses," and "nonproductive expenses." Because these three items are related to all products, they can only be indirectly apportioned. There should also be plans for indirect expenses. These expenses are then apportioned to product cost according to definite standards (generally with reference to the wages of the workers producing the products). We should point out that indirect expenses are largely fixed, and most of them do not change with output. Therefore, when output increases, the indirect expenses apportioned to each unit of product will be reduced, and the unit cost of product can be reduced.

The total cost items of marketed commodities are classified by how each expenditure is used. Therefore, the same expenses, such as fuel expenses, can be listed under different cost items. Fuels used in the production process should be listed under the item of "fuels used in technical processes." Fuels used for heating the workshops should be listed under the item of "workshop operating expenses." These classifications are designed to supervise systematically economies in the use of raw and processed materials and of funds in enterprises and workshops and also to keep track of the unit cost of products.

2) Total cost of comparable products. The main purpose of formulating product cost plans is to reduce costs. The task of cost reduction is simply given by a comparison between the planned product cost and last year's cost. Therefore, the total cost of comparable products refers to the cost of those products which were produced last year and will still be produced in the plan period. To determine the total cost of comparable products and the task of cost reduction, we must solve the following three problems:

First, the problem of product comparability. Planned cost reduction can only be related to comparable products. The larger the proportion of comparable products, the larger the economies derived from cost reduction. Therefore, it is very important in industrial product cost planning to determine correctly the comparability of products and to enlarge the proportion of comparable products.

Comparable products refer to the products which were produced last year or in previous years by the industrial enterprises. Sometimes, there may have been changes in the raw and processed materials, technical processes, assembly, quality, and names of some products from previous years; these products may still be regarded as comparable products as long as their basic specifications are unchanged. Some products may only have been trial produced in the previous year rather than having been produced on a large scale. These products should not be regarded as comparable products. For those industrial activities whose objects and concrete content change frequently, the products should never be regarded as comparable.

Second, the problem of uniform output levels. Planned cost reductions for comparable products should be calculated on the basis of identical output levels. Total product costs at different levels of output cannot be compared. The way to solve this problem is that the total cost of the comparable products in the previous period should be calculated on the basis of the unit cost and planned output of the previous period. These figures should then be compared with the planned total cost computed on the basis of the planned unit cost and planned output.

Third, the problem of constant prices between two years. Cost reductions are a comprehensive reflection of the work quality of the enterprises. However, the level of product cost is, to a large extent, not determined by the subjective efforts of the enterprises. It is primarily influenced by the changes in prices of raw and processed materials and of fuels. Therefore, when calculating planned cost reductions, the effects on the level of planned costs due to changes in price levels and other factors should be analyzed and discounted so that the efforts of the enterprises to reduce costs can be assessed on the basis of constant prices and other objective factors.

3) The rate of and the amount of cost reductions for comparable products. There are two major targets in the industrial product cost plan. One is the percentage rate of cost reduction. The other is the value amount of cost reduction. Sometimes, these two targets change in the same direction. For example, with constant output levels, the higher the rate of cost reduction, the larger the amount of cost reduction. The reverse is also true. However, sometimes they do not change in the same direction. For example, when output increases, the amount of cost reduction will increase, but the rate of cost reduction can be constant. Furthermore, suppose the product variety changes so that the output proportion of a product with a higher rate of cost reduction is increased in the total output and the total output is decreasing. In this case, the rate of cost reduction may increase, while the amount of cost reduction decreases. Since the amount of cost reduction varies with the output level, the rate of cost reduction should be the basis for formulating plans. The amount of cost reduction, like the several targets above, merely serves as a reference.

2. Transport Cost Plans (Including Railroad, River, and Maritime Transport)

The railroad and water transport cost planning tables include the following three targets: (a) the total amount of operating expenses (total transport cost); (b) the cost per thousand converted ton-kilometers (ton-nautical miles in maritime transport); and (c) rate and amount of cost reduction.

a. Total operating expenses (total transport costs). This includes all the expenses of passenger and freight transport. To enable transport expenses to reflect concretely every business activity of the transport enterprises and to facilitate planning and supervision, in the plans, the expenses are classified by their uses. The cost items listed for railroad transport include: (1) wages; (2) expenses for supplementary wages; (3) fuels; (4) mid-year and year-end repair of locomotives and cars; (5) depreciation; and (6) other expenses. Water transport expense items include: (1) wages; (2) expenses for supplementary wages; (3) small and medium repairs; (4) wintering expenses; (5) port agent expenses; (6) depreciation; and (7) others. The determination of these expense items should be calculated on the basis of the transport plan, the labor plan, and all the technical and economic norms. We should point out that the depreciation listed among the transport expenses only refers to the depreciation of those fixed assets related to the major business activities. Thus, it should not include the fixed assets belonging to the cultural and livelihood service units,* health organizations, marketing organizations, purchasing organizations, or mess halls.

b. Cost per thousand converted ton-kilometers (ton-nautical miles in maritime transport). This is the most important target in the transport cost plan. Why must we call it converted ton-kilometers and not just ton-kilometers? This is because we have both freight transport and passenger transport. The unit for freight transport is the ton-kilometer, and the unit for passenger transport is person-kilometer. To facilitate uniform accounting, the two different units must be converted into one common unit. Under these circumstances, it is specified that one person-kilometer in passenger transport is converted into one ton-kilometer in freight

---

*This presumably refers to the livelihood supply shops operated by the Ministry of Railroads that were mentioned in Lecture 10: "Labor and Wage Planning Tables," pp. 206-220, above. — N. R. L.

transport. After conversion, it is called a converted ton-kilometer.

c. Rate and amount of cost reduction. The rate of cost reduction reflects the performance of the transport enterprise in cost reduction. The rate of cost reduction is computed by comparing the unit cost in the base period with the unit cost in the plan period. For example, suppose the unit cost in the base period is 10 yuan and the unit cost in the plan period is 9.5 yuan. Then the rate of reduction is:

$$(1 - \frac{9.5}{10}) \times 100 = 5\%.$$

The relationship between the rate and amount of cost reduction in transport cost plans is the same as that in industrial product cost plans.

3. Commodity Circulation Expense Plan

There are three major targets in the commodity circulation expense planning tables: (a) total commodity circulation expenses; (b) rate of circulation expenses (also known as the expense level); (c) the rate of reduction of circulation expenses.

a. Total commodity circulation expenses. This is an important indicator of the performance of commercial enterprises. From the total circulation expenses and each of its items, we can see the consumption of manpower and material and financial resources by the commercial enterprises in the process of commodity circulation. The quality of operation and management in the commercial enterprise can thus be reflected. The total product circulation outlay is composed of the expenses incurred by each commercial enterprise in each link (transport, storage, marketing, and so forth) of commodity exchange. They are classified into fifteen items: (1) transport expenses; (2) loading, unloading, and transfer expenses; (3) storage expenses; (4) sorting and grading expenses; (5) packaging expenses; (6) insurance premiums; (7) commodity spoilage; (8) inspection and paperwork expenses; (9) interest charges; (10) wages; (11) expenses for supplementary wages; (12) depreciation; (13) marketing of cheap and easily worn out products; (14) cadre-training expenses; and (15) operating and management expenses.

We should point out that not all expenses incurred by the commercial enterprises are included in the total commodity circulation expenses. The following expenses are not necessary for the commodity circulation process and therefore do not belong to commodity circulation expenses: (1) agents' fees paid to other commercial organs for purchasing and marketing services that are more properly regarded as price differentials between purchases and sales; (2) all processing expenses involved in changing the nature of the commodities and commissions paid to other branches for processing; (3) fines and damages paid by commercial enterprises because of contract violations.

b. Rate of circulation expenses. This is a percentage ratio between the total commodity circulation expenses and the net amount of commodity circulation. It mainly reflects the relationship between the circulation expenses and the amount of commodity exchange. Because the natures of the commodities handled by the commercial enterprises vary, the rate of circulation expenses also varies. For example, coal used as fuel has a higher rate of circulation expenses than gasoline. This is because: (1) The selling price of coal is low, and hence the ratio of circulation expenses to the selling price is high. (2) Coal is largely sold on a retail basis. The length of marketing time is long, and the sale outlets are many. Therefore, interest charges, insurance premiums, and operating and management expenses are higher. (3) The marketing network for coal is spread out over the whole country. Hence, the transport expenses are high.

c. The rate of reduction of circulation expenses. This is an important indicator of the performance of the commercial enterprises in terms of expense reduction. It is computed by calculating the circulation expenses in the base and plan periods. For example, if the circulation expense rate were 10 percent in the base period and 9 percent in the plan period, the differential in the expense rate would be 1 percent. Thus, the reduction rate of circulation outlay would be:

$$\frac{1}{10} \times 100 = 10\%.$$

LECTURE 13: MATERIAL-TECHNICAL SUPPLY PLANNING TABLES

Sun Hui-ch'ing*

I. The Concept of Material-Technical Supply Planning

Material-technical supply is the supply of materials and equipment.[†] The material-technical supply plan is a component of the whole national economic plan. Because there are many, many kinds of social products, we cannot include all of them in the material-technical supply plan. However, producer goods of major importance to the national economy must be included in order to achieve planned distribution, that is, unified distribution. The task of material-technical supply planning is to continuously and adequately supply each sector of the national economy with the necessary producer goods (namely, raw materials, processed materials, fuels, power, equipment and tools, and so forth) on a planned basis and guarantee the continuous and steady operation of all enterprises and construction units in order to fulfill and overfulfill the production plan and the capital construction plan, increase product quality, mobilize internal potential, and accelerate the turnover of working capital. The material-technical supply plan must be closely coordinated with the production plan, the capital construction plan, the import-export plan, the marketing plan, and the plan for state reserves.

II. The Scope of Material-Technical Supply Planning

The number of producer goods included in the material-technical

---

*Sun Hui-ch'ing, "Wu-tzu chi-shu kung-ying chi-hua piao-ke." CHCC, 1955, No. 1, pp. 38-41.

†See Chou Shu-chün, "The Material-Technical Supply Plan," pp. 49-60, above, for an explanation of the kinds of materials and equipment covered by the material-technical supply plan. — N.R.L.

240

supply plan is determined by the index of materials subject to unified distribution. This index is compiled according to the production, consumption, and supply characteristics of each product and their roles in the national economy. The products in the index are classified into three categories. The first category consists of materials subject to unified state allocation (or, briefly, materials under unified distribution). This category of materials is of major importance to the national economy and is included in the national balance. These resources are needed by many consuming branches and are subject to state management. The implementation of their production plans and material-technical supply plans have to be approved by the State Council after the State Economic Commission has comprehensively balanced them. The second category consists of materials subject to unified distribution by each central industrial ministry (or, briefly, material resources under ministerial management). These materials are quite important to the national economy. The branches in which they are produced and consumed are relatively centralized, and they must also be balanced on a national basis. They are subject to unified distribution by the ministries. Their material-technical supply plans must be comprehensively balanced by the marketing bureaus of each industrial ministry, and they are implemented after being approved by the ministries in charge. At present, this category of materials also includes products subject to balanced distribution by the management bureaus of each industrial ministry. The third category consists of materials subject to local balanced distribution. These materials are basically produced by local industries and supply local needs. Their material-technical supply plans are implemented after being approved by the people's councils of the provinces, municipalities, and autonomous regions. The index of materials subject to unified distribution changes with the economic conditions in each plan year and with the requirements of state plan management. In addition, there are many locally produced and marketed products that are not included in the material-technical supply plans.

The units that manage requests for materials subject to unified distribution are the central ministries and the people's councils of the provinces, the municipalities under the jurisdiction of the central government, and the autonomous regions. The basic-level requesting units are the basic-level enterprise (operating) units. However, not all basic-level enterprise (operating) units can be listed as basic-level requesting units when we consider the eco-

nomic conditions for organizing supply and their varying competence in planning work. Moreover, not even all the ministries can
be listed as units that manage requests. Only some of them can be
listed as units that manage requests and basic-level requesting
units. All materials subject to unified distribution that are required by each requesting unit must have material-technical supply plans formulated, and they must be applied for and distributed
through the proper request channels. All materials subject to unified distribution which are required by enterprise (operating) units
which are not listed as requesting units are included in the marketed commodity circulation plans of the commercial branches.
The commercial branches formulate their material-technical supply plans to apply for distribution from the management departments.

The procedures for formulating the material-technical supply
plans are as follows: Draft plans are first formulated by basic-
level production enterprises and construction units and are then
checked and aggregated by the units that manage requests. Materials subject to the unified distribution of each central industrial ministry must be approved by the industrial ministry in
charge. Materials subject to unified state distribution must be
approved by the State Council after they have been comprehensively balanced by the State Economic Commission.

At the same time that the approved material-technical supply
plans are sent down to each unit that manages requests, they are
also sent down to the marketing management branches for each
product. The consuming units then send in a detailed order based
on the approved distribution. Each marketing branch then balances
supply and demand according to the variety, specifications, delivery time, and delivery destination specified for each product in
the detailed orders. Orders for goods are organized, and contracts for goods delivery are signed on the basis of this balance.
The needed materials are either delivered to the consuming units
by the producing plants or mines or the offices of various marketing branches, or they are picked up from the producing plants or
mines by the consuming units.

III. Material-Technical Supply Planning Tables and Their System of Targets

Material-technical supply planning tables are tools for formulating material-technical supply plans. They are composed of request

242

forms and calculation tables. Each requesting unit uses the request forms to reflect the quantity of materials and equipment that they require, their normal reserves, and their supplementary needs; they use the calculation tables to reflect the basis for determining the quantity of materials and equipment required.

The Various Targets in the Materials and Equipment Request Forms

The materials and equipment request forms are composed of the following targets:

1. The quantity needed for use. The quantity of materials and equipment needed for use are classified by their uses into production and operational needs, needs related to the construction and installation projects of capital construction, supply and marketing needs, and export needs.

First, the quantity needed for production and operational uses. They are an important part of the overall needs. They are generally divided into three categories: the quantities needed for production; for operation and maintenance; and for major repairs.

a. The quantity needed for production uses refers to materials consumed in the production process. They include consumption directly and indirectly related to production. Specifically, they include the following:

1) All raw and processed materials which directly constitute the physical component of the product after having been transformed by the production process. For example, the electrolytic copper used to produce electrical cables, the iron and steel used to manufacture machines, the timber used to make furniture, and so forth.

2) All raw and processed materials which are applied to other materials in the production process to change their physical and chemical properties. For example, coal used to smelt coke, synthetic ammonia and sulphuric acid used to produce ammonium sulphate, scrap steel and pig iron used to smelt steel, and so on.

3) Electrical equipment needed for assembling products. For example, the electric motor and the ball bearings needed to assemble an automatic lathe, and the diesel engine needed to assemble a drilling machine, and so forth.

4) Fuels used in the production process. For example, the coke used to smelt iron, coal gas used to smelt steel, coal used to generate electricity, coal used in locomotives, gasoline and

diesel oil used in automobiles, and so forth.

5) Raw and processed materials, fuels, and so forth consumed in trial manufacturing new products.

b. The quantity needed for operational and maintenance uses include materials required for regular maintenance and repair of the normal wear and tear on fixed assets, for the operation and management of the production enterprise, for creating normal working conditions, and for packaging and decorating products in the production process. For example, materials and equipment needed to repair and replace railway tracks, replace parts of electric mechanical equipment, repair buildings, and add heating, ventilation, air conditioning, and safety equipment, and sheet metal and wooden boards used to package products.

c. The quantity needed for major repair uses refer to materials and equipment required for periodic major repairs of production equipment, transport facilities, and plants and housing as required in the major repair plan.

In addition, the quantity needed for production and operational uses also include the materials and equipment required to implement technical organization measures and labor protection and to make their own tools.

Second, the quantity needed for construction and installation uses in capital construction. These are also a major part of the total needs. They include the materials and equipment needed for the construction and installation projects of capital construction. That is to say, they include materials required on the work site, for prefabricating structures and parts which are ultimately used in construction and installation projects, and for the operation and maintenance of the construction enterprises themselves (such as tools, construction equipment, and so forth).

Third, the quantity needed for market purposes. At present, the producer goods products supplied through the market are not only complex and large in quantity, but they are supplied to a broad range of users. The quantity needed for market purposes includes the production needs of privately operated enterprises and handicraftsmen, the livelihood needs of the urban and rural population, the maintenance of buildings used for scientific research, teaching and experiments, and by agencies and organizations, and those needs of local enterprises that have not been included within any requesting unit.

The quantity needed for market purposes is generally determined on the basis of the need for each kind of materials and equipment in past years while taking into account the concrete conditions (including changes in the sources of supply) during the plan year.

Fourth, the quantity needed for export purposes. The quantity of exported materials and equipment is determined by the trade agreements signed with other countries.

2. The quantity needed for normal reserves. Normal reserves are the set amount of materials and equipment required to ensure uninterrupted operation of production enterprises.

The quantity needed for normal reserves is the product of the reserve norm (expressed in number of days) and the quantity of average daily needs. If the production and consumption of an enterprise fluctuate very little from month to month or from quarter to quarter, then the quantity of average daily needs can be calculated on an annual basis; if there are large fluctuations from quarter to quarter in the production and consumption of the enterprise, then the quantity of average daily needs in the fourth quarter can be used as a basis. The normal reserve needs of the branches also include turnover reserves of the supply office.

3. The size of the projected balance at the beginning of the year. This is an important constituent of internal materials and is determined by the projected performance of the material-technical supply plan in the base year.

4. The quantity of requested distribution. This refers to the quantity of materials and equipment applied for from the state. This is the major source for filling the needs.

From the various targets in the materials and equipment request form, we can see that it is nothing but a branch balance table showing the availability of, and need for, materials and equipment.

Quantity needed for use + Quantity needed for normal reserves = Estimated size of positive balance at beginning of year + Quantity of requested distribution.

The Targets in the Materials and Equipment Calculation Tables

Materials and equipment calculating tables are appendices to the request forms. Their major targets are: production and operational items or items related to capital construction, construction and installation projects, the quantity of output or the amount of construction and installation work, norms of consumption (the need for materials and equipment per unit of output or per unit of construction and installation work) and needs. The relationships among these three targets are:

Quantity of output (or amount of construction and installation work) × Norm of consumption = Quantity needed for use.

Since the production technical work process of each product and the consumption process of each material differ, the methods of calculating the needs for materials and equipment are also different. Based on these different characteristics, calculating tables can be classified into the following types.

1. <u>Tables for calculating materials used in production and operation</u>.

These are general purpose tables. With the exception of mandatory special-purpose computing tables, these tables are used to compute the need for every material used in production and operation. For example, these tables are used to compute the amount of coal, petroleum products, metallurgical products, timber, chemical-engineering products, thermal-engineering products, natural rubber, and construction materials used to produce each product.

The major bases for calculating the need for materials used in production and operation are all the targets stipulated among the computing items. The computing items in the calculating tables for materials used in production and operation generally consist of the following.

First, the quantity of materials needed to produce each product. This is determined with reference to the production plan and the materials input-output coefficients for the product. To facilitate checking the production tasks, two classification methods are used to compute the needs. One is to classify all the products as state plan products, ministerial or provincial (municipal) plan products, or other plan products. Among these three types of products, the needs of the state plan products and ministerial or provincial (municipal) plan products are based on the output targets and their consumption norms. Due to the tremendous variety of products involved, the needs of other plan products in general cannot be determined individually. They are determined with reference to the consumption levels of past years and the increase in the value of output. Another method is to determine the items of calculation according to each major use of the material resources. For example, the calculation items of natural rubber are rubber shoes, automobile tires, automobile tire tubes, bicycle tires, miscellaneous rubber products, and so forth.

Among the needs for materials in production are also included the quantity needed for the trial manufacture of new products and

246

the quantity needed to increase products-in-process. The quantity needed for the trial manufacture of new products is determined on the basis of the plan for the trial manufacture of new products and consumption norms. The quantity needed to increase products-in-process is determined on the basis of the quantity of products-in-process and the consumption norms. The amount of products-in-process depends on the production scale of the enterprise, the length of the production cycle, and the quality of the production organization. It is very important for the Ministry of Machine-Building to have accurate figures on the needs related to products-in-process.

Second, the quantity needed for operational and maintenance uses. Due to the many items related to operations and maintenance, the required materials are not all the same. It is therefore relatively difficult to calculate accurately the quantity needed for operations and maintenance uses. They are ordinarily determined by the dynamic comparison method (same as the dynamic relations method, see Chi-hua ching-chi, 1955, No. 3, p. 30)* on the basis of the consumption levels of past years and the economizing tasks in the plan period. However, certain branches can also calculate the quantity needed for operations and maintenance purposes on the basis of the maintenance tasks and the maintenance norms, such as the needs related to maintaining railroad tracks and electric cables.

Third, the quantity needed for major repairs. These are determined on the basis of the major repair expenses or the major repair items and the consumption norms in the major repair plan.

Fourth, the quantity needed for technical organization measures and labor protection. These are determined on the basis of the expenses budgeted for these items or the technical organization measures and labor protection items and the consumption quotas.

Fifth, the quantity needed for the self-manufacture of tools. These are determined on the basis of the output of tools and the consumption norms.

Sixth, the quantity needed for wear and tear. These are determined on the basis of the quantity of materials needed for use and the rate of wear and tear.

Seventh, the amount of recycled resources and scraps utilized refers to the number of containers recycled in the packaging of

*Lecture 3: "Methods in Formulating National Economic Plans," pp. 3-11, above. — N.R.L.

certain products and the amount of scraps used directly in the production of certain products. The amount of recycled resources and scraps used as the equivalent of raw and processed materials should be deducted from the total needs in the calculation table.

2. <u>Tables for calculating the need for furnace metals.</u>*

Furnace metals refer to all the metal raw materials (such as pig iron, scrap steel, scrap iron, copper, lead, zinc, and aluminum) used for casting. Several kinds of furnace metals are combined in certain proportions and smelted into a new metal. The quantity of furnace metals needed to produce cast-metal products is determined on the basis of the production plan for successful castings and the success rate of castings.

Quantity of furnace metals needed for use = Quantity of successful castings ÷ Success rate of castings.

The need for each furnace metal is determined with reference to the proportions required for each type of casting. For example, when producing ten tons of a certain kind of pig-iron casting, the success rate is 60 percent. The need for each metal raw material and furnace material can be determined with reference to the proportion of the ingredients:

	Proportions of furnace metals	Needs (Kg.)
Production plan for successful castings		10,000
Rate of success (%)		60
Need for furnace metals	100	16,666
Of which: pig iron	50	8,333
iron alloy	3	500
scrap steel	6	1,000
scrap iron	41	6,833
Of which: recycled iron (wastage 8%)	32	5,333
scrap iron purchased from outside	9	1,500

Recycled iron refers to scrap iron recycled by the foundry during the production process. The amount of recycled iron is determined by the recycling rate (1 − success rate of castings − wastage in smelting).

Quantity of each metal raw material needed for use = Quantity of furnace metals needed for use × Proportion of given raw metal required = Production plan of successful castings × Consumption norms for metal raw materials.

_____

*Referred to as "furnace charge" in the U.S. foundry industry. — N. R. L.

3. Balance table for scrap iron and steel.

This table is used to calculate the amount of recycled iron and steel and the resources of, and the need for, scrap iron and steel. The resource part of the balance table includes production recycling, metal-processing recycling, depreciation recycling, the amount collected, and the amount purchased.

Scrap iron and steel recycled through production includes:

a. Recycling from blast-furnace production. This refers mainly to the scrap iron remaining in the molten-iron trough and the molten-iron pao [包]. In addition, there is scrap iron from castings and waste products from the furnace.

b. Recycling from steel smelting. This includes recycling of waste products and recycling during the pouring of molten steel.

c. Recycling from the production of steel castings.

The amount of recycling from blast-furnace production, steel smelting, and casting is calculated according to the norm for recycling of each process.

Recycling of scrap iron and steel from metal processing includes: scrap iron and steel produced during the machine processing of steel castings, iron castings, forged steel ingots, structural steel, steel pipes, and metal manufacturing. The norms for recycling scrap iron and steel are determined with reference to the metal utilization coefficients, or the ratio of gross weight to net weight of products.

Scrap iron and steel recycled through depreciation include: the scrapping of obsolete metal fixed assets (machines, structures, and so forth) and spare parts and accessories replaced during major and minor repairs. The amount of recycling from the scrapping of obsolete metal fixed assets is determined with reference to the actual amount of recycling in past years. The amount of depreciation recycling from major and minor repairs on them is determined with reference to the need for iron and steel in repairs. In general, the amount of depreciation recycling is approximately equal to the difference between the total need for iron and steel in repairs and the scrap from machine processing and wastage.

The amount of collected scrap iron and steel refers to the scrap iron and steel collected from furnace slag piles, garbage dumps of plants, and the clean up of plants. It is determined with reference to the actual amount collected in past years.

The amount of scrap iron and steel purchased refers to the amount of each kind of scrap iron and steel purchased from the households by purchasing organs appointed by the state. It is determined with reference to the actual amount in past years.

After the amount of each of the above-mentioned sources of scrap iron and steel has been determined, it is balanced against the need of the branch itself for scrap iron and steel and the amount the branch has left to arrive at the amount of scrap iron and steel to apply for or the amount that can be sent out.

4. Table for calculating the quantities of gasoline, diesel oil, and fuel oil that are needed.

The quantity of petroleum products needed includes oil used by motor vehicles, oil used by tractors, oil used by diesel engines, oil used by boats, and oil used by each kind of machine and boiler.

Oil used by motor vehicles is largely for freight trucks. It is determined on the basis of the volume of freight traffic (in ton-kilometers) in the transport plan and the norm of oil consumption per ton-kilometer. The formula for calculating the norm of oil consumption per ton-kilometer is as follows:

Norm of oil consumption per ton-kilometer (in grams) = Average quantity of oil consumed per kilometer traveled by motor vehicles (in grams) ÷ [Average load capacity per motor vehicle (in tons) × Trip utilization coefficient × Load utilization coefficient].

The trip utilization coefficient is a ratio of the distance traveled with a load to the total distance traveled. It indicates the utilization rate of return trips. The larger the trip utilization rate, the smaller the norm of oil consumption per ton-kilometer.

The load utilization coefficient refers to the ratio of actual load to the load capacity. It indicates the load rate of the automobile. When the motor vehicle carries a heavier load or pulls a trailer, the load utilization coefficient is larger, and the norm of oil consumption per ton-kilometer is lower.

Since the norm of oil consumption for different kinds of motor vehicles differs, we must first calculate those for each different brand and then compute a weighted average oil consumption figure, the load capacity, the trip utilization coefficient, the load utilization coefficient, and the norm of oil consumption per ton-kilometer.

To briefly explain this computation method, we use the following examples:

$$\text{The norm of oil consumption per ton-kilometer} = \frac{258}{3.33 \times 0.95 \times 0.6} = 136 \text{ grams.}$$

Brand of motor vehicle	Number of cars	Load capacity (tons)		Utilization coefficient		The quantity of oil consumption per kilometer		The norm of oil consumption per ton-kilometer (grams)
		per vehicle	all vehicles	load	trip	per vehicle (grams)	all vehicles (kilograms)	
A	1	2	3	4	5	6	7	8
Chieh-fang	200	4	800	0.95	0.6	288	57.6	126
Chi-shih 5	150	3	450	0.95	0.6	258	38.6	182
Chi-shih 51	100	2.5	250	0.95	0.6	200	20	140
Total	450	—	1,500	—	—	—	116.2	—
Weighted average		3.33	—	0.95	0.6	258	—	136

In general, the norm of oil consumption per ton-kilometer only helps the management unit above the transport enterprise calculate needs. It is not suitable for evaluating the actual oil consumption of each vehicle. This is because the size of the trip utilization coefficient and the load utilization coefficient primarily depends on the quality of the organization work of the management branch. To evaluate the actual oil consumption of each vehicle, the oil consumption per vehicle-kilometer is generally used instead.

The oil consumption of transport trucks not subject to transport planning can be determined directly on the basis of the distance (kilometer) traveled and the norm of oil consumption per vehicle-kilometer.

Quantity of oil consumed = Annual average number of vehicles × Vehicle utilization rate × Average distance traveled daily × Oil consumption per kilometer × Number of calendar days in a year.

The oil consumption of other vehicles, such as sedans and motorized bicycles, is determined on the basis of their quantity and the norm of oil consumption.

The quantity of oil consumed by agricultural tractors is determined on the basis of the amount of work on cultivated land and consumption norms (the plowing old land calculation).*

The quantity of oil consumed by boats and all the machines powered by internal combustion engines is generally determined on the basis of the amount of installed power (horsepower), oper-

---

*This conversion is explained in Liu Hsien-kao, "Agricultural Production Planning Tables," CHCC, 1957, No. 4. See above, pp. 179-189, for the translation. — N.R.L.

ating time (hours), and oil consumption norms (oil consumption per horsepower hour).

The quantity of oil consumed by locomotives powered by internal combustion engines is determined on the basis of the transport traffic (ton-kilometers) specified in the transport plan and the norm of oil consumption per ton-kilometer.

Fuel oil used in furnaces is used largely for oil refining, steel smelting, glass production, and electricity generation. The quantity of furnace fuel oil needed is generally determined on the basis of the output level and the consumption norms.

Part of the need for oil is that consumed when testing vehicles (or power machines). This part is determined on the basis of the actual consumption in past years and the number of vehicles (or power machines).

5. Tables to calculate the quantity of electrical equipment needed.

There are generally three kinds of computing tables:

The first kind are tables for calculating the quantity of power machines, electrical equipment, and ball bearings needed to assemble a set of machine products. The quantity of these kinds of equipment that are needed is determined on the basis of the quantity of output (the quantity of assembled sets of products) and the assembly norm per unit of product.

The second kind are tables for calculating the amount of large equipment needed for capital construction. This need is determined on the basis of the approved technical design of the capital construction projects. For example, the need for electricity generation equipment, iron-smelting equipment, steel-smelting equipment, large transformers, chemical engineering equipment, and light industrial equipment are all calculated on the basis of the required increase in capacity. Since the amount of electrical equipment required in the technical design relates to the whole project, we must determine the need for electrical equipment in the plan year on the basis of the rate at which the equipment for each project is installed and put into operation.

The third kind are tables for calculating the quantity of electrical equipment needed for capital construction. This kind of need for equipment is calculated on the basis of the amount of work that has to be completed by the equipment. For example, the amount of communications and transport equipment (locomotives, passenger cars, transport trucks, freight trucks, and so forth) is based on the transport task (ton-kilometers); the number of drilling machines is based on the amount of drilling work (thousand kilometers); the number of earth-digging machines is based on the amount of earth to be dug (cubic meters); the number of tractors is based on the area of cultivated land (mou), and so forth. In calculating the need for such equipment, we must take into account the amount of work that can be done with the equipment existing at the beginning of the year and the equipment that will be repaired or retired during the plan year.

$$\text{Quantity of equipment needed for use} = \frac{\text{Total amount of work during year}}{\text{Annual work norms per machine}} -$$

(Number of machines already in service at beginning of year + Average amount of equipment to be repaired − Average amount of equipment to be retired).

6. Table for calculating the quantity of materials for use in construction and installation projects of capital construction.

There are two methods for calculating the need for such kinds of materials. One method is to compute the physical amount of work; the other is to compute the expenses. In general, the former method is suitable for planning units below the level of the administrative bureau, and the latter is suitable for those above the level of the administrative bureau.

For productive construction, the computation units for the physical amount of work are the weight (tons) as for metal structures, the volume (cubic meters) as for reinforced concrete, earth projects, rock foundations, and brick-laying projects, and the length (kilometers) as for electrical cables, railroad tracks, telecommunications cables, and water supply and drainage pipes and channels. For nonproductive construction, each type of housing is calculated in terms of constructed area (square meters). The need for materials by planning units below the level of the management bureau is generally calculated according to the different projects on the basis of the physical amount of work in the construction and installation projects and the norm of consumption per unit of physical work.

Quantity of materials needed for use = Physical amount of work × Norm of consumption per unit of physical work.

Expenses are the monetary expression of construction and installation work. At present, the computation unit in China for expenses is "ten thousand yuan." The "consumption norm of materials per ten thousand yuan of construction and installation project" (the "ten thousand yuan norm" in brief) is a norm for the consumption of materials expressed in terms of expenses. The need for materials by management bureau planning units is generally determined on the basis of the amount of construction and installation work and the ten thousand yuan quota. For example, suppose the capital construction investment of a certain ministry is 500 million yuan, of which construction and installation represent 60 percent, that is, 300 million yuan, and the norm for the consumption of structural steel per ten thousand yuan is 2 tons. Then the need for structural steel is 60,000 tons.

Quantity of materials needed for use = Amount of construction and installation work (ten thousand yuan) × Norm of consumption per ten thousand yuan of construction and installation.

Because the consumption norms differ for different businesses and different types of construction and installation, when the quantity of materials needed is computed in terms of expenses, we must generally classify them into such categories as productive and nonproductive construction, and within the productive construction category, we must further classify different types of construction according to different types of construction business, while also taking into account the amount of construction and installation by each branch and the average ten thousand yuan quota of the branch. Based on the investment composition of each branch and the ten thousand yuan quotas for the classifications, the need for materials can be accurately determined.

7. Table for calculating the quantity of materials needed for newly constructed lines.

Newly constructed lines include railroad tracks, electric cables, telecommunications cables, and water supply and drainage projects for urban public utilities. The materials required for this are part of those required for construction and installation. Because the materials needed for line projects can be directly calculated on the basis of the amount of work (length of line), they are computed separately and included as part of the need in construction and installation. The table to calculate the need for materials in newly constructed lines is an appendix to the composite table for calculating the need for materials in construction and installation.

8. Table for calculating the quantity of seamless steel pipes needed in geological prospecting.

The seamless steel pipes required for geological prospecting include drilling pipes, sleeve pipes, thimbles, rock core tubes, and seamless steel pipes required by the geological-drilling branch for assembling drilling machines. The amount of seamless steel pipes required for geological prospecting is determined on the basis of the amount of drilling done (meters) and the norm of consumption per meter drilled according to different types of mineral deposits.

Fourteen tables have been specified for the 1958 material-technical supply plan; two are request forms, eleven are calculating tables, and one is a detailed table for the materials and equipment required by above-quota construction units. The 1958 tables and targets are greatly simplified compared with those of 1957, but this simplification does not imply a lowering of the standards for material-technical supply planning. In the 1958 tables, although the production reserve quota plan and the analysis of the projected consumption of materials in the base year have been eliminated, such work should still be done at the basic level when the material-technical supply plans are formulated. Because only a few major targets are specified and some tables for specialized activities have been eliminated from the 1958 material-technical supply tables, they may not correspond to the needs of specialized activities under some branches. Therefore, the 1958 tables provide that each ministry and province (municipality) can, whenever necessary and feasible, prepare tables that are more suited to the needs of their own branches, while satisfying the requirements of these basic targets and under the principles of uniformity and centralization. The supplementary tables and targets prepared by each ministry and province (municipality) should also be sent to the higher level along with the material-technical supply plans.

LECTURE 14: CULTURAL, EDUCATIONAL, AND HEALTH SERVICES PLANNING TABLES

Huang Chih-yin*

I. The Basic Task and the Designed Scope of Cultural, Educational, and Health Services Planning

The cultural, educational, and health services plan is part of the national economic plan. It is a plan that reflects the increase in people's cultural standard of living. Its basic tasks are determined by the present political and economic tasks of the state. Its basic tasks are: (1) to train all kinds of manpower for the state, the most important being industrial technicians and scientific researchers; and (2) to improve gradually the cultural life of the working people on the basis of developing production and increasing labor productivity. To make the development of cultural, educational, and health services match the needs of the state and the people, when formulating the cultural, educational, and health services plan, we must conduct a comprehensive study taking into account the policies of the Party and state regarding all the cultural, educational, and health services, the degree to which the quantity of state financial resources can be increased, the subjective feasibilities inherent in the development patterns of all the cultural and educational services, the needs of the state and the people for cultural, educational, and health services, and the historical conditions of different services and different regions. To satisfy the daily increasing cultural needs of the people, we must also rely on the masses and mobilize mass enthusiasm for running various mass cultural, educational, and health services in addition to those cultural, educational, and health services operated by the state.

*Huang Chih-yin, "Wen-chiao wei-sheng shih-yeh chi-hua piao-ke." CHCC, 1958, No. 2, pp. 39-41.

The major content of the cultural, educational, and health services plan is to train manpower for the state, to develop scientific research work, to raise the people's cultural standard of living, to satisfy the people's need for education, and to improve the various aspects of the people's physical constitution and health. The scope of the 1958 cultural, educational, and health services plan can be divided into three categories according to the nature of the services: (1) the training of cadres for the government through higher education (including graduate students) and middle-level vocational education and the sending of students abroad to improve their scientific knowledge; (2) improving the people's cultural standard of living through middle and primary schools, kindergarten education and spare-time cultural and educational services for workers and peasants; movies, performing arts, social culture, and publishing and broadcasting services; (3) clinical and health services such as hospitals, rest homes, and all kinds of health organs to improve the people's health. The scope of the plan can also be classified according to the sponsoring branches: The middle and primary education and kindergarten education plan includes all public schools, schools run by the masses on a collective basis, and private schools; the cultural services plan includes cultural services established by cultural branches, labor unions, and other branches; the health services plan includes health services established by the health branches, industrial and other branches, and groups and individuals. The cultural services provided by cinemas and theaters, classified by economic type, include those operated by the state and those jointly operated by the public and private sectors. Theatrical groups include professional civilian groups. In addition, spare-time higher education and middle-level vocational education are also included among educational services.

The cultural, educational, and health services plan does not include the following items: (1) mass cultural and artistic activities, such as amateur cultural and arts groups; (2) public schools run by national minorities, schools for the blind, deaf, and mute, and private remedial cultural and technical schools; (3) health services such as work-site hospitals, convalescent hospitals, private clinics, and private and group-operated obstetrical clinics and midwifery stations; and (4) libraries run by agencies, schools, and various units to satisfy their own needs. In addition, the 1958 planning tables also eliminated the development plan for scientific research institutes and the physical education services plan. They were transferred to the Science Planning Commission and State Sports Commission respectively to arrange for their relevant service targets.

II. The Composition of the Cultural, Educational, and Health Services Planning Tables and Their System of Targets

The composition of the cultural, educational, and health services planning tables is as follows: (1) those belonging to the system of targets concerning the training of specialized manpower are: the planning table for students studying abroad, the planning table for graduate studies, the planning table for higher education, and the planning table for middle-level vocational education; (3) those belonging to the system of targets concerning improving people's cultural standard of living are: the planning table for middle and primary education and kindergarten education, the planning table for worker-peasant spare-time cultural and educational services, the cultural services planning table, the publishing services planning table, and the radio broadcasting planning table; (3) those belonging to the protection of people's health are the planning tables for health services; (4) balance table for middle-school teachers; and (5) computing tables for the health services plan to analyze the content of the health services plan. The functions, content, and methods of calculating the major targets of these tables are explained briefly below.

1. Tables Belonging to the System of Targets concerning the Training of Specialized Manpower

a. Tables related to the higher education plan and the middle-level vocational education plan. The admissions and graduate targets listed in the tables reflect the task of the institutions of higher education and middle-level vocational schools to train engineers, technicians, scientific research personnel, and teachers for every sector of the national economy. The major targets are:

1) Number of admissions. This refers to the number of new first-year students accepted and registered at schools after passing entrance examinations. Because newly admitted students must undergo three, four, five or even six years of vocational or general studies to complete their training and achieve a certain cultural and scientific level and, at the same time, because all the levels of educational services are closely related, the admissions plans

of schools at each level must be arranged according to certain proportions in order to prevent dislocations. Therefore, when determining the admissions plans of higher and middle level vocational schools, we must start from the need of each sector of the national economy for specialists, the further technological improvement of the national economy, the development of new production, and the increase of social labor productivity. Second, they should be coordinated with the development prospects and geographical distribution of each sector of the national economy. Third, repeated balancing between different categories and different vocations, between higher- and middle-level specialists, and among sectors must be based on what is needed and feasible in order to achieve proportional development.

2) Number of graduates. This refers to the number of students who have attained a certain level of political and cultural awareness and scientific knowledge according to the schooling and curriculum requirements of the state and who graduate after passing examinations in the spring or fall. Qualified graduates from institutions of higher education and middle-level vocational schools are specialists who possess a certain level of political awareness and scientific and technical knowledge. The planned number of graduates is determined with reference to the current number of who should graduate minus the number of dropouts.

3) Enrollment at the beginning of the school year, or the number of enrolled students. This target estimates the total number of registered students at schools of each level at the beginning of the school year. This figure could reflect the level attained by students in school, the rate of growth of educational services, and the size of the schools. The method of calculating the number of students at the beginning of the school year is to use the previous year's statistics minus the number of graduates in the current year plus the number of admissions in the current year. The number of dropouts should be based on a suitable dropout rate and deducted from the plan.

4) Index of vocational classifications. The 1958 plan to train higher- and middle-level specialists requires that they be classified into twenty-three major categories. Due to technological innovations and the development of all sectors of the national economy, the professional range of the specialists required increases daily. Higher- and middle-level schools have to add some new vocations and adjust and combine some old vocations to meet the need for specialists.

b. Planning tables for graduate students and students studying abroad. Graduate students are graduates of institutions of higher education and specialized manpower with an equivalent level of academic achievement who have been admitted into the graduate programs of institutions of higher education and scientific research organizations and are to be trained as teachers and scientific researchers in two-, three-, or four-year programs. In addition to ordinary graduate students, the plan to train graduate students includes graduate students sponsored by various units; it does not include foreign students studying in China. Some specialists required by various branches still cannot be trained domestically due to the limitations of our institutions of higher education. A certain number of students have to be sent abroad for training. In the First Five-Year Plan period, our students studying abroad went primarily to the Soviet Union and secondarily to other people's democratic countries. Most of them were graduates of senior high schools. From 1957 on, senior high school graduates were generally not sent abroad. Instead, university graduates and graduate students were sent abroad to study specialties not offered in China.

In addition, spare-time higher education and middle-level vocational education have been included in the plan since 1956. Spare-time higher- and middle-level vocational schools are evening schools or correspondence schools established in regular higher schools, middle-level vocational schools, plants and mines, and government organizations. They are not divorced from production. They recruit cadres, technicians, and skilled workers as part-time students to turn out even more specialists who are familiar with their own specialties and possess practical experience. To train intellectuals of the working class through spare-time education is a major task of spare-time higher and middle-level vocational education.

2. Tables Belonging to the System of Targets concerning Improving People's Cultural Living Standard

a. Planning tables for middle and primary schools and kindergarten education.

The middle and primary education plan is determined with reference to the policy regarding the development of middle and primary school education, the people's need with respect to cultural standards of living, the rate of increase of people's economic standard of living, the rates of growth and proportional relations among schools at each level, state financial resources, and the supply of teachers. The targets regarding the numbers of schools, classes, admissions, graduates, and enrollments at the beginning of the school year in the middle and primary education planning tables reflect the development of educational services at each level. When formulating the plans, we should also have some relatively accurate data for reference, such as the number of children of school age, the percentage of students going on for higher studies, the number of existing teachers, the number of schools, the number of classes, and the actual number of students in each grade.

b. Balance table for middle-level school teachers. The purpose of this table is to calculate the balance between the number of additional teachers needed in middle-level schools and the possible sources of such teachers in order to provide a reliable material guarantee for the middle-level education plan. This way, not only can the numbers of additional teachers needed in middle-level schools be satisfied in terms of quantity, but we can also pay attention to raising the level of quality. The number of additional teachers needed includes the number of teachers required to staff new schools, the number of teachers needed for new classes and expanded curricula, and the number of teachers needed to replace the loss of existing teachers and to retire disqualified teachers. The number of teacher losses can be calculated with reference to past experience. The reasons include retirement, further studies, and promotion. The method of calculating the number of additional teachers needed is:

Number of additional teachers = Number of teachers needed in plan period – Number of existing teachers + Number needed to replace loss of existing teachers.

The need for teachers in the plan period is calculated on the basis of the number of students, the number of classes, the number of existing teachers and their cultural level, the number of teaching hours, and the number of potential resignations (for further study, retirement, and so forth). To calculate the need for middle-level school teachers, we must also make separate calculations for each specialty in addition to knowing the average quota of teachers required for each class. Let us use the following junior middle school example to explain, with the aid of a simple formula, the methods of calculating the total number of teachers needed and the number of teachers needed for each subject (using history and geography as examples):

1) Total number of teachers needed =

$$\frac{\text{Total number of class hours for each subject}}{\text{Number of classes} \times \text{Average teaching load per week per teacher}} \times$$

(Number of students enrolled ÷ Average number of students per class).

2) Number of teachers needed for history and geography = Total number of teachers needed × Proportion of history and geography classes among all classes.

c. Planning tables for worker-peasant spare-time cultural and educational services.

The worker-peasant spare-time cultural and educational services plan includes literacy classes and middle and primary spare-time cultural studies. All the spare-time cultural studies established for cadres, staff and workers, peasants, and urban people in government agencies and organizations, plants, mines, urban neighborhoods, and rural areas should also be included. At present, the objectives of literacy classes are young adults in the fourteen to forty age group, particularly peasants who represent 60 to 70 percent of all the illiterates in China. The literacy standard should be the recognition of 1,500 characters or more. When calculating the enrollment of peasants in spare-time cultural studies, the number of people should be listed in the table as the number between December of one year and January of the next year. Because the busy agricultural seasons and climate are not the same in the south as in the north, whether this rule is equally applicable to all the regions should be studied further. The number of graduates and the student enrollment at the beginning of the school year in spare-time cultural schools and literacy classes for staff and workers and urban people can be calculated the same way as for regular educational services. To formulate a good literacy plan, in addition to following state policy, we must also rely on census and statistical data and do a good job in literacy surveys and propose measures to implement the plan, such as organizing the teaching staff, arranging suitable class hours, and consolidating literacy achievements.

d. Planning tables for cultural services. The cultural services plan includes movie making and translating foreign movies for home audiences, cinemas, movie projection teams, theatrical groups, theaters, libraries, museums, and cultural halls. These targets can be broadly grouped into the three targets of movies, arts, and social-cultural services.

1) Movie services. (a) Movie production. This is divided into movie making and translating foreign movies. The major target of movie making is to produce artistic movies and science education movies. The movie production plan should be based on the state requirements regarding movie production and the productive capacity of movie studios, and it should aim at improving the ideological and artistic standards of movies. Second, we should try our best to organize correctly the labor of creative and technical personnel and fully utilize the productive capacity of the movie studios in order to increase the quality and quantity of movies. The work experiences of advanced movie-making teams should be studied and popularized to save both film and time. (b) Development of a movie projection network. The movie projection network includes movie projection teams, cinemas, and other movie projection units. When formulating a movie projection network development plan, we should take into account the feasibility of capital investment, the productive capacity of the developing and printing workshops, and the production plan of the movie equipment industry (such as films, movie-making machines). The number and size of newly constructed cinemas should be based on the number of people to be served by one cinema and the number of seats to be provided per hundred people. To enable movies to serve the people more fully and to increase the profit rate of projection units, we should adopt measures to increase the seat utilization rate of the cinemas. The movie projection teams do their rounds mainly at work sites and in rural areas. Other movie projection units are run by government agencies and organizations, schools, plants, and mines to project movies for their own audiences rather than for the public. When formulating the movie projection network development plan, we should also formulate the work load plan for the movie projection network. Based on the number of cinemas (movie projection teams and other movie projection units), the average annual number of workdays per movie projection unit, and the number of screenings per day, we can calculate the annual number of screenings, the size of the audiences, and the gross revenue from projection.

2) Performing arts services. These are divided into the two targets of theatrical groups and theaters. Theatrical groups include all types, such as musicals, juggling, puppet shows, shadow shows, plays, operas, song and dance troupes, cultural work

groups, and singing and performing arts groups. However, they do not include performing units such as puppet shows, shadow shows, and juggling in which there are fewer than five performances. When new theaters are built, we must consider increasing their utilization rate.

3) Social-cultural services. These include the targets for public libraries, museums, and cultural halls. These cultural services are instrumental in organizing the spare-time cultural and artistic activities of the masses. Their development should be directed toward meeting regional needs, increasing the number of library holdings, enriching the content of museums, and actively unfolding spare-time cultural and artistic activities.

e. Planning tables for publishing services. The major targets of the publishing services plan are newspapers, magazines, books, and their number of titles, copies per title, and pages. The number of titles refers to the number of different kinds of publications. The number of newspaper and magazine titles refers to the number at the end of the year. The number of book titles refers to the accumulated number of first and subsequent editions during the whole year. Volumes, issues, and copies refer to the quantity of publication. Newspapers are calculated in copies, and magazines and books are calculated in volumes. An individually bound unit is a volume; a fixed-price unit is a copy. The number of pages refers to the amount of paper used for publication. A standard printing sheet measures 787 mm. by 1092 mm. The publishing services plan is closely related to the balance between the amount of paper used and the printing capacity available.

f. Planning tables for broadcasting services. The broadcasting services plan only includes radio broadcasting. Its major targets are the number of radio stations, the amount of broadcasting machinery, and its transmission power. The targets of the wired broadcasting network were not listed in the 1958 planning tables and are to be arranged by the management bureaus of the broadcasting services.

3. Tables Belonging to the System of
   Targets concerning Health Protection

a. Planning tables for health services. The development of clinical and health services is an important aspect of improving the welfare facilities available to the people. The health services planning table includes the number of beds in hospitals and rest homes, the number of health agencies, and the number of doctors as targets, reflecting the importance of increasing health and clinical facilities and implementing the basic policy of health services. In studying and determining the various targets, we must pay attention to the proximity of newly built hospitals and health clinics to population centers, so that the people can easily get to the doctor. At the same time, the following data should be analyzed: (1) natural changes in population, such as the birth and death rates; (2) the incidence of all kinds of diseases; (3) the conditions of existing clinical and health agencies and the training of existing medical personnel; (4) the working conditions and living standards of the working people; (5) the norm of workdays per year and work hours per day for each doctor; and (6) the turnover rate of beds. The major targets of the health services plan are as follows:

1) The number of beds in hospitals and rest homes. This target reflects the capacity of hospitals and rest homes and is calculated on the basis of the number at the end of the year. Hospital beds include those of comprehensive hospitals, Chinese-medicine hospitals, hospitals affiliated with medical schools, hospitals for infectious diseases, mental hospitals, tuberculosis hospitals, leprosy hospitals, obstetric hospitals (including mother and baby clinics), children's hospitals, other specialized hospitals, hsien health clinics, jointly operated hospitals, and private hospitals. Beds in rest homes include those for tuberculosis, those at hot springs, and general rest homes and convalescent hospitals. However, they do not include beds in spare-time and evening rest homes or army rest homes. The need for hospital and rest-home beds can be estimated by the following formula:

$$\text{Number of beds needed} = \frac{\begin{array}{l}\text{Size of population to be served} \times \text{Proportion} \\ \text{of total number of people to be served} \\ \text{that will be hospitalized}\end{array}}{\text{Turnover rate per bed}}.$$

2) Clinics. This is a composite target including regular clinics, out-patient departments, district [ch'ü] health clinics, and jointly operated clinics which provide diagnosis and treatment at the grass-roots level. Clinics should have full-time and part-time doctors serving designated areas so that the diseases of the local residents can be treated and prevented promptly. To calculate the need for out-patient doctors, the following formula can be used:

Number of out-patient doctors needed = Average number of visits to clinics per person per year × Population to be served ÷ Number of business days in out-patient clinics per year ÷ Number of out-patients per day per year.

3) Doctors. This target calculates the number of doctors practicing Chinese and Western medicine. The number of doctors that are needed can be determined based on the number of beds and the number of out-patients each doctor can take care of and other similar standard work-load indicators. The specialties and number of doctors that are needed for a given number of people can also be determined with reference to the incidence of diseases per thousand people and the coefficient of reduction of these incidences. At the same time, a balance table listing the need for, and possible sources of, doctors can be calculated as a reference for health services planning. The required number of doctors shown in the balance table should take into account the doctors that are needed in newly established hospital organizations of the health system, the need for additional doctors in existing hospitals where the number of doctors is insufficient, and the need for additional specialized teaching doctors in higher- and middle-level medical and pharmacy schools. The sources of doctors include graduates of higher-level medical schools, doctors who leave production for training or study in their spare time, doctors absorbed from private practice, and other sources. In addition, the further organization and mobilization of the large number of doctors practicing Chinese medicine is also extremely important to the balance of doctors.

4) Prevention and vaccination agencies include specialized prevention and treatment clinics, vaccination stations, and vaccination teams.

In addition, there are targets for mother and baby clinics and the treatment of schistosomiasis and malaria.

The majority of the targets in the health services planning tables include the organizations and beds established by the Ministry of Public Health, industrial and other ministries, and those that are cooperatively or privately established. (1) Those that are established by the Ministry of Public Health refer to public health services at all levels belonging to the Ministry of Public Health system. They include the health services of the Red Cross Society and the Antituberculosis Association and health services affiliated with industrial enterprises, government agencies and organizations, and medical schools under the leadership of the health department system. (2) Those established by industrial and other ministries refer to health services belonging to central and local industrial and other branches. They include health services run by the state, joint public and private industrial and non-industrial enterprises, government agencies, groups, institutions of higher education, banks, cooperative headquarters, and all kinds of cooperatives. They also include health services run jointly by two or more enterprises and health services established by the people using pooled resources. (3) Joint establishments refer to health services established by two or more individual medical personnel, such as joint hospitals, joint clinics, and so forth. (4) Private establishments refer to all private hospital beds and doctors in private clinics.

Standards for classifying municipal districts and county districts in the planning tables: Municipal districts refer to health services established within districts under the jurisdiction of municipalities of various levels.* County districts refer to health services established within the districts under county jurisdiction.

b. The calculating table for the health services plan. The purpose of this table is to facilitate the analysis of various factors affecting the annual increase of beds in hospitals and rest homes. From the results of implementing health services plans in past years, we can see that the number of newly constructed beds completed in the year when investment is first made represents only a part of the total projected number, particularly for large projects. There are also transfers of beds among departments. Through the calculating tables, the above changes can be explained and used for reference when the plan is being checked.

---

*Referring to provincial level, special district level, and county level municipalities. — N. R. L.

About the Editor

A graduate of the University of Wisconsin, Nicholas R. Lardy received his M.A. and Ph.D. in economics from the University of Michigan. He has been an assistant professor of economics at Yale University since 1975. Dr. Lardy spent the spring and summer of 1978 in Asia under the auspices of an American Council of Learned Societies Fellowship for Language and Advanced Training in East Asia.

A contributor of numerous articles to economics and area-studies journals, he is the author of Economic Growth and Distribution in China (forthcoming).